The Welfare Assembly Line

The Welfare Assembly Line

PUBLIC SERVANTS IN THE
SUFFERING CITY

Josh Seim

UNIVERSITY OF CALIFORNIA PRESS

University of California Press

Oakland, California

Library of Congress Cataloging-in-Publication Data

Names: Seim, Joshua David author

Title: The welfare assembly line : public servants in the suffering city /
  Josh Seim.

Description: Oakland, California : University of California Press,
  [2026] | Includes bibliographical references and index.

Identifiers: LCCN 2025025573 (print) | LCCN 2025025574 (ebook) |
  ISBN 9780520404151 cloth | ISBN 9780520404168 paperback |
  ISBN 9780520404175 ebook

Subjects: LCSH: Los Angeles County (Calif.). Department of Public
  Social Services—Officials and employees—Case studies | Public
  welfare—California—Los Angeles County—Officials and
  employees—Case studies | Women in the civil service—California—
  Los Angeles County—Case studies | Public welfare administration—
  California—Los Angeles County—Case studies | Division of labor—
  California—Los Angeles County—Case studies | Minority
  women—Employment—California—Los Angeles County—Case
  studies | LCGFT: Case studies

Classification: LCC HV99.L7 .S45 2026 (print) | LCC HV99.L7
  (ebook) | DDC 362.509794/94—dc23/eng/20250909

LC record available at https://lccn.loc.gov/2025025573

LC ebook record available at https://lccn.loc.gov/2025025574

GPSR Authorized Representative: Easy Access System Europe,
Mustamäe tee 50, 10621 Tallinn, Estonia, gpsr.requests@easproject
.com

34 33 32 31 30 29 28 27 26 25
10 9 8 7 6 5 4 3 2 1

For Cole, June, and Nora

Contents

Tables

Author's Note

The Welfare Assembly Line is a theory-driven case study of one of the largest locally administered public benefits bureaucracies in the United States: the Los Angeles County Department of Public Social Services. I use the real names of offices and neighborhoods. Pseudonyms, however, are used for all the individuals I shadowed and interviewed for this project.

Administrators at the department have mandated that I include the following disclaimer:

> While the research to complete this book was authorized by the Los Angeles County ("County") Department of Public Social Services (the "Department"), the views expressed within are solely those of the author and do not necessarily reflect the County nor the Department's official policies, procedures, or customs. Further, the Department does not endorse or guarantee the accuracy of all information presented in this publication and is not responsible for any outcomes arising from its content. Moreover, the Department is committed to serving all of our customers with respect and assisting them in obtaining the benefits they are eligible for.

Acknowledgments

This book would not have been possible without the generosity of many people. I am especially grateful to all the workers who allowed me to shadow and interview them for this project. Special thanks must be given to the administrators at DPSS who permitted me to conduct an in-depth study on the labor process in their offices. Union organizers at SEIU 721 were also kind enough to chat with me on multiple occasions and provide advice.

I am indebted to the many academics who gave feedback at various stages in my research: Sarah Babb, Alex Barnard, Robin Bartram, Latrica Best, David Brady, Erin Devorah Carreon, Liz Chiarello, Alexa Damaska, Anthony DiMario, Kelley Fong, Michael Gibson-Light, Neil Gong, Armando Lara-Millán, Zachary Levenson, Michael McCarthy, Erin McDonnell, Sara Moorman, Ann Owens, Henrik Palasani-Minassians, Allison Pugh, Natasha Sarkisian, Lacee Satcher, Julie Schor, and Michaela Simmons. I was also lucky to present and workshop key parts of this book with scholars in the Work, Health, Aging, Family, and Life Course (WHAFL) working group at Boston College, the Public Sector Organizational Effectiveness workshop at the University of Notre Dame, the Better Government Lab at Georgetown University, the American Anthropological Association meeting in Seattle, Washington, in 2022, the Law and Society Association meeting in San Juan, Puerto Rico, in 2023, and the International Labor Process Conference in Glasgow, Scotland, in 2023.

The support I received from UC Press was also critical. Naomi Schneider and her team believed in this project at a very early stage. The contract I received provided some much-needed motivation and encouragement. I am also grateful to Glynnis Koike for the beautiful cover art, Artemis Brod for the expert copyediting, and PJ Heim for the meticulous indexing.

Research expenses for this book were primarily covered by some very generous faculty "start-up" funds provided by Boston College. I feel incredibly lucky to work at a university that supports faculty research in concrete, material ways. I also received funding through the FirstGen program at UC Press.

Above all, I am grateful for my family, especially my wife, Brenna. I can't imagine a more supportive partner. From providing nitty-gritty editing advice to talking me down from my near panic attacks over site access and interview recruitment, Brenna has always been there for me without question. Since we were eighteen years old, she has been a constant force of encouragement in my life, and I know I simply wouldn't be where I am today without her.

And then there are my kids—Cole, June, and Nora. Thank you for *mostly* being patient while I worked on this project. But most of all, thank you for enticing me away from my research with wrestling, video games, arts and crafts, ice cream parlor trips, and so much more. This book is for you.

Glossary of Key Terms and Acronyms

CALFRESH California's implementation of the federal Supplemental Nutritional Assistance Program (SNAP). CalFresh is often colloquially referred to as "food stamps."

CALSAWS California Statewide Automated Welfare System, the core case management software used by frontline staff at DPSS.

CALWORKS California Work Opportunity and Responsibility to Kids, a cash aid program for families with children funded in large part by the federal Temporary Assistance for Needy Families (TANF) program. Adult recipients in Los Angeles County are typically mandated to participate in the GAIN program.

DPSS The Los Angeles County Department of Public Social Services, one of the largest local welfare departments in the nation and the primary empirical case for this book. Some of DPSS's largest programs include Medi-Cal, CalFresh, CalWORKs, and General Relief. DPSS also administers the bulk of GAIN case management services and all of START case management services.

ELIGIBILITY WORKER DPSS employee who makes initial or continuing eligibility determinations for means-tested programs like Medi-Cal, CalFresh, CalWORKs, and General Relief. Eligibility workers are usually assigned to work one to three specific programs on either the "intake" or "approval" side.

GAIN Greater Avenues for Independence, a mandatory welfare-to-work program for parents receiving CalWORKs. GAIN, however, predates CalWORKs and TANF and began as a state workfare program for AFDC (Aid to Families with Dependent Children) parents in the mid-1980s. The majority of GAIN programming is administered directly by DPSS, but services in the San Fernando and Antelope valleys are contracted to Maximus, a for-profit government services company based in Virginia.

GENERAL RELIEF A county-funded cash aid program that is generally reserved for extremely poor adults without children. Recipients are typically mandated to participate in the START program.

MEDI-CAL California's implementation of Medicaid, a federal means-tested public health insurance program.

SEIU 721 Services Employee International Union 721, the labor union that presently represents frontline workers at DPSS. DPSS workers were previously covered by Local 535 and Local 660.

START (FORMERLY GROW) Skills and Training to Achieve Readiness for Tomorrow (formerly, General Relief Opportunities for Work), a mandatory welfare-to-work program for those receiving General Relief. Much of this program is modeled after GAIN.

WTW WORKER A welfare-to-work worker who handles cases within the GAIN or START programs. Despite their formal titles ("GAIN Services Worker" and "START Services Worker"), WTW workers do not really administer services directly; instead they refer their subjects to a range of contracted programs. I sometimes call these individuals "GAIN workers" and "START workers."

Introduction

Sunshine, Noir, and Bureaucracy in the Suffering City

Perhaps more so than most major metropolises, Los Angeles is a place of intense contradiction. As urban theorist Mike Davis puts it, "The ultimate world-historical significance—and oddity—of Los Angeles is that it has come to play the double role of utopia *and* dystopia for advanced capitalism."[1] It is a site of what Davis calls *sunshine and noir*. On the one hand, Los Angeles symbolizes a kind of sun-splashed paradise for those who stand to reap the most from its beauty and opportunity. On the other hand, it exists as a common backdrop for narratives of suffering in the United States and beyond.

The paradoxical mixture of sunshine and noir also functions as an apt description of social polarization in Los Angeles. We can see this, for example, when homeless encampments run parallel to multimillion-dollar houses in Venice Beach, capturing the ire of reactionary commentators across the nation.[2] We can also see this in a bifurcating labor market that has increasingly thinned out middle-income jobs—pulling few toward security and many toward precarity.[3] And while it is a non-white majority county and has long been framed as a sparkling and radiant symbol of multiculturalism, Los Angeles is also gripped by persistent racism. Even with exceptionally high levels of ethnoracial diversity, an undeniable whiteness colors high-wage jobs and affluent neighborhoods in the county.[4]

If Los Angeles wealth, with its celebrity glam, hill-perched mansions, and corporate office skyscrapers, best captures the dreamy optimism of the capitalist city, then Los Angeles poverty might best capture the nightmarish pessimism of that same location. Indeed, we have long known, since at least the writings of Friedrich Engels on Manchester, W. E. B. Du Bois on Philadelphia, and Jane Addams on Chicago, that suffering tends to obey a kind of social gravity within cities.[5] Agony and insecurity tend to be pulled toward the bottom of interlocking social hierarchies.

And there is a solid base of poverty in Los Angeles to attract significant suffering. According to one study, the poverty rate in Los Angeles County is 15.5 percent, the highest in California.[6] But the magnitude of Los Angeles poverty is only part of the noir. The state—here broadly understood as a differentiated and frequently contested field of political and productive relations of governance—often handles the poor in cruel ways. Given its extensive legacy of incarcerating the destitute and marginal, historian Kelly Lytle Hernández has appropriately renamed the City of Angels the *City of Inmates*.[7] And, as sociologist Loïc Wacquant notes, in the late twentieth century, Los Angeles County became "the largest penal colony in the Western world" just as county welfare became stingier and more punitive, taking the form of workfare (e.g., mandating recipients work, seek a job, or increase their employability).[8]

Even so, there is at least *some* sunshine to consider here too. The governance of poverty in Los Angeles is not purely punitive. While this book will confirm that workfare persists, especially for a highly visible minority of cash aid recipients, I generally reject the claim that Los Angeles is even a remotely suitable case of what others have called the "post-welfare city."[9] Welfare has certainly changed in the county and nation—perhaps even "ended as we know it"—but we do not live in the absence of public assistance for the poor. Whether to reproduce labor power, neutralize social unrest, express state legitimacy, or simply reduce suffering for its own sake, welfare operations today still attenuate the forces of material deprivation in important ways.[10] They do so in a nation where, as poverty scholar David Brady reminds us, welfare generosity, Leftist collective political actors, and civil society coalitions for egalitarianism are low relative to peer nations.[11] Welfare may be stingy, but there is much to be protected—especially amidst the cruelty of right-wing populism.

Without safety net programs like CalFresh (food stamps), Supplemental Security Income (for the elderly and disabled poor), and earned income and child tax credits, the poverty rate in Los Angeles would be a whopping 26 percent.[12] And this is to say nothing about the assistance offered through General Relief, a cash aid program that covers over 122,000 residents; CalWORKs, another cash aid program covering nearly 280,000; and Medi-Cal (Medicaid), a massive public health insurance program covering roughly 3.5 million.[13] The average benefit amount per case, which usually includes multiple individuals in a household, may be small. Per month, this is approximately $1,077 for CalWORKs, $314 for CalFresh, and a measly $221 for General Relief.[14] But for many toward the bottom of the economic hierarchy in Los Angeles, these small amounts of aid do alleviate hardship.

And a good number of these programs are distributed through welfare offices, which, in California, remain responsible not only for CalWORKs and General Relief but also for CalFresh and Medi-Cal. In fact, *over a third of Los Angeles County residents today receive some form of assistance from its local benefits bureaucracy, the Los Angeles County Department of Public Social Services (DPSS).*[15]

This is quite an amazing fact when considering the larger scholarship on poverty governance in the United States. Many social scientists would have you believe that welfare departments have been cast to the dustbin of American history, along with the poor houses, the asylums, and the sanitariums of the twentieth century. There are those, like Wacquant, who assume prisons and jails have overshadowed, and even substituted, a retrenching and increasingly punitive welfare system.[16] Then there are those who credit other kinds of welfare state expansions, like tax credits, disability claims, and even ambulance services, with filling a void. Sociologist Sarah Halpern-Meekin and her team of researchers, for example, argue that H&R Block offices and the like have emerged, in a "postwelfare world," as the new spaces for receiving relief in an era where the Earned Income Tax Credit has eclipsed other cash transfers.[17] Likewise, medical anthropologist Helena Hansen and her team argue that disability claims, which are linked to the diagnostic power of medical professionals, have essentially medicalized poverty governance and siphoned much of the poor from welfare offices to clinics.[18] Even I have been guilty of propagating the myth of withering welfare offices. In my first book—*Bandage, Sort, and Hustle: Ambulance Crews on the Front Lines of Urban Suffering*—I claimed that because traditional benefits have become more stingy and disciplinary, the poor are turning less to welfare offices and more to emergency medical systems for aid.[19]

But, as this book will demonstrate, these other scholars and I were off the mark. The welfare office did *not* shrink to irrelevance. It receded from public and scholarly view, but its reach actually grew significantly in the twenty-first century. It is certainly true that cash aid has declined. But even at its peak, the population on cash aid in the US was less than half the size of those receiving Medicaid and just over half the size on food stamps anyway.[20] The number of families receiving "welfare checks" may have radically shrunk in the past three decades, but these other larger benefits programs have mostly grown. At DPSS, this means that over four million people today receive some kind of benefits from welfare offices—though far fewer than that ever visit such sites in person. Instead, most interface with semiautomated call centers and online applications, both of which are handled by people on cubicle-divided work floors.

The enduring relevance of welfare offices is made possible through *bureaucracy*, a social structure that surely provokes its own dreams and nightmares. The latter probably pop into your mind immediately. Bureaucracy is, as sociologist Erin McDonnell puts it, "practically a four-letter word" in the West.[21] There are certainly many reasons to curse its existence: red tape, long queues, steep hierarchy, frigid officials, and so on. I can assure you that such horrors can be easily found at any welfare office in Los Angeles.

But, as sociologist Max Weber famously argued, bureaucracies are often exceptionally effective and efficient.[22] This is true not only for administrators but also for clients. Much can and should be said about how Los Angeles welfare offices require those seeking aid to navigate a series of often opaque and exclusionary rules and regulations—what public policy scholars Pamela Herd and Donald Moynihan call "administrative burdens."[23] But we should also acknowledge the rationalization that allows merely fourteen thousand employees at DPSS to aid more than four million people.

As one of thirty-eight departments in the Los Angeles County government, DPSS is itself embedded in a larger bureaucratic field that is characteristically massive in its size but limited in its autonomy. The county government largely functions as an "agent" of the California and federal governments.[24] This means that county administrators—including not only those department heads who oversee frontline policy labor but also the Board of Supervisors who oversee department leadership—budget and spend public funds that "come with strings attached."[25] From 500 West Temple Street, where the county supervisors meet, the strings extend to the north. State officials in Sacramento, themselves under the watchful eye of the feds in Washington, DC, enable and constrain Los Angeles bureaucracy with both rules and resources.

Sacramento's power over Los Angeles only became more intense after a taxpayer revolt in 1978, which Davis playfully called the "Watts Riot of the Middle Classes."[26] That year, California voters passed Proposition 13, which severely limited the capacity of counties to levy property taxes, making the counties all generally more dependent on state funds (and on federal funds filtered through the state).[27] For many voters, Prop 13 was understood to be a direct and intentional assault on what was framed as a bloated welfare system.[28] And while state-county funding "realignments" in 1991 and 2011 increased county flexibility in spending on select programs, it is still the case that *most* of the Los Angeles County budget is funded from state and federal sources.[29] This is especially true for DPSS, which funds most of its programs with federal and state funds handed down with attached strings from Sacramento.[30]

In this regard, DPSS might be thought of as an administrative mailman—or perhaps a bureaucratic midwife—that helps "deliver" a series of major state and federal means-tested aid programs to the poor and suffering in Los Angeles. Management has essentially no control over how their programs are funded and regulated. Instead, they are tasked with efficiently handling the purse they are given.

And their largest controllable resource is staffing.[31] County welfare administrators are given significant, but certainly not total, authority to organize the labor process—that is, the manner in which labor is actually executed. These higher-level bureaucrats are structurally motivated to increase the amount of productivity they can extract from those beneath them. Doing so may not generate a profit, but it can bring the agency closer to the often-vague goal of fiscal responsibility and help demonstrate its legitimacy. As sociologist Armando Lara-Millán has demonstrated in his study of county hospitals and jails in Los Angeles, the pressure to pursue such an objective has only sharpened under the intensifying contradiction of budgetary austerity and legal demand.[32] Local bureaucracies are increasingly mandated to serve more people with fewer resources. Squeezing more productivity from the front lines is a primary response to that dilemma.

What I am calling the *welfare assembly line* has been essential to DPSS's strategy. While not at all unique to this agency, this is a promising case for studying how the frontline labor of policy administration has been increasingly specialized, standardized, and automated. Throughout its roughly sixty-year history, this department has systematically reduced workers' control over the products and processes of their labor in the name of efficiency. Those who depend on the agency for assistance are handled by workers distributed along bureaucratic conveyor belts arranged to squeeze out as much productivity as possible.

But this is not a story best told as simple noir. The twist is that there are many reasons to be optimistic about the welfare assembly line in sunny Los Angeles. Not only does it facilitate a mass production of benefits (albeit paltry ones), it also somewhat paradoxically yields security for workers (albeit in relative terms). This book explicates these contradictions of the welfare assembly line by examining an intertwined practice: the labor process.

The Welfare Assembly Line

In fall 2021, hundreds of welfare workers rallied outside DPSS headquarters in the City of Industry, twenty miles east of downtown Los Angeles. This mass showing—made mostly of Black and brown women—blew whistles, rang cow bells, and belted chants like "More Care, Less Stress in DPSS!" and "Don't Crush Our Human Touch!"[33] Management had recently restructured the labor process so that many of the department's caseworkers essentially became taskworkers. Rather than assign whole cases (individual clients and families) to single employees, management implemented a system in their district offices to divide cases into discrete tasks that could be distributed across an array of workers. This came with intensified surveillance, micromanagement, and the alienation of labor. Several carried a union-printed sign with a bold message: "Social Services *is NOT* an Assembly Line!"[34]

But these signs were a bit misleading, at least technically. An assembly-line model for implementing social services has existed in Los Angeles welfare offices for at least a half century. Assembly lines can take multiple forms, but they are essentially production systems characterized by the sequential division of tasks, largely facilitated by machinery. On the one hand, welfare in Los Angeles operates like a manufacturing assembly line: workers are stationed to work on bits and pieces of larger inanimate wholes. On the other hand, it resembles a fast-food assembly line, on which workers interact with living clients in a highly specialized and systematized manner.

The work of determining, monitoring, and sanctioning recipients has long been organized by a heavily automated system that pushes cases and tasks across disciplined units of specialized employees. This work, especially since the late 1960s, has become less professionalized and more proletarianized, as a kind of craft social work was eclipsed by a more industrialized form of state production. For generations now, welfare recipients—and more accurately the documents and records attached to them—have traveled along bureaucratic conveyor belts.

It is certainly true that the work has generally become more standardized, automated, and divided in recent years, but the welfare assembly line is not new or something to soon be completed. It is already here and shows no sign of disappearing—especially as managers struggle to square rising client numbers with a relatively stagnant staffing budget. A more accurate—but perhaps not as catchy—slogan would be "Social Services *should NOT be* an Assembly Line!"

There are two major sublines in the Los Angeles welfare factory: a large one for servicing benefit "customers" and a much smaller one for servicing welfare-to-work "participants." The former positions units of "eligibility workers" on crisscrossing conveyor belts where they test and retest the means of those seeking food stamps, health insurance, and cash assistance. This is a true "people-processing" assembly line focused on quickly and accurately determining eligibility for aid. More than six thousand eligibility workers and roughly one thousand supervisors are stationed here.[35] The latter positions units of welfare-to-work (WTW) workers in a slower and shorter network of conveyor belts for promoting and policing employment-focused activities. This is, at least officially, a "people-changing" line focused on generating client self-sufficiency; but, in practice, it is mostly a "people-processing" line that runs at a slower speed with less automation and specialization. Only about one thousand DPSS employees and just a couple hundred supervisors are stationed here.[36] On both lines, workers find themselves toiling away at an endless stream of specialized tasks and cases.[37]

This does not mean the workers in this book are doing the same kind of labor as those in a Ford plant or a McDonald's restaurant. As frontline public servants, the practical component of their labor process involves distinct materials that yield unique ethical concerns. The relational component of their work, which includes decidedly different consumers and managers, is also unique.

But welfare workers' limited autonomy in production makes them more like assembly-line laborers than the "discretionary" actors generally assumed in the scholarship on frontline public administration.[38] Welfare workers in Los Angeles and beyond may be frontline workers who materialize policy at the street level. However, the front lines in this case take the form of assembly lines. They work less in a so-called street-level bureaucracy and more in a policy factory.

Under these conditions, welfare workers in Los Angeles have been increasingly stretched thin. In the 1970s, DPSS employed about the same number of people as it does currently, roughly fourteen thousand.[39] Yet it had far fewer cases, around a million in comparison to roughly four times that number today.[40] Advancements in the welfare assembly line, namely its machinery and the manner in which it organizes a division of labor, has made district office workers more productive. The relatively small expansion of welfare-to-work programming also helped stretch welfare workers across a regime of not only workfare but also what we might characterize as medfare, schoolfare, and housefare. Much of their job has them connecting clients to a range of not only job training programs but also things like medical screenings, GED courses, and domestic violence services. This, too, is made possible through an assembly line of specialized workers focused on efficiently matching recipients to a range of services in a fragmented safety net. Finally, welfare workers have been stretched over the bottom of the bureaucratic pyramid in larger units and under fewer supervisors. This does not mean that direct managerial power has declined but rather that it has become more automatic and efficient, as occurs with essentially all assembly lines.

But rather than finding it totally alienating and monotonous, many of those who grind on the welfare assembly line also recognize some of its efficiencies and continue to find meaning in aiding the poor. Indeed, the stretching just mentioned has amplified contradictions not only in the materialization of welfare policy but also in the labor process. First, a growing client-to-worker ratio results in these workers being increasingly connected to but also disconnected from those they aid. They are, in other words, connected to more people through phones, online applications, and the like, but at the cost of less intimate relations. Second, in being stretched across the safety net, these workers help sustain a wide but largely weak network of assistance. They distribute small amounts of aid to a lot of people.

Finally, under the direct pressures of management to increase labor productivity, workers are more efficient yet more estranged. Like Los Angeles more generally, the welfare assembly line is a site of intense contradiction.

Means Testers and Program Brokers

The Welfare Assembly Line is a theory-driven case study of welfare work in Los Angeles, California. I draw on a range of data. I first completed ethnographic fieldwork across five DPSS offices in which I shadowed forty-six workers in their cubicles. The access I obtained within these spaces was rare and incredibly valuable. But it was also limited. Despite my pleas otherwise, DPSS administrators only allowed me to shadow workers during a six-month period in late 2021 and early 2022. I wasn't given a clear reason for my severed access, but I suspect it was due to concerns that my observations were distracting workers and slowing the assembly line down.

Heartbroken, I turned to the archives. I dug through all the publicly available boxes of files that seemed relevant for a study of the frontline labor process since the department's emergence from another bureau in 1966. This brought me into libraries and museums across Los Angeles, Pasadena, Northridge, Sacramento, and even Detroit, as I examined not only internal documents from DPSS but also reports, memos, and more for the elected officials, higher-level bureaucrats, union organizers, and civil society actors who attempted to shape frontline welfare work in Los Angeles.

Then, after realizing that neither the fieldwork nor the archives would yield sufficient insight into the subjective experiences of workers, I conducted eighty-seven in-depth interviews with sixty current and former welfare workers in 2023 and 2024. These conversations provided much-needed insights into the motivations and justifications of frontline workers and helped fill many gaps in my understanding of the labor process. The point was not to survey this nonrandom sample but to a) better understand processes identified in the fieldwork and archives and b) better account for the perceptions (rather than just the practices) of workers. Combined, the interview and observation samples include 106 individuals.

Finally, I relied on an assortment of supplemental materials. I conducted fieldwork at two major California welfare management conferences in 2023 and 2024, during which I attended a variety of presentations and workshops. I reviewed additional archival material including relevant news articles, Board of Supervisors meeting transcripts, and internal DPSS documents obtained through California Public Records Act requests. Beyond the formally conducted interviews, I also held dozens of informal conversations with workers, managers, vendors, and other actors who played important roles in the organization of the welfare office labor process. Additional details on method are provided in the appendix.

The Welfare Assembly Line focuses primarily on two kinds of frontline workers at DPSS, eligibility workers and WTW workers (table 1). The former work in district offices and call centers and they tend to test and retest clients' eligibility for a range of benefits. The latter work in the welfare-to-work offices and act less as means testers and more as program brokers. This much smaller group of workers are charged, at least on paper, with fostering self-sufficient clients, and they do this through referrals to job trainings, GED classes, mental health treatments, domestic violence counseling, and more. Again, eligibility workers are focused more on people-processing interventions, while WTW workers are focused more on people-changing ones. The former now work under a taskwork regime, while the latter continue to labor in a more traditional casework system. Where eligibility workers confront clients generally framed as "customers," the WTW workers confront clients generally framed as "participants."[41] Eligibility workers are more proletarianized than the WTW

TABLE 1 Means testers and program brokers

	Eligibility workers	WTW workers
Focus	People processing	People changing
Organization	Taskwork	Casework
Client type	Customer	Participant
Official definition[a]	"Makes initial and continuing eligibility determinations for grants and public assistance programs' applicants and participants"	"Develop and monitor individualized employment plans for (welfare-to-work) program participants and identifies and provides support services to (welfare-to-work) participants"

[a]Definitions from DPSS job advertisements posted on GovernmentJobs.com in 2020 (GAIN Services Worker) and 2024 (Eligibility Worker II).

workers, but both work under high levels of specialization, standardization, and automation. Both, in other words, are subject to a kind of assembly-line production.

I examine these workers and their labor processes across six chapters. Chapter 1 offers a quick tour of frontline welfare operations in contemporary Los Angeles, showcasing both eligibility workers and WTW workers in the agency. The differences between these two groups are important, but the similarities are arguably more interesting. Both lack significant autonomy in the labor process—which is not to say they have no autonomy whatsoever. Rather than finding so-called street-level bureaucrats exercising wide, substantive discretion over policy implementation, we find mostly screen-level bureaucrats toiling away as means testers and program brokers. Their work is not completely void of creativity or agency, but much of it is standardized and coupled with automation. This justifies a theoretical reconstruction of frontline welfare workers as *proletarianized public servants* characterized by the narrow and superficial discretion they exercise during the labor process.

As chapter 2 makes clear, however, proletarianization does not beget total misery. Many of the workers I met, even the veteran ones who experienced significant declines in their autonomy during their tenure, were generally grateful to hold a "good county job." I show how welfare work in Los Angeles tends to come with relatively high material and moral value in a labor market increasingly filled with insecure and meaningless jobs. Getting a county job in Los Angeles is desirable in large part because of its Fordist-like security in a post-Fordist economy. But, where Fordism did not necessarily come with a sense of civic or public duty, good county jobs often do, and this can add to the benefits of the work. I argue that proletarianization in the welfare office has eroded the material and moral goodness of the occupation. Nonetheless, county welfare work is still largely seen by employees as good, and to a large extent this explains why workers remain committed to their jobs.

Chapters 3 and 4 more deeply examine eligibility work and WTW work respectively. Together, these chapters illustrate how a double market logic has shaped two major sublines in the welfare factory: one focused on increasing convenience for benefit "customers," who are handled by eligibility workers, and another focused on promoting employability among the "participants" handled by WTW workers. Both logics motivate managers to squeeze more productivity out of their workers. Administrators, who face their own resource constraints and legal pressures, stretch frontline work by advancing a division of labor and introducing more machinery into the productive process. In addition to showing how standardization, automation, and specialization shape these jobs, I illustrate how workers nonetheless find meaning and purpose in their work. Indeed, I am careful not to exaggerate the noir of the welfare assembly line. While stretched thin, many of these workers still articulate the sunshine of their good county jobs.

The next two chapters compare the sublines for eligibility workers and WTW workers on some key themes beyond people processing and people changing. Chapter 5 directs our attention toward exercises of disciplinary power, a key component of both welfare administration and assembly-line production. The eligibility workers tend to be subject to more explicit techniques of disciplinary power than the WTW workers, but the latter tend to expose their subjects to more disciplinary techniques than the former. This helps motivate my distinction between "administrative discipline" (more common on people-processing assembly lines) and "paternalistic discipline" (more common on people-changing assembly lines). This variable responsibilization of workers and clients also helps contextualize narrow and superficial discretion among proletarianized public servants in the suffering city.

Chapter 6 focuses specifically on how workers across these bureaucratic conveyor belts are variably connected to and disconnected from their clients. Where the people-processing activities that are more common in eligibility work tend to fuel worker-client disconnections, the people-changing efforts that feature more regularly in WTW work tend to foster worker-client connections. Both eligibility and WTW work nonetheless involve a mixture of connective and disconnective relations and these shape narrow and superficial discretion in important ways.

This book ends with a short concluding chapter that considers the theoretical implications of this study as well as how we might reimagine welfare offices. Rather than envision a world without these spaces, we should strive toward one where conditions are better for both clients and workers. Critical to this should be an effort to appropriate, rather than abolish, the welfare assembly line. Finding ways to give workers and clients more control over the frontline provision of welfare should be essential.

1   *The Policy Factory*

"Welcome to South Central!" Deputy Diaz greeted me with a chipper tone as I entered a welfare office in Watts. I made my way in through the employee doors in the back of the austere brick structure, on the side opposite the front lobby. I snuck into the gated parking lot by rudely tailgating a worker who opened the gate for themselves.

This was not my first time in a welfare office. I spent many hours in just such a space in Spokane, Washington, when I was a young kid. I remember goofing around in the lobby with other children. I also remember my mom crying in a cubicle. Mostly though, I remember being bored out of my mind. Then, shortly after I graduated college, my wife and I entered a welfare office in Portland, Oregon, to submit an application for food stamps. We ended up qualifying for six months of assistance—but only after a caseworker sent me on an embarrassing errand. I had to get the professor I was working for at the time to sign some paperwork "proving" that I met a twenty-hour-a-week employment requirement. A few years later, I found myself in welfare offices in Oakland, California, on two separate occasions: first to help my wife enroll in "pregnancy-only" health insurance and then to keep our children covered during my final years of graduate school. While such a pernicious label is not typically imposed on white men like me, I guess you could say I was one link in an intergenerational chain of "welfare dependency."

Still, I had never entered a welfare office from the back. I was nervous and felt particularly out of place. Luckily, Deputy Diaz was expecting me. Someone from headquarters notified her earlier in the week that I, "a professor," was coming to shadow frontline workers.

I had come to study "street-level bureaucrats," a label political scientist Michael Lipsky used to describe the frontline executants of public policy.[1] His 1980 book *Street-Level Bureaucracy* had become a personal favorite of mine.[2] In it, Lipsky argued that a range of frontline workers—including teachers, cops, physicians, and welfare caseworkers—"make policy" through their direct relations with the subjects beneath them and the managers above them.

Far from being simple cogs in bureaucratic machines, Lipsky argued that these kinds of workers exercise "wide discretion in decisions about [the] citizens with whom they interact."[3] Street-level bureaucrats, he insisted, make important, if significantly constrained, decisions. As he put it, "street-level bureaucrats have considerable discretion in determining the nature, amount, and quality of benefits and sanctions provided by their agencies."[4] Speaking specifically of welfare agencies, Lipsky noted, "While eligibility for public service benefits often may seem cut-and-dried, a considerable part of eligibility is in fact problematic. Rules and regulations provide only a measure of guidance in determining eligibility."[5] Frontline worker discretion, he insisted, is essential even when street-level bureaucracies rely on standardization and automation. On this point Lipsky was especially clear: "The fact is that we *must* have people making decisions and treating other citizens in the public services. We are not prepared as a society to abandon decisions about people and discretionary intervention to machines and programmed formats."[6]

Lipsky did not argue that street-level bureaucrats have *total* agency in the frontline production of policy. He acknowledged that factors such as funding, protocols, and client demands both enable and constrain policy administration in important ways. From political assaults on welfare systems to shifting cultural narratives of poverty in America, he recognized that street-level bureaucrats and the agencies they worked within were significantly shaped by external forces.[7]

But Lipsky was nonetheless insistent that we cannot understand policies and programs like cash aid and food stamps without considering the "relative autonomy" of street-level bureaucrats.[8] It is their discretionary actions which "add up" to policy.[9] Speaking of frontline welfare workers in particular, Lipsky noted that they "may exercise discretion in determining client access to benefits, even though their discretion is *formally* circumscribed by rules and relatively close supervision."[10]

I spared Deputy Diaz many of these details, not because I wanted to be deceptive but because I did not want to bore or annoy her. I simply told her that it was not enough for me to study how welfare policy is conceived by lawmakers and protocol writers. I also needed to see how welfare is *worked* at street-level.

Taskwork in the District Offices

The deputy assured me I had come to the right place. The South Central District Office—one of the busiest in DPSS—was exactly where I needed to be to gain these insights. I also came to the right person. Ms. Diaz explained that, as a deputy, she oversees multiple units of eligibility workers, each led by supervisors who report to her directly. These are the mostly hidden workers who determine who qualifies for programs like CalWORKs (cash aid for families with children), CalFresh (food stamps), Medi-Cal (Medicaid), and General Relief (cash aid typically for individuals or couples without children). My nervousness soon morphed into excitement.

Ms. Diaz kindly escorted me to where I could best see the labor of eligibility determination in action. I assumed we would walk straight to the front of the building—*toward the street*. Surely, I thought, the lobby and its proximate booths and desks must be where we would find most of these workers making policy.

To my surprise, Ms. Diaz took me up an elevator to a floor where clients are forbidden. We walked down a hall past multiple rooms packed with cubicles before eventually turning into one of these rooms. Inside, I counted nearly two dozen cubicles, each dually illuminated by fluorescent light bulbs and the California sun peeking through some small windows. Only about half of the cubicles were occupied at the time. Ms. Diaz explained that a few workers had been assigned lobby duty downstairs and a few more were working remotely from home. It was nonetheless in cubicles like these that Ms. Diaz assured me I could best see welfare work.

In these cubicles, I found not the street-level bureaucrats of Lipsky's original conceptualization but, if anything, *screen-level bureaucrats*.[11] The workers—all brown and Black women in this particular room on this particular day—spent most of their time doing data entry on their computers to determine who was eligible for aid and at what specific amounts. They certainly interacted with those on welfare, but they mostly did so from a distance. The front lines primarily took the form of *phone lines*. Indeed, this place reminded me more of a call center than a welfare office.

A few days later, I sat with Cassandra, a twenty-five-year-old Black woman, in one of these cubicles as she processed a series of benefit redeterminations for CalWORKs, the state's cash assistance program for poor parents with minor children. Not once in her shift did Cassandra meet a client in person. Instead, she spoke to dozens over the phone through a headset, which freed her hands to click through drop-down menus and tab through windows on her computer at furious speeds.

For most of the time I spent with her, Cassandra responded to calls distributed to her by an automated phone tree. In one of these calls, a CalWORKs recipient phoned to confirm receipt of some paperwork she submitted online. Cassandra pulled the woman's file on her computer, browsed some photos of paystubs and bank statements, and assured her the documents in question had been received. She told the woman another worker would process the material at another time, ended the call, typed a short comment in the case notes, and quickly readied herself for the next call by clicking a button indicating her availability on the line.

I then watched as she handled another call, this time for a CalWORKs recipient who had received an automatic text message notifying her to call DPSS to redetermine her eligibility for the program. Cassandra asked a battery of standardized questions guided by the digital worksheet on her computer: "Anyone in the house born outside the US?" "Are children between sixteen to eighteen attending school regularly?" "Anyone recently lose their job or get reduced hours?" "Anyone in violation of probation or parole?" "Do you receive child support?" "Do you own any vehicles?" I couldn't hear the woman's answers on the other end of the line due to the headset, but I could see the responses Cassandra was logging on her computer.

After putting the client on a brief hold and reviewing the documents she recently submitted through the department's mobile app, Cassandra determined that the woman must submit a vehicle registration (to assess whether the value exceeds a resource limit) as well as some updated paystubs for her adult son and daughter who live in the house. As it turned out, the woman *had* submitted said paystubs, both from large corporate retail companies, but unfortunately they were for the wrong month. The "system," as Cassandra would later put it to me, prevented her from further processing the redetermination. "You have ten days from today to do this [submit documents]," she told the woman. "If you don't, your case will terminate. . . . If the case terminates, you'll have to reapply." Before ending the conversation, Cassandra collected a telephonic signature from the woman by reading a short script and asking her to state her full name and the last four digits of her social security number.

When the call concluded, Cassandra again updated the case notes on her computer and then quickly readied herself for another call. I was enthralled. "You work so fast," I said. "Thank you," responded Cassandra with a proud smile. She explained that an accelerated pace makes the time go faster.

I wondered where the discretion was in this process. Perhaps I was just too mesmerized to see it. But, as I would soon conclude by closely shadowing more workers in this office and others like them at district offices in West Lake in the center of Los Angeles and in El Monte in the San Gabriel Valley, there simply was not much discretion to be found. Eligibility workers were not entirely without autonomy. Cassandra's pacing, for example, was to some significant degree within her control. But they did not exercise nearly as much discretion as Lipsky assumed the frontline workers in his analysis did. In fact, what struck me as immediately surprising was how *little* autonomy they exercised in "determining the nature, amount, and quality of benefits and sanctions."[12]

I watched as eligibility workers like Cassandra tested their subjects' means by drawing on information obtained from scripted interviews, rigidly constructed forms, and formalized record systems. This work is not without significant skill. As they would explain to me, it takes months if not years of practice to feel a strong sense of competency in the cubicles. This is work that requires critical thinking and is no doubt mentally exhausting.

But it is also tedious. These workers spend *most* of their time feeding both subjective data (e.g., client self-reported family status) and objective data (e.g., paystubs) into the California Statewide

Automated Welfare System (CalSAWS) on their computers. They push and pull a series of computerized levers to determine if their clients qualify for benefits. They work in what political scientist Virginia Eubanks calls the "digital poorhouse," a modern regime of poverty governance made of automated eligibility determination systems, massive databases, and other technologies for sorting out who is (and is not) deemed worthy of assistance.[13]

Contrary to Lipsky's expectations, there is not much liberty in determining the quantity or quality of public assistance when these workers plug highly specific forms of information into their computers. Once the data is entered, they click a button to run an "eligibility determination benefit calculation." That button "spit outs," as one worker explained, a precise answer as to what benefits a client is entitled to. And, if this was not enough to have me questioning everything I thought I knew about frontline policy work, I watched as the vast majority of these eligibility workers submitted these semiautomatically calculated determinations to their unit supervisors for review and authorization. If worker autonomy is relative, as Lipsky insists, then in this case it was relatively low.

These workers are more policy materializers than policymakers.[14] As one DPSS administrator put it, these workers are tasked with "enforcing" and "adhering to" to policy.[15] Still, it was clear to me that their work was essential. Without them aid would not be distributed or denied, and policy would only exist on paper. Their productive acts, whether in line with or in deviation from written protocol, are what essentially "add up" to welfare policy in the district offices. And, like essentially all workers, they nonetheless have *some* autonomy in the labor process—that is, the manner in which their work is carried out. The eligibility workers who so kindly allowed me to observe and interview them for this book may not approximate the archetypal street-level bureaucrat, but they were not simply appendages of machines.[16]

I would come to learn that their discretion is more narrow than it is wide and more superficial than substantive. Sure, they cannot personally decide who gets aid, but they can find little ways to "work with" those they find especially deserving of extra attention and assistance. They can take what sociologist Robin Bartram calls "stabs at justice," albeit in limited and mostly shallow ways.[17] On the flipside, they can "nitpick" those they find undeserving—namely, those they see as ungrateful, deceptive, negligent, dependent, or lazy. They also develop creative ways to handle a seemingly infinite wave of clientele and mitigate the managerial pressures to hustle through the day's tasks.

I use the word *tasks* very intentionally. You might assume, as I did, that those laboring in Deputy Diaz's units are caseworkers, workers with assigned clients whose cases they work over time. But they're not. Sure, they work on cases—documented records of individuals and families—but they do not hold caseloads. As noted in the introduction, management at DPSS ditched the traditional caseload regime typical in welfare bureaucracies and replaced it with a more flexible task-based regime for essentially all eligibility workers in 2021. It was an idea they had flirted with for more than fifty years as they simultaneously advanced the division of labor and introduced more machinery into the welfare shopfloor. Now, rather than attach workers to cases, management splits cases into lots of little tasks that can then be assigned to different workers depending on need.

This meant that instead of watching as eligibility workers struggled to stay on top of their caseloads, I watched as they worked an endless stream of tasks: interview client A, verify paperwork for client B, process online application for client C. Meanwhile, each case was being worked on by multiple workers. As organizers for the Services Employee International Union (SEIU) Local 721, the union covering these workers, put it, this kind of regime organizes welfare services as "an assembly line."[18]

Casework in the Welfare-to-Work Offices

I wondered if things would be different in the county's so-called welfare-to-work offices. District offices like the ones I studied in Watts, West Lake, and El Monte more closely approximate what social welfare scholar Yeheskel Hasenfeld calls "people-processing organizations."[19] The manifest function of these spaces is to churn through applicants to determine who does and does not officially qualify for various forms of public benefits. The much smaller welfare-to-work offices, in contrast, are at least ostensibly designed to be "people-changing organizations."[20] The official objective in these spaces is to transform cash aid recipients into "self-sufficient" worker-citizens. While research suggests such efforts do little to challenge poverty, they do seem to increase employability in low-wage and highly precarious forms of work and fuel an overall thinning of the client list.[21] Certainly, I reasoned, the work must be different in these spaces.

A couple months later, I entered a GAIN office in an industrial neighborhood just south of Compton to observe workers materializing a different kind of policy. GAIN is a cute, clever, or cheesy acronym—depending on who you ask—for "Greater Avenues for Independence." This is a program generally mandated for all so-called able-bodied parents on CalWORKs. GAIN is the Los Angeles County Government's effort to fulfill a state and federally imposed duty to promote employability and discourage welfare use.

I shadowed GAIN services workers like Isabel, a thirty-year-old Latina woman. Unlike the eligibility workers in the district office, she possessed a caseload of clients. Her job was to promote and police client participation with welfare-to-work contracts, ancillary aid, and sanctions for noncompliance—although, due to the COVID-19 pandemic, sanctions were paused at the time. "Are you looking forward to the sanctions returning?" I asked while sitting in her cubicle. "Yes and no," she said. "Some clearly need [negative] incentives."

Even so, Isabel had more than enough work to keep her busy. I watched as she worked her caseload. She asked her clients a series of questions not only about their work histories but also their health, housing, education, and more to gauge their "employment barriers." This was done to determine what kinds of program-approved activities, resources, and exemptions would be most appropriate in order for clients to remain compliant with state and federal rules for parents receiving means-tested cash assistance. I watched as she linked a handful of GAIN participants to program-approved activities like a four-week job club. "They help with resume, job search, and booking interviews," Isabel said over the phone to one of her clients who was about to enroll in the job club run by a third-party nonprofit. "It's a good program. They'll help you succeed." I also watched as she provided funds for a laptop to one client (to enable remote participation in job club), a bus pass to another (to enable transportation to work), and even some funds for a work uniform to one who just secured a new job.

WTW workers like Isabel are focused on making *workfare*. They also assemble some supplemental policies that might best be labeled *schoolfare*, *medfare*, and *housefare*. Thus, in addition to things like job club, WTW workers in the GAIN program frequently refer their subjects to GED programs, mental health treatments, domestic violence counseling, and other activities. By and large, such referrals come with explicit mandates that clients learn, heal, and stabilize for the sake of becoming employable. WTW workers incentivize their subjects with both carrots and sticks. They issue bits and pieces of "ancillary" assistance in the form of money and vouchers for gas, textbooks, daycare, rent, clothing, and more to enable compliance across activities of workfare, schoolfare, medfare, and housefare. And, under non-pandemic times, they impose "sanctions," or more typically, the explicit threat of sanctions, to promote participation in these activities.

The work in this GAIN office, as well as in another one I observed to the east, in Monterey Park, was certainly different from what I encountered in the district offices. I also shadowed WTW workers in the county's smaller START (Skills and Training to Achieve Readiness for Tomorrow) program, which is a mandatory workfare initiative for General Relief recipients.[22] It was in these smaller and more specialized spaces that I found caseworkers. In contrast to the taskworkers in the district offices, the vast majority of GAIN and START workers possessed their own caseloads—usually around two hundred per GAIN worker and 550 per START worker. All the WTW workers I shadowed were former eligibility workers, and each of them described their current relations with clients as more "intensive." This work necessitated deeper connections with subjects and more autonomy from management.

These differences were all relative though. I still struggled to find the highly discretionary frontline policymakers described by Lipsky. The WTW workers shared a lot of similarities with their eligibility worker counterparts. Like Cassandra, Isabel was mostly relegated to doing work over the computer and telephone. The GAIN and START workers were more program brokers than means testers, which came with more discretion, but this was still a far cry from the kind of breadth of autonomy assumed in street-level bureaucracy theory. And while it became clear to me that the GAIN and START WTW workers were micromanaged less than the eligibility workers, they still materialized policy through a fairly narrow discretionary field. They also worked with highly standardized tools and procedures and were closely supervised by management. Such standardization and surveillance are not as intense for the WTW workers as they are for the eligibility workers, but they curb discretion in similar ways.

Indeed, while Isabel possesses a caseload and is tasked with "getting to know" her clients in a deeper way than Cassandra, much of her job at GAIN still involves her pushing and pulling digital levers in

CalSAWS. Rather than work on screens for determining eligibility, Isabel mostly works on screens for monitoring and incentivizing her clients' activities for the welfare-to-work program. But the job is still heavily standardized. Written policies and protocols largely determine which specific questions she asks her clients and which sanctions she gives in response. The job is also very specialized. As a "general flow" and "approval side" GAIN worker, Isabel is stationed on a complex welfare-to-work production line separating intake and approval sequences on the one hand and levels of intensive intervention on the other (e.g., general flow units, specialized supportive services units, and family stabilization units, each involving higher levels of case management). And like her counterparts in the district offices, she is expected to quickly churn through her assignments to stay on top of her workload.

As sociologist Celeste Watkins-Hayes argues in *The New Welfare Bureaucrats*, contemporary welfare work bends increasingly toward missions of "efficiency engineering."[23] This is true, she argues, not only for the content of the labor but also for the identities of workers. Even after President Bill Clinton and other champions of late twentieth-century welfare reforms attempted to mix more people-changing activities into the people-processing machinery of American welfare offices, workers are largely oriented to efficiently grind through cases and tasks. All are stationed, so to speak, on welfare assembly lines focused on a mass production of policy.[24]

Watkins-Hayes does not just offer an account of welfare workers after the 1990s welfare reforms. She pushes us to think of street-level bureaucrats in a new way. Her book is as much a theoretical update as it is a historical one, as it both complements and complicates Lipsky's *Street-Level Bureaucracy*. It maintains the core claim that policy is materialized at the street level, while pushing for a new theorization of discretionary action and worker disposition. Watkins-Hayes departs from Lipsky most explicitly by arguing that street-level bureaucrats must be more broadly "situated."[25] It is not enough, she argues, to account for the positioning of these workers inside their agencies. We must also locate them—along with their practices and perceptions—within the broader structures of capitalism, racism, and sexism. This focus on "situated bureaucrats" in turn motivates her analysis not only of racialized and gendered labor but also of different discretionary styles. The "efficiency engineer" identity was the strongest among the workers she studied in Massachusetts, but she also observed some street-level bureaucrats who adopted a kind of optimistic "social worker" orientation and others who adopted a more pessimistic "bureaucratic survivalists" orientation.[26] In broadening a focus on workers' social location while simultaneously deepening a focus on their identities, Watkins-Hayes reconstructed street-level bureaucracy theory for the better.[27]

That said, I wondered early in my fieldwork if I was examining something substantially different than what Watkins-Hayes had studied. Perhaps I was looking at even *newer* welfare bureaucrats. I struggled to find workers who I could cleanly classify as "efficiency engineers," "social workers," and "bureaucratic survivalists." To me these seemed more like contradictory dispositions that *all* the workers I was studying carried to various degrees—with the efficiency engineering orientation being dominant not only across but also within workers. Some circumstances may motivate employees to "work with clients" (loosely approximating the identity of social worker) and other circumstances may motivate workers to minimally invest in their work (loosely approximating the bureaucratic survivalist identity), but I found that the work of both means testing and program brokering directed welfare workers toward efficiency engineering regardless. I also wondered how her notion of *situated* bureaucrats could be updated to account for these workers' positioning on the welfare assembly line—a productive structure largely overshadowed in her account of identity.

Herein lies the beauty of *theory-driven case studies.*[28] I entered welfare offices with my favorite theories in mind. By *favorite*, I do not refer to personal taste but to analytic leaning. I started the research for this book with the works of Lipsky, Watkins-Hayes, and *many* more already in my head. Just as my lived experiences in welfare offices shaped my worldview and oriented my expectations, so too did my training in sociology. But my goal was never to simply reproduce or reject theory. I set out to reconstruct theory in light of my fieldwork—which I also combined with historical research, in-depth interviews, and more. All of this was done in effort to link the lived experiences of welfare workers in Los Angeles to larger structural forces in what C. Wright Mills famously called "the sociological imagination."[29]

Proletarianized Public Servants

So, there I was, in Los Angeles welfare offices, examining what I assumed would be a quintessential case of street-level bureaucracy. But I had to squint hard to see workers in the way this theory described. I started to seriously question the trademark concept of discretion and considered how these workers might best be characterized by their lack of control. I began to see them less as street-level bureaucrats and more as *proletarianized public servants.*

Here, proletarianization is broadly understood as the intensification of work as something "more routinized and degraded" and something involving "less autonomy" for the worker.[30] While the concept of proletarianization has traditionally been used to explain a conversion of various populations into wage laborers, I am more inspired by those who have used the concept to explain a general erosion in worker control over not only the products but also the *processes* of their labor.[31] As sociologist Martin Oppenheimer puts it, this erosion is typically marked by an extensive division of labor, high managerial power, and high levels of wage dependence among work-ers.[32] I argue that a theory of proletarianization offers more explana-tory power than a theory of street-level bureaucracy when trying to make sense of frontline work in contemporary public benefits bu-reaucracies like DPSS.

In light of my research, I depart from Lipsky with three critiques. First, his model exaggerated the significance of discretion at the time in which it emerged. When I dug into the archives to understand DPSS work in the 1970s, I found workers with more discretion than those I observed in 2021 and 2022, but I certainly did not find workers exercising the breadth of agency that classical street-level bureauc-racy theory assumes. Workers at the department I studied never re-ally had much substantive control over who was determined to be deserving or undeserving of benefits or sanctions, and such sorting has long been standardized in significant ways.[33] Second, street-level bureaucracy theory provided few insights into how worker autonomy might erode over time, but erosion was exactly what I was finding in my research. Not only was discretion narrower than one would as-sume, but it was also narrowing under direct pressure from manag-ers.[34] Third, discretionary action was not exclusively, let alone primarily, what was "adding up" to policy in my case. Rather it was the *labor process*, independent of discretion, that was materializing policy.

Indeed, this should be our starting point. The labor process is a core Marxist concept that has itself been extended to other theoreti-cal traditions.[35] Its broad appeal is rooted in its broad applicability. The labor process simply refers to how the capacity to work ("labor power") is converted into actual productive activity ("labor").[36] It is in this conversion that policy is materialized.

All labor processes are simultaneously *practical* and *relational*.[37] The practical component of the labor process refers to how workers utilize instruments of production to transform the world. With respect to welfare work, we can see this when eligibility workers use their computers to determine benefit amounts or when WTW workers write mandatory referrals to job clubs. Such transformations may be micro, momentary, and mundane, but they are transformations nonetheless. And they are made possible through the social relations of and in production—the relations that workers enter into during the productive process. For welfare workers, this means accounting not only for their relations with the clients beneath them but also for their relations with the other workers at their sides and with their managers above. Together, the practical and relational components of the labor process direct and channel the conversion of labor power into actual labor. Like all workers, those in welfare offices are simultaneously enabled and constrained by the material they encounter, the tools at their disposal, and their complex relations with others at the site of production.

As Watkins-Hayes argues, we must adequately "situate" these workers. It is not enough to locate frontline labor within their formal organizations. We must also locate them within a broader social space ordered by divisions in race, gender, and more if we hope to fully understand how they materialize policy. But I take this argument a step further and insist that we also situate these workers and their labor processes within a *mode of production*. While rarely framed as such, frontline public servants tend to labor under capitalism.

To be clear, said workers may not contribute to the accumulation of capital. They may not even obviously supplement this accumulation by supplying private firms with low-wage labor via workfare programs like GAIN and START. Indeed, their work might contradict capital accumulation in important ways. But all public bureaucracies under democratic capitalist nations are, and have always been, rooted to an essential feature of capitalism: the commodification of labor power.

Be they teachers in a local school district, correctional officers at a state-run prison, social workers at a publicly contracted nonprofit organization, or nurses at a for-profit health care clinic, essentially all public and quasi-public servants sell their labor power to employers in order to live. These employers, in turn, organize the policy shop-floor to translate that labor power into productive activity. Whether motivated by the pursuit of profit, fiscal responsibility, public accountability, expressions of organizational legitimacy, or some other objective, these employers generally try to increase the amount of labor effort they extract from their employees. And, as noted in the introduction, this is especially true for those administrators that confront the contradictory pressures of budget austerity and legal demand.[38]

We must certainly be careful not to conflate the organizational logics of private firms and public administration. But it is generally the case that, through a wave of market-oriented reforms, public service bureaucracies in the West have become *more capitalistic* in the past fifty or so years.[39] Such operations have become increasingly privatized, and more administrators are drawing clear inspiration from the private sector, labeling these efforts "new public management."[40]

Examining public services as a labor process does not mean we have to fall into a pit of class reductionism. Welfare work, as we already know, is also deeply gendered and racialized. This labor has long been doubly feminized as a kind of care work on the one hand a kind of clerical work on the other. Such jobs, as Watkins-Hayes demonstrates, have also been increasingly occupied by Black and brown women.[41] This has correlated not only with the expansion of affirmative action initiatives and calls from welfare rights activists to diversify the department but also increased labor standardization and surveillance.[42] A focus on the labor process can help us better understand the gendered and racialized dynamics of welfare offices because such an approach pushes us to examine the complex social relations that enable and constrain frontline public services.

A focus on the labor process also does not mean we need to flounder in the internal dynamics of the shopfloor. Studying the relational component of the labor process necessitates a consideration of external forces. Situating frontline workers within structures of capitalism, racism, and sexism is part of this. So too is accounting for struggles over policy as written, for these *political relations* shape but do not overdetermine *productive relations* on the frontlines.[43] Put another way, the conception of policy shapes the execution of policy, and many such conceptions transcend the immediate authority of management. The "state," as sociologist Lynne Haney puts it, is a "layered entity, comprised of multiple and even conflicting apparatuses" and is best understood as a "composite of subsystems that can be in sync or at odds with one another."[44] Administrators like Deputy Diaz do not set the income limits for aid programs; nor do they have much say in how most basic procedures should be followed on the front lines. A series of guidelines, often generated in complex political struggles that not only involve state officials but also social scientists, journalists, activists, and more, orient both workers on the front lines and their managers.

In treating the frontline production of policy as a labor process, we are well positioned to see welfare workers in Los Angeles as *proletarianized public servants*. Indeed, this is a more accurate conceptualization of the kinds of work I encountered in DPSS offices. I met workers defined less by their autonomy and more by their overall lack of influence over the products and processes of their work. Where a theory of street-level bureaucrats assumes discretion, a theory of proletarianized public servants assumes a lack of worker control. But just as Lipsky does not claim that workers have total discretion, I am not arguing that workers have zero control.[45] The differences between the two frameworks are important but relative. They are best thought of as points on a continuum.

TABLE 2 Two poles of frontline policy work

	Street-level bureaucrats	Proletarianized public servants
Quantitative discretion	Wide	Narrow
Qualitative discretion	Substantive	Superficial

Table 2 summarizes some key differences between street-level bureaucrats and proletarianized public servants. The primary distinctions rest with that all important concept of discretion—and more specifically a discretion in and over the labor process. We can distinguish this in quantitative terms (i.e., how much discretion) and qualitative terms (i.e., what kind of discretion). Where street-level bureaucrats exercise wide discretion over substantive distributions of benefits and sanctions, proletarianized public servants exercise a narrow discretion over more superficial matters. Worker autonomy, under the latter, concerns seemingly more trivial issues like pacing and interaction techniques. But together with standardized action, such discretionary conduct "adds up" to policy. Indeed, I assume all workers have some significant agency in the labor process but that their agency varies depending on the practical and relational components of that process.

In Los Angeles welfare offices, where managers are legally required to facilitate a mass production of aid with limited resources for administration, the general strategy has been to proletarianize labor on the front lines. Stretching the productive capacity of workers along a welfare assembly line has been central to those efforts.

In sum, welfare workers in the suffering city find themselves not so much in a street-level bureaucracy as on the shop floor of a *policy factory*. Before digging into the labor processes linked to its assembly line, the next chapter highlights another surprise. Why, considering the proletarianized conditions of their work, do so many workers generally see their jobs as "good"?

2   *The Good County Job*

In addition to shadowing welfare workers in their cubicles, I spoke with dozens over the phone.[1] Many of those who were actively working for DPSS at the time called me on their lunch breaks or shortly after they clocked out of work for the night. Several phoned from their cars as they slowly crawled through rush hour traffic. A few even spoke to me as they played with their kids or went grocery shopping after a long day. Talking to the "researcher guy" was something that could be easily folded into their personal tasks after a shift.

This was, in my view, a great time to chat with these women and men about work. They would often apologize for "venting" about their days, and I would, in turn, assure them I was very interested in their frustrations. Almost all of them complained about opaque procedures, cumbersome software, and micromanagement. "It's being under control," Elizabeth, a forty-five-year-old white eligibility worker explained to me during one of her long commutes home. "[Managers] are counting every minute, every second you are working. . . . It's frustrating." Several also complained of impatient, hostile, and sometimes even violent clients. "He told me, 'You're just a stupid, ignorant n-word,'" said Amber, a forty-two-year-old Black eligibility worker, recalling a recent encounter she had on the phone with a CalFresh recipient. She continued, "It's usually the ones that, and I hate to say it—it's the meth heads."

Yet despite their *many* complaints, the majority of the workers I spoke to told me they were generally grateful to hold a "good job." Tre, a forty-five-year-old Black eligibility worker, described his occupation in this way: "I just think the stability of it all. I feel like the benefits, I mean, we have some of the best medical and dental benefits. I feel like that alone makes it a good job, and then it's rewarding. It's like you're giving back, you're helping people." This was a persistent theme in the interviews, as well as in the conversations I held with workers in the field. For those I met, working at DPSS was generally seen as "good," firstly because of its material value and secondly because of its moral value.

Consider the material benefits. With eligibility workers making around $59,000 a year and WTW workers making around $64,000 a year, the earnings are modest in a county where the median household income is $83,000.[2] But the benefits (especially the retirement and the health and dental for dependents), schedule (Monday through Friday with increased opportunities for remote work), and job security (termination and layoffs are rare) help make the job relatively desirable in a labor market loaded with "bad jobs."[3]

For many Black and brown Angelenos in particular, government agencies like DPSS have provided key avenues for secure employment. As sociologist Orly Clergé notes, the "good government job" has been critical to expanding opportunities for upward mobility for many US-born racial minorities, but especially African Americans.[4] Indeed, DPSS has disproportionately employed Black labor since the late 1960s.[5] And while the department had initially hired relatively low numbers of Latino workers, affirmative action initiatives helped alleviate this throughout the succeeding decades.[6] Today, well over half of the DPSS payroll are either Latino (46 percent, roughly the same share as the county population) or Black (18 percent, about double the county rate).[7] That is generally consistent with county government jobs overall, but DPSS employs a higher percentage of women—77 percent compared 60 percent across the county.[8] At least on the labor side of the desk, the welfare cubicle does appear to increase security for groups historically marginalized in the labor market.

But it is not just material security that makes a DPSS job good. Most of the workers who spoke to me also emphasized, like Tre did, the *moral* value of their work. Even though it is common to question the legitimacy of clients' poverty and suffering, many workers told me it "felt good" to link people to various forms of aid. And while I was initially skeptical of these comments, thinking they were "just talk," I came to understand the overall sentiment to be authentic. I also came to learn that the moral value of the work came from more than just aiding those who were seen as worthy. The welfare office is a place to do "good work" even when the "good clients" are absent or distant. From salvaging some virtue in their increasingly depersonalized encounters with clients to realizing a particular dignity in executing routine bureaucratic procedures, welfare work is understood by many to be "more than just a job."

Faith, a thirty-four-year-old Black eligibility worker, is especially happy to hold a "good county job." While she complained of excessive supervisors from above and impudent clients from below, these downsides of the job were largely outweighed by the upsides. When I asked why she initially applied to DPSS three years earlier, she said, "Stability, the benefits, the longevity people get in the county and then they retire. That was my goal." And while the moral justifications were secondary to these material considerations, Faith was also quick to remind me that she finds meaning and purpose in helping people—or at least the "people that genuinely need it." Faith described her interactions with clients—be it over the phone or in person—as mostly "chill" and quite often "pleasant." She regrets that the kind of aid she distributes is so small, but she takes pride in knowing she provides significant support to her clients. "I really enjoy what I do," she told me. "When I wake up in the morning, I just pray that God use me and let me help somebody that really needs it." And, like several of the workers I spoke to, Faith explained that she also took pride in doing good paperwork, keeping a good pace, and being an overall "good employee."

This chapter examines the "goodness" of county welfare work. Those I met generally understood their work to be good relative to assumed and experienced alternatives in a labor market characterized by insecurity and inconsequence. This helps explain, among other things, why these workers tolerate much of the proletarianization detailed in the succeeding chapters.

Cubicle Dreamin'

No one really "falls into" welfare work. There are a number of hurdles to applying for a job at the county generally and DPSS specifically. Applicants must pass civil servant tests, and then they usually wait months until they get a call back. Resumes, references, and relatability are generally less important for landing a DPSS job than simply having patience.

But patience generally assumes a goal: a desirable, even if uncertain, reason to wait. For applicants who spend hours in the lobby, the goal is often to meet a worker in a cubicle for the purposes of starting, continuing, or increasing benefits. For those applying for a job at DPSS, the goal is also to access the cubicle, albeit as a paid employee.

Workers set their sights on DPSS employment for many reasons. Roughly half of those I spoke to were enticed by the job descriptions posted on GovernmentJobs.com and other hiring platforms. Several workers told me they were looking for any general BA-level county job and DPSS was hiring at that time. I was surprised that only a few of them told me they were explicitly looking to do human service work. I learned that many were casting a wider net beyond county employment and were drawn to the entry-level eligibility worker job postings because of its salary, hours, and benefits. It is reasonable to assume, then, that larger racialized and gendered divisions in labor explain why so many welfare workers are women of color. Some exogenous sorting effects, shaped not only by market conditions but also by the cultural meanings attached to clerical and caring occupations, likely explain who would be motivated to apply for welfare work after reading a job ad.

Yet, for every worker who told me they learned about the job through online ads, there seemed to be another one who identified alternative sources that motivated their pursuit of the cubicle. Many learned of the job through family or friends already or previously employed by the department. These contacts could not vouch for them in the formal application process since this was a highly centralized procedure out of reach of the offices where the frontline workers spend their time. They also did not seem to provide detailed tips to applicants on how to pass the pre-employment tests. Rather, the value of knowing someone in DPSS was much simpler. These network ties help aspiring employees learn that the job exists.

"My mom worked for the county," Talisa, a Black eligibility worker in her early thirties told me. "She kind of just encouraged [applying] and then that's how I ended up here." Andrea, a Latina worker around the same age, told me her mother was also an eligibility worker, and she accompanied her to work on a couple of occasions when she was a teenager. "It was really fun," she said describing a bring-your-child-to-work event, "[management] would show us around, they would ask us what we wanted to be when we grew up, and then for lunch they would take us out." This experience did not, in and of itself, inspire Andrea as a teenager to become an eligibility worker, but the memories did warm her up to the idea when she was looking for employment after graduating from California State University.

I also met a handful of workers who said they were at least partially inspired to seek employment at DPSS because they themselves had been clients—either as adults or as children. Pam, a white eligibility worker in her mid-fifties, had been raised by a single mother who was "on welfare back when they had actual paper food stamps." However, she first thought of applying for a DPSS job after she herself "had to go on welfare" in the county as a young parent. Likewise, Arsen, an Armenian man in his late thirties, was inspired to seek employment at the agency after having encountered it as a recipient shortly after he immigrated to the US. It was through these encounters that workers like Pam and Arsen first learned of the agency and witnessed snippets of the frontline labor process. I also met a handful of workers who told me they obtained employment at DPSS through their mandated participation in welfare-to-work programs.

Regardless of the motivation, once their sights were set on DPSS employment, these workers had to navigate a long and confusing processes to get hired. After submitting an application, they had to take an in-person test on reading comprehension, data interpretation, basic arithmetic, and other general topics. Then they waited. And waited.

One worker described this moment as "limbo," but Faith referenced something worse: "Working for the county is definitely rewarding. Once you're finally in, you're in, but getting in is, I don't want to compare it to hell, but it's a challenge." She was nonetheless confident the struggle, and above all the patience, would be worth it. Having been exposed to county bureaucracies during her time as a temp worker with a third-party staffing agency, she knew the county would be a good place to work. Faith was not interested in DPSS specifically; she wanted any county job because they're generally known to be good. Referencing another employer in Southern California known for its relatively good benefits, she told me, "I prayed for either the county or Kaiser [Permanente]."

Praying is understandable, especially when seeking a job at DPSS. There is no interview for an entry-level eligibility worker position, and no one from headquarters ever seems to call applicants' references. While knowing someone already employed at the agency can certainly help ease the nerves, there are no obvious ways a current employee can really help a friend or loved one get a job. There's no one for them to put in a good word to. And workers at street level have essentially no insight into who is making hiring decisions or when they do so. The best advice they can give to the applicant is to be patient. No insight or strategy will speed up the often three-to-four-month waiting period between the test and the potential job offer.

While in this hellish space, some turn to forums on Reddit to share information about application timeline, test scores, and words of encouragement. Reddit is also a place for current workers to communicate with aspiring ones—and therefore to temper expectations. "Department is stretched thin," posted one user. "If I knew the state of the job before working, I would never have accepted."[9] Another posted, "I'm a new [eligibility worker] and have been suffering," before detailing their struggles getting various medical accommodations.[10]

But much like my interviews with DPSS workers, many of the comments were optimistic. "Guys, there's going to be lots of work as an [eligibility worker]," posted one user. "Lots of work means job security though."[11] Responding to a question about the intensity of the work, the same user posted, "The benefits of working in DPSS/county outweighs the workload. You can also say the workload is heavy out there in the private industry. It's all relative." On another forum, a different user was even more buoyant. "I just want to say that being an [eligibility worker] has been one of the best decisions in my life."[12]

Landing a cubicle job at DPSS may not be anyone's lifelong dream. But there appears to be no shortage of people seeking employment at the department. Rather than see the cubicle as a nightmarish pit that sucks the souls out of workers, many dream of entering it because of its *relative* value.[13]

Relative Security

Marrying the County

Getting a good county job often leads to long-term employment.[14] As one worker jokingly said to me in a district office breakroom, "I'm married to the county." We were exchanging pleasantries during the lunch hour and chitchatting about her plans to stay at the agency until retirement. The symbolic links to the domestic sphere did not escape me in this moment. This woman made this comment after she pulled food out of the microwave and before she scrubbed some dishes in the sink. But if this was a marriage, it was less one of romance than of dependency. She did not say she "loved" her job, just that she was resolved to keep it.

This was a passing exchange in the breakroom, but it spoke to a pattern I heard throughout my many conversations with frontline welfare workers. DPSS employees are committed to their work because of its *relative security*.

Relative is the key word. Workers frequently compared their current positions to their former ones during our conversations. Previous jobs at Ikea, Starbucks, Home Depot, Ralphs Grocery, Bath & Body Works, Bank of America, Olive Garden, and various mom-and-pop restaurants served as common reference points to weigh against the value of the good county job. In addition to better pay, workers repeatedly told me about the county's good benefits including good retirement, good healthcare, and good dental. Relatively strong coverage for dependents was also regularly cited as proof for the goodness of the job.

Lucas, a twenty-eight-year-old Latino eligibility worker, explained why he was drawn to the job after working at Lowes,

> So, at Lowe's, it all depended on sales. My position specifically was a sales specialist. So, I mean, I was always pressured to go out and look for sales. I had a quota to meet. If I didn't meet the quota, I got talked to. And if sales weren't doing so good, they started cutting hours. So, it wasn't consistent. There wasn't no consistency in terms of the hours worked, the pay that you received, stuff like that. And on top of that, the benefits weren't so great either. So, when my mom [an eligibility worker] told me about DPSS, I hopped on it immediately. When I initially applied for DPSS, I thought about the benefits. I had a daughter on the way at the time, so I was more so attracted to the benefits side of it in terms of just coverage, the benefits that my mom received. And in terms of doctor visits and stuff like that, there was hardly anything that she had to pay out of pocket when it came to taking us to the doctor. So that's what I was mostly excited about. And not only that, but job security and consistency.

Like Lucas, others told me that, especially in comparison to "dead-end" retail and restaurant jobs, the county's opportunities for raises and long-term employment was especially attractive. Then, of course, there are the hours. In addition to mostly working standard business hours, DPSS employees do not have to worry about just-in-time scheduling common in retail and restaurant jobs.[15] This makes childcare arrangements significantly easier for working parents. Some employees understandably complained about the austere conditions of their workplaces, and several reminded me that things are better in the welfare office than in the store or eatery. One eligibility worker, for example, told me that she especially appreciates her "sit-down" job after years of working on her feet in retail.

While perhaps not to the same extent as the good Fordist jobs of the mid-twentieth century, today's good government jobs seem to elicit comparably high levels of commitment from workers. Management at both are motivated to extract more labor effort from their employees for the sake of productivity. But neither rely on despotism. Workers in so-called good jobs often find reason to work hard and they generally consent to the conditions of their employment. As with those employed in the Ford bureaucracy of 1950s Detroit, those employed in the welfare factory in 2020s Los Angeles are significantly motivated by job security. Fordism, as social theorist Zygmunt Bauman argues, ties employees and employers together in a kind of "marriage" defined by long-term commitments and assumptions of mutual dependency.[16]

According to sociologist Michael Burawoy, the sanctity of this marriage was at least partially maintained in Fordist factories by the combination of an "internal labor market" and an "internal state."[17] Rather than rely solely on the externalization of economic forces (e.g., slack job markets) and political power (e.g., employer-biased regulations) to motivate workers onto the shopfloor, Fordist employers internalized these to foster labor engagement for the sake of mass production. Something similar can be observed in the Los Angeles welfare department.

Internal Labor Market

In much of the private sector, these marriages have dissolved in favor of hookups and cohabitation; they constitute shorter term and more flexible relations between employees and employers.[18] However, in the public sector, long-term commitments remain relatively common in large part because of the preservation (and sometimes expansion) of internal labor markets.

An internal labor market at DPSS commits frontline workers to the job through real possibilities of both vertical and horizontal mobility. Indeed, this market is shaped less like a ladder and more like a pyramid. Approximately 80 percent of the payroll are frontline workers, 11 percent are middle-ranked supervisors, and 9 percent are upper-level managers.[19] Lateral moves not only within these broad categories but also within the same occupation can bring significant quality of life improvements. Several workers told me, for example, that they have or are currently shopping for the same jobs in different offices to minimize their commutes. Others are interested in staying in their current offices but would like new units where the tasks are presumed to be easier (e.g., the less stressful workloads in "approval side" units compared to those in "intake side" units). Some aspire to move to similar units under the watch of less demanding supervisors.

While no doubt important, lateral mobility in a "transfer market" seems less important than the possibilities of upward mobility in a "promotional market." This was especially true for the younger employees I spoke with, such as Basma, a twenty-seven-year-old Middle Eastern eligibility worker. After less than two years in the role, she told me she was focused on advancing into a supervisor position and, eventually, into upper management.

These aspirations are fairly realistic relative to what these workers generally experienced in the private sector. Department managers have long recognized the value of hiring for mid- and upper-level positions "from within."[20] I did not meet a unit supervisor who did not first work as an eligibility worker. I also never met a deputy or higher-level manager that did not enter the position with years of experience in county government.

The profile of supervisors and managers also give workers hope that promotions are not particularly biased in terms of race or gender. Indeed, these demographics are remarkably stable up and down the pyramid. Roughly half of frontline labor (45 percent), supervisors (50 percent), and managers (51 percent) are Latino. The percentages of white, Black, and Asian employees are also stable, with each group accounting for less than a fifth of these general positions. And while the bottom of the pyramid is certainly more feminized than the top, women constitute the majority at all levels (79 percent of frontline workers, 75 percent of supervisors, and 69 percent of upper managers).[21]

We must certainly be careful not to overstate the goodness here. Feminized labor is still generally paid less in the county government, and there are still reasons to suspect that a color line cuts through the pyramid in important ways.[22] In fact, just a few years ago, a jury awarded a Black former eligibility worker $3.5 million after management retaliated against her for speaking out against racial segregation in her district office.[23] Consistent with this, Talisa told me that she and other Black workers feel the "predominantly Hispanic" managers in their branch favor white and Latino workers. This may not shape promotions, she told me, but she suspected that it shaped the distribution of work. She insisted that Black workers were sorted into more demanding units and supervised more intensely. Even so, she still considered her DPSS job to be generally good because it provided opportunities for upward mobility.

Second only to managerial positions, many of the eligibility workers I spoke with aspired to move into workfare programming. Indeed, all the WTW workers I shadowed in South Los Angeles and Monterey Park started out as eligibility workers. Getting into a GAIN or START cubicle inside DPSS often requires a significant commitment to the agency. For example, Rocío, a Latina woman around forty years of age, worked her way up from eligibility worker to WTW worker in eight years. Workers like her are the living proof of internal promotion—not only for me but for the eligibility workers who told me they're working to ascend the pyramid. And, of course, many WTW workers have interests in climbing further up. Rocío was eventually promoted to GAIN supervisor, and the last time I spoke with her, she told me she would continue to look out for other promotional opportunities.

It is important to note that the internal labor market extends beyond DPSS. It is bounded by the county not the agency.[24] Workers receive regular announcements of job postings in other departments, and several told me they had aspirations to move "out and up" into higher paid positions in the departments of Mental Health, Child and Family Services, Public Health, Aging and Disability, and more. As Shandra, a Black eligibility worker in her early thirties, explained, now that she had a "foot into the county" she hoped her hard work would increase opportunities for "branching out" into higher paying county jobs.

Internal State

An internal state can also commit workers to the job. Burawoy defines an internal state as "the set of institutions that organize, transform, or repress struggles over relations in productions and relations of production at the level of the enterprise."[25] Before Fordism, these institutions were mostly controlled by despotic managers. In many firms today they're regulated through human resource departments and related entities that largely serve to protect the interests of employers. But under Fordism, internal states were shaped in large part through trade unions and collective bargaining more generally. Consistent with this, public sector unionism today, which is strong relative to the massive deunionization of the private sector, bestows rights, institutionalizes paths for grievance, and helps mitigate labor oppression.[26] This is generally true even with concession-driven unions that inspire limited engagement from rank-and-file members.

In Los Angeles welfare offices, an internal state was primarily consolidated in the mid-1960s as part of a larger wave of public sector unionization throughout the region and nation.[27] Employees for what was then called the Bureau of Public Assistance organized a strike in 1964 that led to the Services Employees International Union (SEIU) chartering Local 535.[28] Within just a couple of years, the union represented public social services employees across multiple counties including Alameda, Contra Costa, Marin, and Santa Barbara.[29] While often described as a "social worker union," Local 535 covered frontline welfare staff more generally.[30]

In these early years of unionization, organizing efforts were partially fueled by coalitions between frontline welfare workers and welfare rights activists.[31] While there was no doubt tension between these groups, especially when the latter understandably accused the former of discrimination, this alliance made sense. Both parties shared basic interests in expanding, or at least protecting, the safety net. Organized labor showed up to protest benefit cuts and welfare rights activists showed up to protest rising caseloads.[32]

When the Bureau of Public Assistance was rebranded as DPSS in 1966, welfare workers were already unionized and an internal state was essentially preestablished.[33] Indeed, DPSS has always been a union shop bureaucracy. An internal state has long regulated working conditions from "caseloads to coffee-breaks."[34] Most employees would later be covered by Local 660, until Local 721—now the county government's largest union—took over in 2006.[35] Eventually, the alignments with welfare rights activists waned (as did the larger social movement) and workers began to align more with other frontline public servants like nurses in their organizing efforts.[36] They did not, however, lose sight of what mattered most to them as workers: material security.

That said, the internal state refers less to the union specifically and more to the *relationship* between organized labor and management. Unions may exert real pressure on management and shape the conditions of the labor process, but they also make concessions. In this case, throughout the history of DPSS, organized labor frequently accepted increased caseloads, new automations, and reduced discretion in exchange for material security.[37] For example, in a comment to the Board of Supervisors in 2015, union leader and eligibility worker Rita Josephbek called not only for increased hiring but also welcomed improved and expanded automation to increase efficiency.[38] Seen in this light, unions help solidify worker commitment not just to the job but also to its shifting conditions. Like many organized workers under Fordism, frontline welfare labor in Los Angeles accepted proletarianization in exchange for relative security.

While my conversations with workers suggest that the internal labor market attaches them to the job more than the internal state does, the latter is certainly important. Many, like Brianna, a forty-one-year-old Black worker and former retail employee, recognize that the material goodness of their current jobs is tied to collective bargaining. "It's nice to be part of union," she told me before explaining how pay and benefits are higher in her current job because of unionization. Still, the union was certainly not seen as perfect. "I will say," Brianna continued before describing some recent increases in out-of-pocket medical costs for workers, "I wish the bargaining was better." A few other employees stressed disappointment in absent, careless, and management-sympathetic shop stewards. But the typical sentiment I encountered was one of gratitude. The workers I met were generally grateful for the union's efforts to increase pay and benefits. And, although the union often makes concessions on workload and automation, they also frequently fight these conditions, and many workers see and appreciate that.

The most grateful, however, were those like Julia, a twenty-six-year-old Latina worker, who relied on the union to obtain individual accommodations. She turned to her union steward to challenge management for erroneously denying a medical leave. "[Management] paid more attention to me when the union got involved," she told me. Julia was confident that without the union her request would have been denied. Though she does not show up to union rallies, she appreciates the rights afforded to her through her union job. Moments like these remind workers how good it is to have a shop steward nearby.

Much of what made Fordist jobs good relative to post-Fordist jobs is what makes county jobs good relative to private sector employment: security. This is accomplished in large part by both internal labor markets and internal states. While these markets and states have been hollowed out in many private firms, they remain relatively intact within public bureaucracies like DPSS. While we must be careful not to romanticize mid-century employment relations—and we should remember that marriages can be abusive—the comparison and metaphor are useful.

Relative Calling

More Than a Job

Even with relatively strong internal labor markets and states, which are features we tend to associate with monopoly capitalism in the mid-twentieth century, we should not exaggerate the similarities between Fordism and good government jobs. Not only are the motivations and justifications for productivity different, so too is the practical component of the labor process. This is especially true for those who are employed as frontline policy workers.

To put things more plainly, frontline public servants are not industrial employees. They work directly with people in welfare offices, jails, hospitals, classrooms, and more. This integrates additional moral aspects into the work. Factory workers may not see the objects of their work as particularly worthy or unworthy of their labor, but those in public services generally do. The latter also frequently articulate a sense of vocation or mission in their work. And while the mission may not always be about alleviating human suffering—especially when accounting for the bureaucracies of the penal state—it does seem to concern broad goals of civic duty, or what policy scholars frequently call "public service motivation."[39] Workers in highly professionalized occupations in education, law, and medicine often express having this motivation, but so do workers in highly proletarianized forms of policy work.

Workers stationed on the welfare assembly line tend to carry what might best be labeled a *relative calling*—a sense of vocation and mission that distinguishes their job from others. This, too, is an important feature of the good county job. While I never spoke to anyone who seems to do welfare work "for its own sake," most identified some moral value in the work they do relative to the alternatives. It is not just that DPSS provides better benefits and hours than Home Depot, Olive Garden, Bank of America, and other previous employers. Working at DPSS is simply more "meaningful."

Often central to this is a sense that one is aiding not only the authentically needy but also the authentically grateful. Natalie, a thirty-two-year-old Latina eligibility worker, for example, told me what she found most rewarding about her job. She said, "When I get one of those cases where I can tell that they really do need the—I mean, a lot of these people do need help—but I can tell they're just genuinely grateful for my help. That always makes me feel good." Roxanne, a twenty-seven-year-old Black eligibility worker echoed this sentiment when I asked her the same question. She said, "I would say helping people who actually need to be helped—helping the ninety-year-olds who can't do their paperwork or helping a mom with kids who needs health insurance. Just seeing them and them thanking us for actually taking the time to help them. That's pretty rewarding."

Indeed, the goodness of the job comes not only from its security but also from a general sense that the work benefits the deserving and grateful poor. I found this to also be generally true in the GAIN and START cubicles. Even those few workers who articulated ambivalent, sometimes outright pessimistic, opinions about the county's "welfare-to-work" mission told me it felt good to help connect their clients to services and ancillary aid.

As Sydney, a Black eligibility worker around forty-five years of age, explained in reference to her previous job, something just generally feels "better" about helping DPSS clients than helping retail customers. For sure, frustrations run high when workers suspect they are being "played" by their clients or when those clients seem especially "entitled." But there are generally enough rewarding encounters with them—even over the phone lines—to characterize DPSS work as "more than just a job."

Bureaucracy as a Life Order

Realizing a kind of moral value from frontline welfare work is not, however, limited to rewarding moments with deserving and grateful clients. A sense of good work can also be reaped through interactions with those seen as undeserving or ungrateful. Workers taught me that a certain kind of moral achievement can be realized, for example, by "keeping one's cool" and maintaining a "good face."

Yet, in my experience, most see the bulk of their clients existing somewhere between deserving and undeserving and between grateful and ungrateful. The standard client, if there is one, is mundane and forgettable. Workers generally encounter them as tabs and boxes on CalSAWS and as voices in their headsets. Yet there can be a relative glory in the grind. It is better to do routine work that helps those in need than sell jeans or serve food to the more fortunate.

There are reasons to take this a step further. A sense of morality can be realized not just in welfare bureaucracy but also in bureaucracy in general. There is a goodness to be found in the basic routines and rhythms of bureaucratic work. My interviews did not make this clear, but my observations did. For example, while I was shadowing Jon, a Latino WTW worker, he explained how he found some satisfaction in "boosting files." This has nothing to do with issuing aid directly; it refers to a series of acts for printing, organizing, and paperclipping case documents and preparing them for digital imaging. There is just something about neatly organizing the papers that he finds mentally and manually satisfying. As Jon put it, the "organization freak" in him appreciates these little moments.

But he is not really a freak. Other workers I shadowed also told me they took satisfaction in particular bureaucratic routines. Many, for example, took pride in assembling "good case notes," even though this involved little actual authorship. Most copied and pasted short narratives, changed a few key words, and then maybe added a sentence or two. At first blush I assumed there was no craft here, and perhaps there generally wasn't. Yet workers frequently explained that they reveled in constructing good notes and emphasized their frustration with the "sloppy" or "empty" notes of some of their peers. Then there were those who took pride in responding swiftly and confidently to any task supervisors threw at them. This is not because they are robots or bootlickers but because it is the "right" thing to do in officialdom. Doing good work, as I learned while shadowing workers in their cubicles, doesn't just mean helping clients; it also involves generally obeying bureaucratic authority, even when it contradicts one's personal opinions.

I understand this runs counter to many of our commonsensical visions of bureaucracy as neutral at best and dehumanizing at worst. We often misrecognize the official objectives of formal impersonality as moral bankruptcy, but as sociologist Paul du Gay notes in his deep reading of Max Weber, the bureau is best understood not just as an iron cage of cold instrumentalism but also (and perhaps more so) "as a distinct life order with its own ethos."[40] For one thing, an effort to realize an ideal of impersonality *is* a moral stance. That stance may certainly be flawed and rest on false assumptions of universality and objectivity, but it is coupled with a Western liberal ethic emphasizing formal democracy, the rule of law, and so on. Public bureaus like DPSS are not zones of amorality. Instead, for the frontline workers that make and remake them daily, they are sites of *relative* morality not unlike other life orders in a highly differentiated society.[41]

The relative calling captures both the specific and general virtues of welfare work realized in a labor market characterized not just by material but also by moral insecurity. On the one hand, there is a welfare-specific ethos that emphasizes a mission of "poverty alleviation." While this was frequently tempered by preferences to help the deserving and grateful poor, most of the workers I met said they liked how their jobs had them helping people in need even if through a screen. On the other hand, workers can also find meaning in generalized visions of good bureaucratic labor. From the moral accomplishment of keeping one's cool to the minor satisfactions of doing good paperwork, materializing policy at ground level can provide opportunities to realize a sense of dignity under conditions we often caricaturize as dehumanizing. And while the distinctions between this and a more general work ethic under capitalism is admittedly blurry, the peculiarities of officialdom suggest there is a unique life order to consider inside bureaucracy.

Materiality over Morality

The relative calling is no doubt significant. This book would be incomplete without an account of the moral dimensions of frontline public service work. But there is very little reason to conclude that this elicits as much consent from workers as relative security. The good county job is mostly good because of its material benefits.

This became especially clear to me after I interviewed fifteen current and former WTW workers from the San Fernando and Antelope valleys. Unlike those I shadowed in South Los Angeles and El Monte, the GAIN workers up north are not county employees. They are instead employed by Maximus, a government services company.[42] Chapter 4 will detail some of the history behind this splitting of workfare case management services in the county. For now, the primary point I want to convey is what I learned from these current and former employees of Maximus: privatized welfare work is relatively bad. As one report published by SEIU 660 put it in 1991, "Privatization turns good jobs which pay decent wages and benefits into 'working poor' jobs, eroding the pool of good jobs available to minority workers and reducing the income they bring back to the communities where they live."[43]

"They had us do so much," Valentina, a twenty-six-year-old Latina worker, said to me when reflecting on her recent employment in a privatized GAIN office. "And we were underpaid. Josh, it was terrible." Like other GAIN workers in Palmdale, Valentina was paid less than county GAIN workers. Although unionized and placed on a stable nine-to-five schedule, she made $16 an hour for a job that the county pays double for (about $35 an hour).[44]

Some of these privatized WTW workers say they get paid less for the same work, but that is not entirely accurate. Few of them seem to realize that they actually do *more* work than those in county-run GAIN offices. Where many county GAIN workers reported caseloads of around one to two hundred, those in privatized GAIN said they were often expected to handle closer to three hundred cases. And, because contracting added in additional layers of auditing, those in the privatized offices are expected to complete more paperwork than those in the county-run GAIN offices. The expectations for regularly contacting participants are also higher in the privatized offices—an effect of stringent expectations of contractual compliance.

Where eligibility workers throughout the county often aspire to be GAIN workers, the inverse appears to be true in those territories where GAIN operations are privatized. In the Palmdale and Burbank GAIN offices, many Maximus employees aspire to obtain a good county job at DPSS. They dream of a DPSS cubicle. Yet despite their experience, they do not qualify for county GAIN work. Their best bet is to get hired as eligibility workers. That was what Valentina did. "When I went to DPSS," she told me, "a lot of the workers were like 'Oh, you were a GAIN worker, you must have [been] *demoted.*'"

She frequently explained to her new DPSS coworkers how privatized GAIN is different and worse than county GAIN. Sure, she lost some autonomy in the shift from casework to taskwork. Valentina even told me that she "loved" working with GAIN participants and misses it in many respects. But none of this was enough to arouse any significant feelings of regret. The shift from privatized WTW worker to county eligibility worker was, in her case, an obvious economic upgrade.

Valentina's trajectory was not unique. I met a handful of eligibility workers who started out as privatized GAIN workers. And while they agree that GAIN work, even when contracted, comes with more autonomy and purpose, there is widespread consensus: it is better to be a county means tester than a privatized program broker. That is because the former comes with more material security: namely better pay and better benefits.

Increased security was also frequently cited as a motivation and justification for leaving DPSS for other county agencies. Carolina, a thirty-year-old Latina worker, left DPSS for a county job at another human services agency doing, as she put it, "less important" human services labor, providing superficial referrals. Among other things, she frequently directs her new clients to the very district office where she was employed as an eligibility worker. She misses her cubicle there because she was able to "actually issue aid" to her clients. But any moral decline in the kind of labor done was significantly countered by the material advancements. Her current job provides better hours, expanded remote work opportunities, and, most importantly, better pay.

So, while much can and should be said about the vocational commitments of these workers, we must not fool ourselves into thinking they clock into work primarily out of a moral commitment. I am convinced that most do develop authentic, albeit limited, missions of poverty alleviation. I am also convinced they develop a particular moral sensibility linked to generic bureaucratic procedure. But neither orientation is what primarily keeps them returning to the welfare assembly line. A relative security outweighs a relative calling. Indeed, frontline welfare work may not be "just a job," but it is *primarily* one.

Internal Decline

Let's not let the sunshine of the good county job blind us. There is, as I suggested in the introduction, a kind of noir to occupying a cubicle in officialdom. While du Gay is right that the public bureau is not the dehumanizing, soul-sucking hellscape we often assume it is, there is still a kernel of truth within our knee-jerk suspicions of bureaucratic power. There is good reason, as DPSS employees themselves learn through their arduous experiences of getting hired, learning protocols, and requesting time off, to seriously question the rationality of bureaucracy.

It is not that frontline public service work is neutral; it is contradictory. It is meaningful and meaningless, warm and cold, humanizing and dehumanizing. But these contradictions are not necessarily balanced, and they are certainly not static. Bureaucratic noir, especially for frontline labor, is increasing relative to the sunshine. The "goodness" of frontline welfare work is eroding.

Even with relatively stable internal labor markets and internal states, material security has declined on the frontlines. In 1974, for example, a newly hired eligibility worker could expect to earn roughly $9,500 a year, which, in 2024 dollars, was approximately $58,000.[45] That is about 12 percent higher than the current starting salary of around $52,000.[46] Making the deal sweeter for management but sourer for labor, this real wage deflation has been coupled with a credential inflation. Most who get the job today need to have a bachelor's degree whereas fifty years ago an associate's degree or lower was typical.[47]

The good county job may be better than what is available in the private sector, but again, the security it provides is relative. Union leaders have routinely reminded the bosses of their bosses—the Los Angeles County Board of Supervisors—how the material security of their job in particular has waned. "We eligibility workers struggle to make ends meet," stated Julia Marin, a shop steward, during a 2015 county Board of Supervisors meeting packed with union members. She continued, "Many of us live from paycheck to paycheck and are unable to save for our future, such as our children's college education and/or unexpected living expenses."[48]

Union officials often appeal to the Board to not only improve but also preserve the material security of good county jobs in reference to deteriorating conditions in the private sector. In a 2003 board meeting, for example, eligibility worker Shirley Carter protested cuts to health insurance benefits,

There are picket lines in all grocery stores all over town. Our hearts and support go to the UFCW [United Food and Commercial Workers, a union covering many grocery store employees] who, like us [*audience cheers*], are fighting to protect their health benefits. Their employers are ruthless, in the pursuit of better stock prices and larger profits, they want to destroy their workers' benefits. We are grateful that we work, we hope, for a more caring and progressive employer. Surely LA County won't follow the ruthless employers down the road of ending workers' benefits, reducing our pay and forcing us out of the middle class. Except we have a better definition for middle class than a $600,000 house. We just want to—[*audience cheers*]—we just trying to pay light bill, gas bill, and make it from the fifteenth to the thirtieth, and we're not succeeding [*enthusiastic cheers and applause*]. Surely, our county will lead the way by example, showing private employees how a decent, considerate, and public spirit employer behaves. Surely, you will act in a manner that lets the public and your workers know that our efforts and dedication are appreciated, that the work we do is vital to the people of this county and that preserving the middle-class jobs in LA County is your top priority. You must understand, we expect this, we expect more, we deserve it, we demand it. Thank you. [*Enthusiastic cheers and applause*][49]

The moral benefits of the job have also declined. Casework has given way to taskwork in the district offices, reducing workers' already limited control over the labor process. More on that in chapter 3. Meanwhile, the preservation of casework in the welfare-to-work cubicles have been coupled with an intensified rationalization of "black box" referrals, sanctions, and ancillary aid. More on that in chapter 4. While it may be true that workers can find meaning and purpose in even the most mundane bureaucratic procedure, routinization still increases workers' alienation in the productive process.

Put differently, a narrowing of worker discretion increases the repulsiveness of labor. The standardization and specialization of the welfare assembly line has made it harder for workers to find "rewarding moments" with their supposedly deserving and grateful clients. Further, these conditions have made it harder for workers to realize a sense of vocation within the bureaucracy. Among other things, formalized expertise on the frontlines has given way to discrete tasks that require less formalized training.[50]

These changes are part and parcel of a larger trend that scholars of public sector work have been observing: the so-called good government job is becoming less secure. As sociologists George Wilson and Vincent Roscigno demonstrate, such occupations are generating more precarity and providing fewer opportunities for upward mobility for Black workers in particular.[51] A managerial movement that embraces a "business model" in the public sector is, as they argue, undermining a labor market niche that has provided relative security for workers who have been historically marginalized in the private sector. Welfare work in Los Angeles is still relatively good, but, as one senior DPSS employee said to me while she typed away on her computer, "It's not as good as it used to be." Just as Fordist jobs gave way to more insecure forms of private sector employment, good government jobs are giving way to mediocrity in the public sector.

Still, welfare work is generally seen as a good job—especially when compared to the more economically and ethically limiting positions found at the bottom of the bifurcating labor market. Workers' frequent references to low-end retail and restaurant work made this clear, but so too did their references to bad government jobs. Carolina, for example, noted that DPSS work was far more secure than the teacher's aide job she quit. She could "at least live" as an eligibility worker.

The next two chapters delve into the labor of means testing and program brokering. Workers across both of these cubicles have been increasingly stretched thin on the welfare assembly line, and this has eroded the goodness of the job. But as many workers have reminded me, and as I have tried to make clear in this chapter, a frontline job in the policy factory is still *relatively* good. This perspective, which is shaped not just by workers' experience in the labor process but also in the labor market, helps explain how so many can stomach their increased proletarianization.

3   Seeing Customers

Public aid for the poor in the United States is notoriously stingy, and Los Angeles is no exception.[1] The average monthly check for Angeleno families on CalWORKs, the state's key Temporary Assistance for Needy Families (TANF) program, is a pitiful $1,077.[2] Individuals who get a General Relief check, the county's other main cash assistance program for extremely poor adults, receive only $221 a month (down from $341 in 1992, or $777 in 2024 dollars).[3] Households receiving CalFresh, the state's Supplemental Nutrition Assistance Program (SNAP), get, on average, just $314 a month to help with their grocery bills.[4] And while the economic relief generated by Medi-Cal benefits, the state's Medicaid program, is harder to quantify, things like enrollment "churn" and patient "share of cost" policies make this program difficult to praise relative to universal coverage in other Western capitalist democracies.[5]

Yet stingy welfare does not necessarily mean small welfare. In Los Angeles, the crumbs may be paltry, but they reach plenty. DPSS distributes small amounts of aid to a lot of people. In fact, in 2025 the department aided over four million people in a county of nearly ten million.[6] Medi-Cal is by far DPSS's largest program, covering roughly 3.5 million people in 2024. CalFresh covers less than half of this (1.6 million). Both Medi-Cal and CalFresh dwarf the two main cash assistance programs, CalWORKs and General Relief, which cover only about 250,000 and 100,000 people respectively. Between these two programs is In-Home Supportive Services (IHSS), a federal-, state-, and county-funded program for providing personal care to aged and disabled Medi-Cal recipients that covers about 240,000 people.[7]

While more than a third of Los Angeles County residents are means-tested welfare recipients, they are almost never labeled as such. As one recent department report put it, "We serve over 4.2 million *customers*."[8] I first learned of this terminology when attending a conference in 2019, where then–DPSS director Antonia Jiménez spoke at a keynote panel to a variety of public workers, agency managers, activists, and academics.[9] In her brief presentation held at a golf resort in Montebello, California, she mentioned that instead of referring to their clients as "recipients" or "applicants," DPSS calls them "customers." The latter, she insisted, was a more dignified and fitting title.

This shift from recipients to customers makes sense when considering larger changes to the state. As historian Lizabeth Cohen notes, the late twentieth century came with an increased focus on "government customers" in the US, and this paired well with an increased emphasis on government efficiency and accountability.[10] It was also in the 1990s, during federal welfare reform, that DPSS began explicitly and publicly referring to their subjects as "customers."[11]

Indeed, the welfare state was not just refashioned into a workfare state, it was also refashioned into a *customer service state*.[12] The poor are not only framed as worker-citizens but also as consumer-citizens. Rather than being seen as passive recipients, they are depicted as active customers. Such subjects may not actually purchase anything, and they may not have other options in a marketplace of benefits, but they "consume" health insurance, food stamps, and cash aid.[13]

And these customers do so through their interactions with front-line means testers. Officially called "eligibility workers," these employees determine and redetermine people's qualifications for aid. Today they look less like the kind of frontline workers described by Michael Lipsky and more like the customer service representatives you likely encounter quite frequently in your daily life.[14] Like bank tellers, call center workers, and retail sales associates, these frontline workers have comparatively little discretion over the kind of services they can provide. Their discretion, as noted in chapter 1, is more narrow than wide and more superficial than substantive. They are less street-level bureaucrats than they are proletarianized public servants.

This chapter examines the labor process of eligibility work. I begin with a close examination of one worker's routine to give some sense of what this job entails. It's certainly a lot more complicated than just determining eligibility or processing applications. I then unpack what is essential to this job: legibility. More than anything, eligibility workers make customers interpretable to the administrative machinery of the welfare office. While such work has forever existed in DPSS, I show that it has been increasingly stretched thin by managerial efforts to intensify productivity. Such efforts, I argue, have transformed the welfare office into something reminiscent of fast-food service.

Camila's World

Who's Next?

While many eligibility workers today have been relegated to "screen-level" rather than "street-level" work on the welfare assembly line, most who are assigned to district offices are still expected to work with customers in person. In fact, I saw eligibility workers interact with customers in the flesh far more than I saw the WTW workers do so with their participants (more on that in the next chapter). So long as customers are required to submit and resubmit themselves to the scrutiny of means testing, the department will need eligibility workers who can navigate both the screen and the street.

The working world of Camila, a thirty-three-year-old Latina eligibility worker at the Metro North office, might best illustrate this. Many district office eligibility workers are assigned "lobby duty" one week at a time every month or so, but Camila occupies a relatively unique role as a "dedicated lobby worker." Her fluency in both English and Spanish makes her an ideal candidate for this more flexible station on the welfare assembly line. Positioned in a ground-floor cubicle near the front entrance, she specializes in both intake and approval side determination for CalWORKs, CalFresh, Medi-Cal, and a very small Cash Assistance Program for Immigrants (CAPI) that covers roughly seven thousand elderly, blind, and disabled legal immigrants ineligible for Supplemental Security Income. While she certainly spends much of her time examining and updating the CalSAWS screens like any eligibility worker, she does so for customers who are there in person.

That said, Camila's supervisors prefer she handle as many customers as she can without actually inviting them into the building. The point is to reduce congestion in the lobby. While the pandemic intensified the practice of making customers wait outside, this was not a new routine, especially in this office with a relatively small waiting area. This means Camila spends much of her time walking back and forth from her lobby cubicle to the front entrance of the building. She doesn't run, but she does walk briskly.

When I first followed Camila on her route, my eyes struggled to adjust. The sudden shifts between the fluorescent interior and the sunny exterior were strong enough to have me second guessing my steps. But I eventually got used to the space, and more specifically to Camila's well-worn path.

Each time she stepped outside, Camila met a line of bodies that snaked along the side of the building. Sometimes I estimated twenty bodies in this line, while at other times it seemed closer to fifty. It was often hard to tell since the tail creeped around the corner beyond my view.

This human snake included wheelchair-bound elderly folks and stroller-bound babies. A quick glance suggested it was a reasonable sampling of what we know about public assistance subjects more generally: disproportionately female and disproportionately Black and brown. But there were still plenty of men and certainly a lot of white people. All, with the exception of a couple of kids running and jumping to the side, looked miserable or numb as they patiently waited their turn in the slow creeping snake.

Camila always greeted the head with a simple question: "Who's next?" I watched as she served a range of customers. She helped a woman file a claim for approximately $450 of stolen food stamps before she added a newborn to another woman's Medi-Cal case. Later she checked the status of a CalWORKs recertification for a woman before she helped a man replace a lost EBT (electronic benefits transfer) card. Camila also aided customers who journeyed to the office to challenge what they claimed to be erroneous changes to their benefits. At the edge of tears, one woman insisted she turned in the right documents at the right time but was still being discontinued from CalFresh. And because this office serves a number CAPI customers, I was not surprised to see Camila also help elderly people with some of the complicated paperwork required for this particular program.

Camila was able to handle all of these tasks by running back to her cubicle and leaving customers outside. After doing some screen-level work checking on information already entered to CalSAWS, adding new data brought in by customers, (re)calculating benefits, and so on, she would then reemerge from the building with good, bad, or no news before asking again, "Who's next?"

Touching Cases

Camila often juggled tasks across two or more cases at a time. That is because when she returned to her cubicle after resolving one customer's issue, she usually updated CalSAWS with a journal entry before attending to the next customer's issue. By overlapping the completion of one task with the initiation of another, Camila was able to reduce the number of trips between the street and the screen. Making things more complicated, it was not unusual for Michelle, Camila's supervisor, to stop by the cubicle and drop off some additional tasks that she too was gathering from the human snake outside. It was certainly a lot to follow as an ethnographer, but I did my best to quickly jot notes about Camila's world.

Among the many things that caught my eye was a large banner that Camila passed every time she reentered the building. Nailed to the wall far above our heads, it read, "Quality Standards: Efficiency, Accuracy, Courtesy, Knowledge, Seamlessness." I wondered what the customers in line would say about this. I doubted a man who complained to Camila about his long wait would find the office staff to be very efficient or courteous. Likewise, given that several people in the line were there to challenge what they believed to be erroneous changes to their benefits, I was sure many would question the points about accuracy, knowledge, and seamlessness.

But from my point of view, Camila did seem to embody these standards. She was efficient, at least within the constraints of her assignments and duties, multitasking to keep pace with the perpetually regenerating snake of customers outside. Camila was also accurate, or at least she strove to be, as she knew that a supervisor was going to verify all of her calculations and determinations. And while some workers I shadowed were rude and condescending toward customers, I found Camila to be especially warm and friendly—not only to customers but to fellow workers, supervisors, and me. More than anything though, I found Camila to be a knowledgeable and seamless worker. She knew many complex protocols and procedures by heart, and this enabled her to string together disparate tasks to help keep the assembly line flowing.[15] A conveyor belt of customer problems rolled before her, and her job was basically to clear the queue and keep things moving. She was not doing casework but rather handling tasks linked to cases worked by many eligibility workers before her and many after her.

The only thing that seemed to break Camila's flow were my nosy questions. Through such questioning, I learned what Camila likes most about her job: relative autonomy. And *relative* is the key word. Before she found herself running between screens and streets in a busy district office, she worked at DPSS's Customer Service Center. This is a particular kind of call center where eligibility workers tend to handle calls on the main department hotline. They mostly answer customer questions beyond what can be answered through automated voice recognition software and telephone keypad inputs.[16] When necessary, they then transfer calls to other workers on more specialized branches in the call tree. While those workers in other DPSS call centers do many of the same things that district office workers do, those in the main Customer Service Center look more like phone operators than means testers. "I hated it," Camila told me. "I couldn't really touch cases .... I couldn't add people, things like that.... Now, I can change whatever I want."

While this was clearly an exaggeration since no eligibility worker can change *whatever* they want, I understood what she was saying. I had heard others say something similar. There is some intrinsic value in "touching cases"—that is, in transforming the world—albeit it in minor ways. Case touching gives eligibility work more meaning, or at least a bit more weight and sense of consequence. It has workers changing, rather than just reading, screens. While she cannot change whatever she wants, Camila nonetheless appreciates her current assignment relative to her past one.

She may not hold or possess cases under the taskwork regime, but she can at least *touch* them as she runs between the screen and the street. While veteran eligibility workers may generally see this as trivial, Camila does not take it for granted. It enables her to realize some sense of consequence and autonomy in a context where casework is dead and discretion is wounded.

The Other Side of the Runaround

Much has been written about the poor being sent on "runarounds" and being bogged down by "administrative burdens."[17] Depending on the specific aid program, DPSS customers are often sent on errands to retrieve and submit paystubs, rental agreements, school attendance records, doctor's notes, and more.[18] Indeed, many of those in the human snake that Camila was taming stood not only with frowns on their faces but folders in their hands. Many were there to submit documents that other eligibility workers had told them to retrieve previously. As Herd and Moynihan note, such burdens are costly for clients and citizens. They include "learning costs" (e.g., effort in searching and navigating complex systems of information), "compliance costs" (e.g., effort in adhering to complex rules and requirements), and "psychological costs" (e.g., stresses from navigating said complexities).[19]

But there is another costly side of the runaround that is rarely acknowledged: the side of labor. Indeed, eligibility workers are generally expected to do some running around of their own. In a way, they each bear their own share of administrative burdens. We see this in Camila's oscillation between screen and street. However, this runaround does not always require physical movement. I saw Camila and other eligibility workers also do a sort of "digital runaround" as they navigated various software applications to determine eligibility in an accurate and timely manner.

And while much of this labor runaround occurs independently of what customers do, there are some ways the latter can inadvertently intensify the runarounds for eligibility workers. A common way customers can fuel the labor runaround is by submitting incomplete, incorrect, or inconsistent paperwork—an easy thing to do when customers are struggling to navigate their own confusing and demanding runarounds. Workers are given tons of documents with irregularities and imperfections that must be addressed before eligibility can be determined. Sometimes workers can reject these tasks outright if the documentation is really messy, but doing this for every piece of flawed paperwork is simply not an option. The assembly line would grind to a halt. Management expects eligibility workers to fill gaps and make repairs. They do this by consulting multiple computer applications (e.g., navigating other databases to fix inconsistencies in CalSAWS). They also do this by calling customers to ask questions about their circumstances and emailing supervisors to ask about policies and procedures.

Just as customers shape the labor runaround, so too do workers shape the customer runaround. Eligibility workers most obviously do this by *giving the runaround*—that is, by issuing "homework" and "errands" to their customers: bring this document, complete this form, do this interview, and so on. Without frontline workers to handle these tasks and then convey the next step, customers would not have many places to run between. Giving the runaround is part and parcel of how these workers materialize policy—and more particularly a set of policies that push administrative burdens onto those who suffer most in the stratified city.

There is often a kind of superficial, rather than substantive, discretion at play when workers give the runaround. Some—I suspect most—adopt a kind of minimalist approach and request as little as possible to get customers through the eligibility determination process. But there are others, much to the annoyance of their peers and supervisors, who intentionally make clients they perceive as deceptive "work for it" by requesting verifications that could otherwise be waived or ignored.

"I'll dig," said Faith, who we met in the last chapter. She takes a bit of pride in requesting excessive verifications from customers she sees as being deceptive. Speaking of a customer who she suspected of lying about whether or not they owned the car they slept in, Faith said, "You came in here on shit. I'm going to meet you. I'm going to meet you at the energy you came in here with, and *now* I'm going to request [vehicle] verification." These kinds of notable exceptions—what public administration scholar Rik Peeters calls "informal" yet "intentional" administrative burdens—aside, eligibility workers do not have much choice but to give their customers the runaround.[20] A lot of this is generally determined by protocol. Most verifications that workers request are needed for eligibility to be determined.

In my experience—no doubt biased by workers who knew I was watching them—discretion tends to be directed toward ways to help, rather than hinder, customers. There are some limited ways workers can ease the administrative burden by *sharing the runaround*. They cannot share the burdens of most customers, but they can and do for many. As a couple of eligibility workers put it, they can "work with customers." They do this by slowing task-based production and taking a few extra minutes to help them navigate their runaround.

Camila did this, for example, when she assisted a middle-aged white man who came to the office with some DPSS paperwork folded in the hat he wore. The customer explained that he lost his EBT card, which held his CalFresh benefits, during a recent homeless encampment sweep. He received a replacement card from the office the day before, but it was not working.

When Camila opened the case on her screen, she learned the man was exceptionally unlucky. He not only lost his card in the sweep; he was also discontinued from CalFresh for failing to submit a semiannual review report known as a SAR 7. Camila was a bit annoyed that the eligibility worker who recently printed the man a new EBT card did not recognize this. She grabbed an empty SAR 7 form and a pen and returned to the streets.

She explained to the customer that he was missing some important documentation. The man did not have a mailing address, and Camila explained that the form was sent to this district office where he was supposed to be routinely checking for mail. The customer was, however, surprised to learn that he could even pick up mail at this office at all. No matter, Camila explained that he should complete the SAR 7 that day and hand it to her directly. She noted that he technically has three days to complete the form, but she strongly recommended that he do it at that moment. Camila also told the man he could interrupt her if he had any questions about what to report.

The customer did not have any such questions, but he did take this as an opportunity to ask about a Department of Motor Vehicles (DMV) voucher. This is special paperwork that DPSS workers can give to customers so that they can receive state identification with waived or reduced fees. Camila explained the procedure for obtaining such a voucher and noted that he would need to get his food stamps reactivated first to qualify. She then took a moment to explain how the voucher application would work if the man eventually made his way to the DMV to replace the identification he lost alongside his original EBT card.

Camila shared this man's runaround. Sure, it was in a minor way. But it wasn't insignificant. And, at least technically speaking, it was not the *least* she could have done. She could have very well handed the man the form and told him to return it within three days. She did not need to volunteer to offer any kind of support while the man completed the paperwork outside. And she did not need to spend the extra couple of minutes explaining how the DMV voucher functions. None of this may have dramatically disrupted the man's runaround, but it probably helped a bit.

The customer was certainly grateful. After completing a few more tasks, Camila eventually collected the SAR 7 form from the man. In addition to thanking Camila for the help, he told us he was "so grateful" for the food stamps and was excited for their return. "I've seen terrible things," he said. "The food stamps have helped a lot." Camila nodded and smiled, but she didn't seem too interested in continuing the conversation. "That's great," she said. "That's what we like to hear. Take care of yourself now!" The customer seemed to get the cue and, while putting his backpack on, he said, "Ok, I see you're super busy. Thank you!" "No problem," responded Camila, "Have a good day, sir."

Camila told me she likes to help customers in this way when she can. But she simply cannot do this for everyone all the time. She admitted to me that she was especially unlikely to walk people through paperwork and procedure when the line outside was particularly long.[21] That is because such circumstances intensify the pressure to work fast. As the line lengthens, workers in the lobby often worry that supervisors will get more anxious and that customers will get more irritable. Caught in the middle, these workers tend to feel an urge to accelerate an already fast pace and hopefully trim the line a bit. As we walked a bit faster back to her cubicle, Camila told me that when it's exceptionally busy, she can't have customers "taking up too much time" like the man she just aided. Giving the runaround is the rule. Sharing it is the exception.

And because it is the exception, eligibility workers tend to reserve it for exceptional customers and circumstances. Other eligibility workers told me how they like to "work with" certain categories of customers. Some mentioned college students, who face unique paperwork challenges in qualifying for food stamps. Others mentioned the elderly and parents of young children. The impoverished old and young, those before or beyond working age, are seen as especially deserving of attention. And some, like Camila, noted that they liked to help "homeless customers" because they are particularly vulnerable to lost paperwork, missing phone calls, and more.

But, alas, they cannot do this for everyone, let alone for entire categories of customers. Eligibility workers like Camila are running between screens and streets as they attempt to complete a range of tasks on the welfare assembly line.

Legibility Work

The label of *eligibility worker* is a bit misleading. These workers do not "make" people eligible for benefits. The actual determination of eligibility is largely distilled to a single act: pushing the "run EDBC" (eligibility determination benefit calculation) button in CalSAWS. This is the button that "spits out" an answer for whether or not someone is eligible for aid and, if so, what kind and at which specific amounts. With this tool, workers do not need to know much about means-tested thresholds, and many admitted that they often don't know what decision will be generated for many if not most of the applications they process. But EDBC cannot be run until the information entered is complete and presumably accurate. Otherwise, CalSAWS will generate an error message. What the workers do is make the case interpretable to CalSAWS so that a EDBC can be run without error. Put another way, the job of the eligibility worker is largely one of making cases legible so that a determination can then be made. Indeed, the vast majority of their time is spent collecting, entering, and editing information on customers.

Workers like Camila are perhaps best described as *legibility workers*. They "see like a state," as political theorist James Scott might phrase it, and this necessitates that they make their subjects legible to the administrative machinery of the welfare office.[22] A central task of statecraft according to Scott is to assemble and arrange populations so that basic tasks like taxation, conscription, and public benefit distribution can be executed. Key to this is an often crude conversion of innate complexity into simplified features.

Reflecting on state power and legibility over two decades later, Scott notes, "What I overlooked while writing [*Seeing Like a State*] is the obvious fact that legibility doesn't come cheap. It requires veritable armies of observers, enumerators, census takers, compilers, statisticians, clerks, scribes, etc."[23] And the exercises of these observers must be "endlessly repeated" to keep pace with the many changes in circumstances for both individuals and populations.[24] "Legibility," as sociologist Max Greenberg aptly notes in his reconstruction of Scott's theory, "is carried out by actors at 'street level.'"[25] Such workers "manage the mess and scrum of daily life into state-sanctioned and locally specific forms."[26] And, within the customer service state, they are expected to do so efficiently and ideally with a smile.

Eligibility workers on this portion of the welfare assembly line reduce the immense complexity of their subjects' lives into a series of simplified texts and digits: name, date of birth, social security number, address, household occupants, income, employability, medical history, and so on. As policy scholar Jeffrey Prottas notes, much of the frontline work of welfare bureaucracies like DPSS "consists of categorizing and processing people as a precondition to their receiving benefits—not unlike an ordinary factory where materials are processed as a precondition to their sale."[27] Camila and her coworkers do the labor of making their subjects not only visible but also readable to the bureaucracy. Indeed, the one thing that "approved" and "denied" customers have in common is that both are rendered legible, and therefore testable, in reference to a series of standards and thresholds.

It is important to note that frontline welfare workers do not encounter raw material. As sociologist Leslie Paik notes, welfare offices and related sites often expect their subjects to 1) appear when asked, 2) fill out paperwork in a certain way, 3) bring certain kinds of documentation, 4) prepare for appointments, and 5) share information with staff.[28] These are all expectations of legibility. Customers must package and submit snippets of their biography and circumstance to workers in ways that are at least partially intelligible to the protocols and procedures of the department. They impose some significant simplification on themselves as they submit fragments of their backgrounds and situations via paper and online forms.

Frontline labor is nonetheless necessary for scrutinizing, organizing, and amending such simplifications. Eligibility workers like Kayla, a Black woman in her late twenties, must do some legibility work. She's assigned to an intake unit for CalFresh and Medi-Cal in the same office as Camila. Unlike Camila, but like most eligibility workers I shadowed, Kayla spends the majority of her time in an upstairs cubicle detached from the lobby. While she gets "lobby duty" once every month or so, most of her work is done on screens and over the phone.

One morning, I watched Kayla process a CalFresh application for a twenty-seven-year-old woman. Kayla needed to call her for an interview, but first she took some time to acquaint herself with the information that the applicant submitted online. A couple things in particular caught her eye. First, the applicant reported living with a thirty-year-old male but he was not listed on the application as someone who would use the food assistance. Second, the woman reported $0 income but $1,000 rent, and that was, in Kayla's words, "questionable." Customers should be poor and suffering—but in a plausible way, to avoid questions of deception and fraud.

Kayla snapped on her headset, opened the Cisco Finesse telephone program on her computer, and called the woman. "I got some questions about your CalFresh application," she explained through her headset. "You got time for an interview?" I could very faintly hear the woman say "yeah" through the headset. "Wahoo!" responded Kayla in her trademark optimistic tone.

She started by asking a battery of questions to fill in some missing information in the application. I couldn't hear the responses when Kayla was clicking and typing rapidly in CalSAWS. But I could read Kayla's screen and, of course, I could hear her side of the conversation.

Kayla asked about the man the applicant lives with. "Is that your boyfriend? . . . He is? Ok. . . . Do you cook and eat together?" Kayla was double-checking to see if the man needed to be on the CalFresh application. It was at this point that Kayla's voice changed. "No?" she said with a tone of suspicion. She then turned to me, rolled her eyes, and we exchanged a quick smile while she continued her inquiry. "But you live together. I'm sure you eat what he's eating." There was a bit of a pause before Kayla concluded matter-of-factly, "We got to count him."

She then asked questions about income. "Are either of you working? . . . " He is? Ok. What kind of work does he do? . . . Self-employment? Sort of? Ok. How much does he make a month?" The customer apparently didn't know because Kayla then said, back in her bubbly voice, "Shoot, we need that."

But before sending the customer on the runaround to report and prove her boyfriend's income, Kayla first needed to add the man to the application. Unfortunately, the customer did not have her boyfriend's social security number memorized. "We need that too," remarked Kayla. "Let me see if there's another way."

While not necessarily obvious to the customer, Kayla then shared her runaround a bit. She could have very well demanded that the customer obtain her boyfriend's social security number and submit it online along with some scans of his state identification card, but Kayla did some extra work to alleviate the woman's forthcoming errands. During the call, she opened up MEDS (Medi-Cal Eligibility Data System), a database that provides quarterly income records and state and federal aid histories linked to social security numbers. She searched the database by name and confirmed the address with the customer. "Ok, this is him," she said while nodding, "We found him . . . . That's good news." Kayla then pulled the social security number off MEDS and entered it into to CalSAWS to discover that he's already in the state benefit database. The man is, as workers frequently phrase it, "known to the system" rather than "new to the system." This helped Kayla populate some other fields in the case (e.g., number of dependents) that would have otherwise fallen on the customer. More importantly, though, it saved the customer from having to upload identification documents for her boyfriend.

Kayla could not, however, avoid giving the woman the runaround entirely. She told the customer that she would need to submit her boyfriend's income. "You live together, so we need his information. We need to know his pay for the last 30 days . . . a paystub or a letter." There was no discussion of how someone who is "self-employed" could furnish a paystub or a letter, but Kayla did say she would physically mail some detailed guidelines on what kinds of documentation qualify. "You have a week to get that to us," she said.[29]

After asking a few additional questions about rent, utilities, savings accounts, and more, Kayla told the woman that she could "follow up with our customer service call center." Indeed, Kayla was not, and would never be, this woman's caseworker. She was simply clearing one of many intake tasks assigned to her that morning. Her job was to make the customer legible enough to progress to the next step in the application processing. It would be up to the next worker assigned this customer's file to push that EDBC button and determine benefit eligibility.

The interview ended with Kayla playing a mandated recording detailing the customer's rights and responsibilities. Kayla then ordered, via CalSAWS, a Request for Verification form known as CW2200, to be mailed to the customer. She modified it on her screen a bit to emphasize that one of the following income verifications needed to be submitted ASAP:

- 30 day paycheck stub(s)
- Letter from employer with gross pay, hours, worked, etc.
- Copy of child support check or payment stub
- Benefits award letter (Social Security/Veterans/Unemployment/Disability, etc.)
- Self-employment tax forms (IRS Schedule C, etc.)
- Receipts for work expenses if you are self-employed
- School grants/loans/financial aid statements
- Sponsor statement form[30]

Kayla was "touching the case" to increase its legibility to the bureaucracy. This task did not conclude with her determining eligibility, but it did render the application more complete. The process of determining eligibility is largely reduced to a click of a mouse. But the EDBC button cannot be pushed until the case is legible. Errors will pop up for incomplete or nonsensical data. Her job is primarily to help make the case intelligible to the bureaucracy.

Put another way, the labor of legibility preconditions the labor of determination. The question of "Who's next?" is less "Who's next to be determined eligible?" than "Who's next to be simplified?" Before the sprint to push the EDBC button in CalSAWS, there's the other side of the runaround: the scramble to make subjects into texts readable in that software. Individuals must be identified before means can be scored, and means must be scored before they can be tested.[31]

Proletarianizing the Means Testers

The Death of Social Work

When the Bureau of Public Assistance became the Department of Public Social Services in 1966, the vast majority of frontline welfare workers throughout California were known as "social workers." They were generally college graduates who passed civil service tests for that particular job category.[32] This did not mean they were necessarily trained or credentialled in the growing academic field of social work, but it did signal a relatively broad scope of practice and high levels of discretion. They were, by all reasonable accounts, street-level bureaucrats.

These social workers held caseloads and were generally expected to test the means of clients (with the aid of clerical staff) and connect a significant number of clients to a range of services and resources.[33] The welfare office, especially after the federal Public Welfare Amendments of 1962, was imagined to be a space to both distribute public benefits and link the poor to a variety of employment, education, housing, and medical services.[34] The labor of means testing was generally done by the same workers who were doing program brokering in the agency.

Then came 1968, a year of remarkable turbulence. Martin Luther King Jr. was assassinated. Protests against the Vietnam War ballooned. Nixon won the presidency. In Los Angeles, Chicano high school students to the east led one of the most significant protests against a racist education system. And, just a few blocks from the Metro North DPSS office, a young Robert F. Kennedy was shot and killed at the Ambassador Hotel.

In the same year, welfare offices were dramatically restructured across California. With approval from the federal government, the state commanded county welfare offices to separate eligibility work from social work—largely in an effort to increase efficiency and reduce costs.

One California legislature committee report in 1989 summarized the shift as such: "Prior to 'separation' social workers did the eligibility functions as well as provide social services. The split was a cost-cutting measure that would allow for relatively few social workers, who had college degrees, to provide adult and child protectives services, employment and training services, information and referral, etc. Eligibility work meant taking applications, processing papers, and determining benefits for public assistance. The great mass of workers would be eligibility workers whose duties were considered basically clerical and required no college degree. Eligibility workers would necessarily be paid less than social workers."[35]

Sociologist Alice Burton notes in her historical ethnography of welfare labor organizing in California that this statewide separation rendered most frontline welfare workers "objectively proletarianized."[36] However, such a loss in worker control was not evenly spread. Discretion narrowed more severely for those relegated to eligibility determination than for those who entered the higher-paid and higher-status positions of "social worker" or "services worker," the latter of which was a more common title in Los Angeles after the separation noted above. Both social workers and services workers were increasingly expected to have graduate degrees in social work, at least in some counties in California.[37] Burton also observes that this separation was racialized; a higher proportion of Black workers were hired for eligibility work, and a higher proportion of white workers were hired for social work.[38]

At DPSS specifically, this separation left offices with a "substantial surplus of Social Workers" who needed to be "transferred," or rather demoted, to "eligibility work."[39] The social worker label was largely reserved in the early decades for those assigned to broker services for the Homemaker Chore Program and a growing division of family and children-related services.[40] The Chore Program was eventually replaced with IHSS, which is now the only major program at DPSS that employs people under the title of social worker (less than 5 percent of the department payroll).[41] These employees hold caseloads and regularly conduct in-home visits with clientele to assess needs, evaluate housing conditions, determine assistance hours, and so on. Children services, on the other hand, was carved off and made a separate county department in 1984, the Department of Children and Family Services.[42] This is the family policing and children's protective services agency in Los Angeles.

Social work was suffocated by pressures to advance the people-processing objectives of welfare offices. In the 1960s, largely as a consequence of advancements made by the civil rights movement, means-tested welfare was declared an "entitlement," which increased the pressure to process applications in a timely and accurate manner.[43] This significantly expanded welfare access to Black and brown families, but it also sharpened budgetary attacks on welfare offices in the succeeding decades. The racialized caricature of the "welfare queen" provided conservative politicians like Ronald Reagan in the 1980s and more centrist ones like Bill Clinton in the 1990s with the rhetorical justification to tighten welfare budgets.[44] Such imagery also fueled an increased focus on detecting fraud, and this intensified frontline legibility work. Workers were expected to scrutinize paperwork and applications more and, for some time around the turn of the millennium, they were even mandated to collect fingerprints from their clients.[45] Talk about customer service!

Each of these pressures—access entitlements, budgetary cuts, and antifraud initiatives—amplified DPSS's people-processing objectives.[46] Who needs a social worker at the DMV or the TSA? State and county welfare administrators reasoned that lesser paid eligibility workers could do the vast majority of the labor for its major aid programs. And once child protective services spun off into its own department, there was little to no need for frontline workers to do the kind of deep case management associated with the title of social worker.

Even the DPSS employees categorized as social workers today hold a mostly symbolic title. Lindsey, a thirty-five-year-old white former Medi-Cal eligibility worker who was promoted to IHSS, was quick to tell me in an interview, "I'm not a clinical or licensed social worker." She explained to me that her job tended to emphasize a quick determination of eligible in-home care hours. Her work in IHSS comes with more autonomy over schedule but not much more discretion over policy. In fact, her IHSS social work job looks a lot like eligibility work. She is primarily tasked with determining the number of in-home care hours her customers qualify for. She does not even connect them to aid directly. "It's *their* responsibility to hire a provider," Lindsey explained to me when talking about her customers. The most she can do is hand them the number to a homecare registry system maintained by a third party.

Social work was buried under the welfare assembly line. Or so it seemed. As I'll detail in the next chapter, the rise of workfare initiatives in the 1980s and 1990s focused, at least ostensibly, on reorienting welfare offices across the state and nation into people-changing bureaucracies.[47] This animated a kind of "mechanized social work" in the form of mandated welfare-to-work programming. For the eligibility workers still in the district offices, however, the people-processing operations were only to become more explicit.

More Division of Labor + More Machinery

It is important to note that even with the fiscal assaults on cash aid programs in the closing decades of the twentieth century, the number of welfare customers has *generally increased* since the birth of DPSS.[48] While attacks on welfare have been real and consequential, they have largely focused on cash aid to poor mothers. This was true even after 1996, which was supposed to "end welfare as we know it." Following the replacement of Aid to Families with Dependent Children (AFDC) with the more draconian Temporary Assistance for Needy Families (TANF, or CalWORKs in California), the number of families with minor children assisted with cash aid in the county dropped from roughly three hundred thousand in 1996 to about one hundred thousand in 2022.[49] However, the number of CalFresh and Medi-Cal customers generally grew.[50] The former fluctuated in size throughout the closing decades of the twentieth century but then majorly expanded during the Great Recession and has remained historically high since (with an additional peak during COVID).[51] The latter generally expanded at a somewhat steadier pace until the Affordable Care Act in 2010 significantly expanded eligibility (and also peaked during COVID).[52] Taken together, these changes have resulted in a net growth of DPSS customers from a little over a million in the mid-1970s (approximately 14 percent of the county population) to over four million today (approximately 44 percent of the county population).[53]

Yet the number of workers did not increase at even remotely the same rate. As noted earlier in this book, the number of employees at DPSS was about the same in the 1970s as it is today—roughly fourteen thousand. This is not, however, a case of stagnation. In fact, with Children and Family Services spinning off into a separate department in the mid-1980s and the county facing a severe budgetary crisis in the 1980s and early 1990s, DPSS staffing dropped to about seven thousand employees in 1995 to cover over 1.5 million recipients.[54] This period of exceptionally "lean times" for the department, which was directly linked to the 1978 taxpayer revolt mentioned in the introduction and to a particularly conservative Board of Supervisors at the time, generated a fairly obvious crisis of legitimacy: workers were stretched too thin and both processing errors and wait times shot up.[55] Journalists, activists, labor organizers, and state auditors chastised the county for understaffing its welfare offices and for falling short on its legal obligations to efficiently distribute federal and state funded aid to those who qualified.[56] This crisis of legitimacy, combined with an improved county budget during an economic boom in the late 1990s, motivated investments in staffing.[57] Hiring freezes and layoffs gave way to hiring surges, and staffing was eventually bumped up to ten thousand in the late 1990s and was fully restored to 1970s levels by 2020.[58] This rebound, however, did not keep pace with the growth in cases.

While the agency was able to redirect its staffing budget toward more eligibility workers (from 30 percent of the payroll in 1974 to 45 percent today), the actual number of eligibility workers increased from approximately 4,000 to 6,300 during this fifty-year period.[59] That is roughly a 58 percent growth in eligibility workers to cover a 300 percent growth in clientele. For welfare administrators, the problem has long been clear: too many customers but not enough workers.[60]

High caseloads have always been a concern within the department, but worry peaked during the rollout of Medicaid expansions after the Affordable Care Act. Yolanda Floyd, an eligibility worker who frequently spoke before the Board of Supervisors, summarized the situation in 2015: "We are drowning in cases. Our lobbies are overflowing. We are unable to maintain the caseloads that we have. In the past, our caseloads were high if we had six hundred. Now we have over two thousand cases. We are unable to provide effective and caring service to our community. We need bodies."[61]

Indeed, more bodies would alleviate the problem. But we should be careful not to blame DPSS administrators for failing to bring more people on. They generally want to hire more workers to relieve pressure on the assembly line.[62] Doing so is often seen by both middle- and top-level managers as an ideal way to reduce processing errors, trim wait times, and improve customer satisfaction. But department budgets often prevent this.[63] Administrators are expected to stretch the frontline thin with minimal reductions to quality service. Luckily for management, there is a classic formula lying at the heart of essentially all assembly lines for doing so: *more division of labor +* *more machinery = more productivity.*[64] Here, increasing productivity refers to what sociologist Erik Olin Wright calls the "appropriation of labor effort."[65] In a welfare office, the stakes may be "fiscal responsibility" or "general efficiency" rather than "profit," but the underlying end is similar: make labor more productive. The means are also frequently comparable: specialization and automation.[66]

We have encountered much of this already. Eligibility workers have long been distinguished not only by the districts they're stationed in but also by the kinds of "specializations" they hold (e.g., CalWORKs, Medi-Cal, and CalFresh) and whether or not they tend to work the intake side or approval side of the welfare assembly line. Kayla, for example, does Medi-Cal and CalFresh approval work for the Metro North District. Camila does dedicated lobby work at that same location. I have also already mentioned a bit about automation in means testing, including workers' heavy use of CalSAWS. But, if increased productivity is dependent on greater specialization and automation, then we should expect specialization and automation to increase over time. And that has generally been the case.

Consider the division of labor. In addition to having workers focus on specific places, programs, and periods, administrators increasingly dedicate workers to particular kinds of processing. There are units of workers today who are exclusively focused, for example, on processing semiannual reports (SAR 7s) for CalFresh and CalWORKs. They essentially handle the processing of one specific and very routine document, which customers must submit in order to keep their benefits. Likewise, there are other dedicated "redetermination" units that focus on specific kinds of approval-side paperwork. As previously noted, some eligibility workers are assigned to units in call centers where their primary job is to field questions from curious customers. DPSS even operates a dedicated Medi-Cal "mail-in office" where eligibility workers are only assigned application processing for this program.

That said, divisions of labor can also be clunky and rigid. Overspecialization can dampen productivity by increasing the number of "handoffs" between workers.[67] That is why, for example, management has continued to cross-train staff even as program specializations have increased. Those trained in CalWORKs and General Relief, for example, tend to also be trained in Medi-Cal and CalFresh and are deceptively known as "universal workers." Some cross-training makes sense operationally given that customers who qualify for these cash aid programs almost always qualify for the other two. Eligibility workers can process CalWORKs and General Relief paperwork while also processing paperwork for the other aid packages. But, because cash aid is rare overall, it makes sense to organize more workers into dedicated CalFresh and Medi-Cal units. Specialization matters, but management has long understood that it should be flexible.

Of course, divisions of labor, whether flexible or not, are just part of the equation. An increased stretching of eligibility work on the welfare assembly line also depends on the continual improvement of machinery. From updating the capacity of "check writing machines" in the 1970s to rolling out the EBT system in the 1990s, welfare managers have perpetually updated automation on the welfare assembly line.[68]

On the one hand, administrators seek technology that increases operational accuracy by helping to lower errors and detect fraud. On the other hand, they seek technology that increases operational efficiency by reducing the time spent updating and managing files. Whereas efforts to maximize operational accuracy tend to intensify the surveillance of the poor, efforts to maximize operational efficiency tend to intensify the productivity of frontline labor. EBT, for example, expanded opportunities to monitor how recipients use their benefits while it also streamlined payment distribution. This technology, as management noted, was good for both "fraud prevention" and "processing efficiency."[69]

Likewise, the evolution of computerized case management at DPSS has expanded the visibility of the poor while also accelerating the pace at which workers can process any given application or recertification.[70] In the mid-1970s, for example, then-director Keith Comrie oversaw the rollout of the Welfare Case Management and Information System (WCMIS).[71] As one department newsletter explained, WCMIS enabled eligibility workers "to simply inquire via a computer terminal located in the district office regarding individual cases and get an immediate response on a TV-like screen."[72] This increased the speed of legibility and thus the efficiency of legibility labor. And the technology was used to justify the elimination of a number of clerical jobs, speed up an otherwise sluggish "welfare paper mill," and increase the number of cases handled per worker.[73] The *Los Angeles Times* headline seemed to write itself: "County Welfare Agency Trims Fat by Computer."[74] In the 1990s, similar justifications of accuracy and efficiency were articulated for the development of a new program called LEADER (Los Angeles Eligibility, Automated Determination, Evaluation, and Reporting).[75] And while that program did not cut jobs immediately, administrators pursued it in part because they believed it would motivate "the attenuation of any required growth in DPSS positions, particularly at the Eligibility Worker and [Eligibility] Supervisor levels."[76] Following LEADER came LRS (LEADER Replacement System) and then eventually CalSAWS—each bringing with them their own increases in accuracy and efficiency.[77]

Eligibility workers' engagement with such technology has been varied and contradictory. On the one hand, there is some evidence that these forces have reduced workers to something like appendages of machines.[78] As an ethnographer this was most apparent to me as I watched dozens of eligibility workers review scans of driver's licenses, paychecks, and other documents that customers submitted online. A common intake task I observed involved workers reading these scans on one window and then simply typing that information in another. In many ways, the digitalization of eligibility determination has reduced their work to simple data entry tasks. As Basma, who we met in the last chapter, explained, "Literally, we are just doing data entry. You give me your information. I put it in the system, and then the system is programmed to determine [eligibility] based on the info it's given."

On the other hand, there is evidence that such workers are not deskilled but rather reskilled or even upskilled by such technology (although not in ways that correspond with wage increases).[79] Eligibility workers labor in an information factory where they look increasingly like what media scholar McKenzie Wark calls "hackers," limitedly creative actors who produce "new information out of old information."[80] The labor of legibility certainly necessitates a kind of information conversion that is more creative than what Basma acknowledges. While workers are often physically stuck in their cubicles (or at-home workstations), they are given powerful tools to creatively complete their tasks. We saw this when Kayla handled the problem of the underreported boyfriend for her CalFresh customer. She and other workers I shadowed proudly showed me their data-entry shortcuts. It was also not uncommon for workers to express awe over their software. Several paused, for example, when they navigated the new Work Number program that DPSS had purchased from Equifax. "Isn't this cool?" one worker said as she navigated the database to "objectively" verify a customer's recent income. My awe, however, mostly came as I watched her and peers "get in the zone" and type and click through their tasks at blistering speeds like hackers in a cyberpunk movie.[81]

Still, this is part of a larger regime that seeks to squeeze more productivity out of workers. The subjective experiences of labor add some nuance we should acknowledge, but let's be clear: Welfare managers, motivated by the contradictory forces sociologist Armando Lara-Millán identifies as budgetary austerity and legal demand, have long struggled to square an increasing customer base with a relatively stagnant number of workers.[82] Their primary strategy has been to advance the division of labor and improve machinery. This only became more obvious in recent years, which I detail next.

The Death of Casework

Since 2021, essentially all eligibility workers have labored not under a casework but a taskwork regime. Most clock into their shifts today to confront not a caseload but a task list. Usually this is a literal list sent by supervisors: complete a CalFresh intake interview for customer A, determine eligibility of Medi-Cal for customer B, finalize semiannual report for CalWORKs customer C, and so on. Other times the list is to be determined by the queue: answer incoming calls on the Medi-Cal approval line, assist General Relief walk-in customers, or retrieve assignments from a digital task bank. Either way, eligibility work tends to be organized according to tasks in the customer service state.

DPSS customers enter offices, call hotlines, and submit documents online not to assigned caseworkers but instead to a collective body of taskworkers. Cases still exist, but they are no longer so central to the organization of frontline labor. Instead, cases are divided into discrete and assignable tasks. Most cases today are now "touched," as workers frequently phrase it, by multiple eligibility workers stretched across different units and sometimes different offices. DPSS customers today do not have assigned eligibility workers, just as you do not have an assigned worker at a Bank of America branch, on the Amazon customer service hotline, or in a Target store.

Key to the shift to taskwork has been the implementation of the "First Contact Resolution (FCR) business model at all district offices," which, according to a report published by DPSS, "is designed to deliver streamlined services to customers."[83] The general idea here, along with an "end-to-end" application-processing initiative implemented in the call centers, is to improve customer satisfaction by reducing their administrative burdens. This necessitates, however, a rupture from the traditional caseload regime so that multiple workers—be they in the district offices or in the call centers—can "touch" any given case. And while there is evidence to suggest such policies can indeed be good for customers, things are not so peachy for workers on the other sides of the desks and screens.[84]

Under the taskwork regime, units are still organized by place, program, and period for most district office workers, but eligibility workers usually share cases within and across units of seven or so workers. Taskwork is even more extreme in the dedicated call centers since cases in those spaces are not even assigned to units or offices. Such workers simply handle calls throughout the county (disrupting divisions in place). Some are even assigned the task of answering customer inquiries across a range of DPSS services (disrupting divisions in program and period).

The shift from assigned cases to assigned tasks is arguably the biggest increase in the division of labor since the separation of means testing and social work in 1968. And the coordination and control of such divisions has necessitated the improvement, or at least the modification, of machinery. Things called "ghost files" were rapidly integrated into CalSAWS. These are files assigned to a *collection* of workers rather than individual employees. Nobody I asked knew why they were called ghost files; it was simply the term used to describe unit-assigned rather than individual-assigned cases. Perhaps it's because they float in a system designed for casework, or maybe it's because they haunt the workers tasked with working bits and pieces of them. Either way, many supervisors distribute daily spreadsheets that assign specific tasks to workers to then be handled in the ghost files. In addition to tweaking computerized case management systems to facilitate shared case touching, new techniques for measuring productivity have been rolled out.

Yardsticks have been replaced with stopwatches. Gone are the days of worrying about workers' caseloads, which were measured with so-called yardsticks (e.g., expected caseload maximums) and tended to grow as the number of customers increased. Now, management is more explicitly focused on the speed in which tasks can be tackled. As one eligibility worker and union organizer noted, "When we met with [former DPSS director] Antonia Jiménez, [administrators] were talking about the First Contact Resolution and then I saw the blueprint that—oh, wait a minute—that says, 'performance expectation.' That's where they were going to start telling me how long it takes to do everything."

This has motivated new technologies for monitoring and measuring productivity, including timers for specific tasks. In one of the customer service call centers, for example, workers are automatically timed and are expected to spend only three minutes between general inquiry calls. "After I end a call," Christina, a twenty-six-year-old Latina eligibility worker in the customer service center, explained, "I have three minutes, and then another call is going to come to me." To be clear, time is elongated on the other side of the line. One "secret shopper" audit study, for example, found that those calling to ask about the Medi-Cal coverage in Los Angeles can expect to wait an hour or so before speaking to an eligibility worker.[85] But the workers who handle these calls are hustling.

As an ethnographer, I was introduced to taskwork as a "cutting edge" model. It was a "new work system," as one union newsletter in 2021 put it, that further turns "social services administration into an assembly line."[86] And, for the workers I shadowed, it felt "brand new" given that it was rolled out on a massive scale across the district offices just a few months before I began fieldwork. I later learned, however, that taskwork was neither a novel nor a particularly new way to organize means testing. Social scientists had observed the emergence of similar regimes in New York, Indiana, Florida, Georgia, Massachusetts, Utah, Washington, and even San Diego.[87] Taskwork in some of these other jurisdictions extend as far back as the 1970s, but most of it emerged in the new millennium.

It is also worth noting that, despite their rhetoric insisting otherwise, the workers in Los Angeles were not completely caught off guard in 2021. In the decade proceeding the massive shift toward taskwork, this regime had begun to creep in, but it was mostly contained in the call centers and some of the reception-based work in the district offices. There was a real concern that taskwork would permeate the core units of eligibility determination. Union organizers called on the county officials to preserve and expand casework as a more dignified organization of the means testing labor process.

One eligibility supervisor, Marcos Alvarez, spoke before the Board of Supervisors in 2017: "Many of the participants [clients] who come to district offices or call the hotline, the call centers, if you will, require the intensive case management work of back-office eligibility workers like myself, many of whose work has been redirected to task-based customer service functions . . . . Roughly one thousand eligibility workers have been assigned to CSCs [customer service call centers] and 10 percent or more of each district office eligibility workers are assigned as CSRs [customer service representatives] . . . . The priority must be to maintain an adequate number of case-carrying EWs [eligibility workers]."[88] This plea was apparently ignored. The only response came from a county supervisor who told Mr. Alvarez that his time to speak had expired. The expansion of taskwork seemed almost inevitable. It was certainly a long-term goal of department managers.

In fact, DPSS seriously considered implementing a taskwork system for means testing more than fifty years ago. One manager in 1973, for example, advocated for a new system where "eligibility workers will no longer be responsible for individual cases."[89] The manager went so far as to pilot such regime in an East Los Angeles office that same year. A department newsletter described the tested model as follows: "The point of the system is to identify the tasks which make up the basic functions and to group them together. This will result in the 'disappearance' of the case-carrying worker. Instead, all cases will be banked and only used by workers as individual actions are required. While the recipient will no longer relate to a single individual, the system as a whole will better serve the recipient's financial needs with more prompt and accurate determinations. The vehicle for this functional model is a series of teams which concentrate on the functions and tasks assigned to their group."[90]

It is unclear why this initial proposal for taskwork was not implemented, but the shift away from casework did eventually come. In fact, the quote above is a fairly accurate description of the organization of eligibility work today. It was a sort of bureaucratic prophecy. The case-carrying eligibility worker has disappeared; cases are banked in units; and recipients, or "customers," no longer relate to a single caseworker. Whether or not this system is better for customers is trickier to determine, but there is good reason to suspect it has increased organizational efficiency. One study of SNAP and TANF administration in New York state, for example, found that the "productivity ratio [output as measured by cases/number of workers needed to produce the output]" was roughly four times higher in counties that employed a task-based regime than in those that employed a case-based one or a mixture of the two.[91]

In the Los Angeles cubicles, the reactions to the shift from casework to taskwork were somewhat mixed but mostly negative. One common theme I heard was that casework made time at work better but time off worse, while taskwork makes time at work worse but time off better. With a caseload, workers are given a bit more autonomy over their work. Sure, caseworkers are still on the welfare assembly line, but they have some sense of control over *their* cases even if they have limited discretion over policy implementation. The downside of this kind of responsibility is that it spills over into their personal time. Eligibility workers had long complained that their vacations and sick leaves were spoiled by the weight of rising caseloads. They would return to their cubicles after long breaks to be greeted by massive amounts of work. Taskwork has largely eliminated these stresses since workers no longer have to worry about "their cases" expiring. But, in exchange for less stressful time off, workers have an increasing sense of dispossession while on the clock, which generally outweighs the benefits of taskwork.

Gloria, a thirty-two-year-old Latina former eligibility worker, recalled how peers reacted to the shift to taskwork,

> A majority of people at first were more than happy because [taskwork] means people would be able to go on vacation and wouldn't have to be stressed out as much. But then the reality hit, and it was more like, wait, now you're having to pick up the slack from somebody else. Because before it was your caseload. If you didn't finish the work, then that's all on you. But now if another worker doesn't finish it, and then you get that task . . . You're [the one] having to fix what the other person did or did not do.

For essentially all the eligibility workers I met who had worked the two systems—including both senior and junior employees—this tradeoff was not enough to justify the transition. When speaking to current and former employees like Gloria more than three years after the transition, most told me they preferred the caseload system over the task-based system even though many believed the latter to be more efficient overall.

This is in large part because increased efficiency came at the cost of a double alienation—first from clients and second from fellow workers. The casework regime provided a venue for more meaningful connections with customers. As Jeremy, a forty-eight-year-old white former eligibility worker, explained, the taskwork system helps administrators "use the workforce efficiently from a time perspective," but the "the caseload [system] is more helpful because you are getting to know people, and they are willing to share more information with you." Like all the other workers I spoke to about this, he felt a real loss of control over the productive process. And this has generally increased alienation between eligibility workers. Taskwork requires more workers to share common materials of labor, but sharing is often a source of frustration. While the work is heavily standardized, there are significant differences in style (e.g., case notes, orders of operations, and discretion over whether to give or share the customer runaround). These stylistic differences can make taskwork particularly frustrating as workers spend time trying to figure out why another worker did what they did on a previous task. And, with cases fully dislodged from individual employee files, horizontal suspicions have increased. Several of the workers I spoke with suspected the task system was increasing *their* workload while incentivizing their peers to be lazy. Andrea, a twenty-seven-year-old Latina former eligibility worker, who has since been promoted in the agency, told me that after completing the tasks assigned for the day, her supervisor would just reassign additional tasks from other workers in the unit to her. This is framed by supervisors as a way to benefit the unit as a whole and help workers who have fallen behind, but it tends to fuel tension and distrust between employees.

But by far the biggest complaints workers have regarding the task system concern the intensification of micromanagement and surveillance. When the task system was rolled out in 2021, it was soon facilitated by new software called Current. This program is made and sold by the Change and Innovation Agency—in this case for roughly three million dollars for two years.[92] Current offers "visibility into all of an agency's systems," alerts "leaders when agency-determined thresholds are triggered and corrective action is needed," and generates "work assignments and delivers them to the right workers at the right time."[93] As I saw it in the field, this software was essentially a supplemental tool for organizing task distribution on the one hand and observing workers' use of time on the other. In many units, eligibility workers were expected to hit a "get next" button on Current to learn which task they should work next on Cal-SAWS. The program would also carefully time workers, measuring how many minutes they spent on a given task and how many minutes they were "idle" between tasks.

No specific topic during my fieldwork sparked more immediate ire than that of Current. Workers generally described the software as an explicit tool of excessive supervision. One said its timer function was literally nightmare-inducing, and another said it was nothing short of a digital "babysitter." Another commented, "It was basically keeping tabs on us, what we're doing all the time," and someone described the program as a means for supervisors to "stalk" workers. Indeed, supervisors frequently checked in with workers whose "status" on Current was in "idle" mode for more than fifteen minutes. Such "idle checks" functioned to remind workers that they needed to finish up their paperwork on the previous task and move on to the next one quickly. I witnessed these checks firsthand in the field and workers repeatedly complained about them in interviews (more on this in chapter 5).

Luckily, Current had a short lifespan at DPSS. Administrators dropped the program in late 2022. A couple of workers I spoke to credited the union with pressuring management to dump Current.

And while this would make sense given that the union officially decried the program along with taskwork more generally, a top-level manager told me they concluded Current to simply be redundant. They figured that the program would be useful to facilitate the shift to task-based work but realized the tool was not needed for efficient task assignment. Plus, CalSAWS and other programs (e.g., Cisco Finesse) already allow supervisors to surveil labor, including the time spent on and between tasks. As Adriana, a thirty-two-year-old Latina eligibility supervisor put it, Current, was "dumb" because CalSAWS allowed her to closely monitor task progress within her unit anyway. Regardless, casework is still dead in the district offices.

The McDonaldization of Welfare

In his massively influential reconstruction of Max Weber, sociologist George Ritzer argues, "The model of rationalization, at least in contemporary America, is no longer the bureaucracy, but might be better thought of as the fast food restaurant."[94] The main characteristics of rationality—efficiency, predictability, calculability, automation, and control over uncertainty—are, for Ritzer, better captured by your local McDonald's than by any public bureau.[95] Ritzer did not consider, however, that instead of eclipsing bureaucratic rationality, many public bureaucracies have themselves undergone a kind of "McDonaldization." Later, social work scholar Donna Dustin extended Ritzer's critique of American rationalization to welfare states across the Atlantic. In *The McDonaldization of Social Work*, Dustin argues that frontline workers in public welfare organizations are increasingly deprofessionalized into something akin to fast food workers in a consumer-oriented state.[96] She showed how the welfare office could be McDonaldized.

I do not know whether Ken Miller, the founder of the Change and Innovation Agency and one of DPSS's many software vendors, ever read Weber, Ritzer, or Dustin. But he too looks to McDonald's as a model of rationalization. For him, however, McDonald's is not a target of critique but rather a source of inspiration. In addition to praising the speed and consistency of McDonald's restaurants, Miller applauds the company's so-called *poka yoke* techniques (a Japanese phrase roughly translating, as Miller puts it, into "idiot-proof").

In his 2019 book, *Extreme Government Makeover*, which a sales representative from his company gave me for free at a welfare management conference, Miller states,

> McDonald's has an interesting workforce challenge. The restaurant chain could try to recruit and retain the best and the brightest, in which case hamburgers would cost twelve bucks apiece. Or they can try to keep hamburgers at sixty-nine cents. To have cheap hamburgers, they have cheap labor. Unfortunately those workers aren't always paying attention. So how do you get consistent, "quality" hamburgers from a workforce that isn't paying attention? *Poka yoke.* When are the French fries done at McDonald's? When the buzzer goes off. There's not a single kid in that restaurant kitchen who knows how to make a French fry. They don't know how long to cook them or at what temperature. All they know is that to make that annoying buzzer stop, they have to hit that red button. Heck, the fries even rise out of the oil automatically. Idiot-proof.[97]

He imagines a world of McDonaldized welfare where most of the work is highly simplified and routinized and so too is the distribution of means-tested benefits. Sociologist Robin Leidner, also drawing on the case of McDonald's, describes this an "extreme standardization" of both products and labor.[98]

Miller does not acknowledge, as sociologist Jill Esbenshade and her team of researchers in San Diego have, that task-based welfare services risks intensifying the labor process, disempowering workers, and deteriorating the quality of services.[99] Rather, Miller praises the taskwork model that is increasingly replacing casework as a force that is "revolutionizing social service agencies" for the better.[100] "The results have been staggering," he claims without citing any specific examples, "As much as 40 percent more customers served, 70 percent faster."[101] Current, the task bank software program Miller's company sold to DPSS may have been canceled, but the "revolution" of taskwork endures. And Miller's company, which he has since sold, is there to help state and county agencies make the transition.

Besides McDonald's, Miller is heavily inspired by Ford. In an earlier book, which was also generously gifted to me by his staff, he draws explicit parallels between the "system of work for a Ford Mustang" and the "system of work for food stamp distribution." Both involve "factories," "widgets," and "customers."[102] For those working the CalFresh assembly line in the welfare factory, the widget is the EBT card and the customer is the food stamp recipient. And both systems are also oriented by specific outcomes of efficiency and quality. Writing to an audience of government administrators, Miller notes, "A profit-making enterprise has to innovate or die because it is driven by the natural force of competition and the necessity of providing a high return to its investors. Are we really that different?"[103]

The McDonald's restaurant, the Ford factory, and the local welfare office. Indeed, what's the difference? Setting aside the fact that employees in the latter tend to view their work as a relative calling, the organization of labor processes in each appears remarkably similar. McDonald's and Ford pursue profit while the welfare office pursues a balanced budget amidst contradictory pressures of austerity and legal demand, but both these ends depend on increased productivity. And an increasing division of labor and the continual improvement of machinery remain a go-to strategy.

Perhaps this all makes sense in a people-processing bureaucracy where, not unlike in the Ford plant or the McDonald's drive-thru, production is expected to be both mass and fast. But what if the welfare office is also summoned to be a people-changing bureaucracy? Would that not require a different kind of welfare assembly line? Would that not assume a different kind of worker and perhaps even a different kind of client? Might it also assume a different kind of welfare state? I tackle these questions and more in the next chapter.

4 *Making Participants*

For a minority of DPSS customers who receive cash assistance—less than 8 percent of working-age adults served by the agency—aid is contingent on participation in employment-oriented case management services.[1] They enter local welfare offices and read "work first" mission statements, enroll in "employment readiness" programming, and sign "welfare-to-work" contracts.

There are reasons to believe that workfare—the conditioning of aid on holding or seeking employment—is at least partially driven by efforts to meet the increasing demand of low-wage precarious work in a post-Fordist labor market. As geographer Jamie Peck puts it in *Workfare States*, "Under conditions of falling wages, chronic underemployment, and job casualization, workfarism maximizes (and effectively mandates) participation in contingent, low-paid work by churning workers back into the bottom of the labor market, or by holding them deliberately 'close' to the labor market in a persistently 'job-ready' state."[2]

Though given the small number of DPSS customers who are actually mandated to participate in welfare-to-work programming, the symbolic motives of workfare may be stronger than the material ones. As a political project, workfare is fueled in large part by efforts to punitively and paternalistically react to the "welfare queen" and other racist and sexist mythologies that emerged following the successes of the civil rights movement. Building on Patricia Hill Collins's writings about the welfare queen stereotype, sociologist Dawn Marie Dow argues the subtext of this controlling image is clear: "Staying at home to raise children is not an appropriate use of African American mothers' time, and if they receive welfare benefits, they should be obligated to work."[3] Thus, rather than simply provide low-wage employers with cheap labor, workfare expresses a cultural commitment to imposing work expectations on particular populations.

Together, these forces conspire to put a highly politicized minority of welfare recipients to work, despite the fact that most working age people who seek means-tested aid tend to be employed on the margins anyway.[4] And while workfare does basically nothing to challenge the structural roots of poverty, research does suggest it pushes people further into formal employment.[5] It succeeds, so to speak, in serving some employers with low-wage labor; more importantly, it serves a reactionary public the *image* of a postwelfare state.

In Los Angeles, workfare exists most explicitly through GAIN and to a lesser extent through START. GAIN stands for Greater Avenues for Independence, while START stands for Skills and Training to Achieve Readiness for Tomorrow. GAIN is the mandated welfare-to-work program for able-bodied parents receiving CalWORKs, but it first emerged across the state of California in the 1980s during the long sunset of AFDC. START is a similar but much smaller work-first program that emerged for those receiving General Relief, and it was modeled heavily on GAIN. Those mandated to participate in GAIN are disproportionately mothers while those mandated to participate in START are disproportionately single men. Like essentially all welfare-to-work participants across the nation, those on GAIN and START are expected to complete weekly "activity hours" in order to remain in good standing in their programs. Falling short on activity hours puts clients at risk of being "sanctioned" and having their cash aid cut or significantly reduced. And both programs assume temporary participation.

Workfare programming does not just concern the labor, or potential labor, of welfare clients. It also necessitates the labor of frontline public servants. And specialized eligibility workers will not cut it. Another kind of frontline laborer is required to promote and police workfare activities. Such a worker must officially focus less on processing people and more on changing them. They must also work a different kind of subject, not office "customers" but program "participants."

These workers—often categorized in program documents as "welfare-to-work workers" (WTW workers)—are scattered throughout Los Angeles. Some can be located in about half of the county's district offices, tucked away in relatively small units specializing in START operations. Most, however, exist in the nearly dozen DPSS-run GAIN offices that are physically detached from these branches. And, as noted in chapter 2, another minority of these workers can be found in privatized GAIN offices in the San Fernando and Antelope valleys.

While all the county-employed GAIN and START workers I met first cut their teeth in the agency as eligibility workers, their jobs as WTW workers were different in terms of both content and context. In addition to handling participants instead of customers, these workers labor under a system of casework rather than taskwork.

The WTW workers who handle GAIN and START cases are officially called "services workers," but the title is a little misleading. Indeed, these workers do not directly train clients for employment; nor do they run workshops for resume building or manage transitional job programs. Instead, they refer their clients to outside organizations that administer workfare programming. This brokering labor is mixed with a kind of diagnostic work, as these workers determine specific referrals (and exemptions), and with a kind of policing work, as they surveil and sanction their participants' performance in referred activities.

But this is still just part of the story. In addition to pipelining their subjects into traditional workfare activities, they connect many to *schoolfare* via GED classes, vocational training, and community college programs. It is also not uncommon for them to link clients to *medfare* via mental health treatments, substance abuse counseling, and temporary disability screening. Additionally, these workers connect clients to *housefare* programming in the form of temporary shelter vouchers, childcare services, domestic violence treatment, and a range of interventions focused on home dynamics.[6]

Nonetheless, the WTW workers find themselves on the welfare assembly line, albeit on a section distinct from what was outlined in the previous chapter. There was no regime of taskwork in the GAIN and START units I encountered, and the WTW workers within them were generally expected to engage with their clients in much deeper ways than their eligibility worker counterparts. However, as a pair of GAIN workers reminded me at a labor rally outside a Los Angeles County Board of Supervisors meeting, assembly line conditions remain alive and well in welfare-to-work programming. The conveyor belts may move a bit slower, and workers may handle cases for longer periods, but this is still work marked by sequential separation, worker specialization, and automation.

This chapter examines the labor of WTW workers in Los Angeles welfare offices.[7] Just as the eligibility worker position was designed to proletarianize welfare staff, so too was the position of the GAIN worker (and its younger sibling position in START). But where eligibility work primarily involves "seeing customers," welfare-to-work programming primarily involves "making participants." The eligibility workers are oriented toward materializing a "customer service state," while the WTW workers are oriented toward materializing a "workfare state"—or at least the image of one. The latter is made possible through a kind of mechanized social work in which case-work is reinvented as a highly standardized system only to be labored by workers with narrowed discretion.

Tracy's World

Black Boxes

Just south of Compton, in an unincorporated area of Los Angeles County, stands a discreet, hedge-covered building with no signage. A flagpole in the front displays a flag with a county seal, but there's nothing to clearly indicate that this is a welfare office. When I arrived in the fall of 2021, I had to pull out my phone and open the DPSS web-site just to triple-check I was in the right place.

But as soon as I stepped inside, it was immediately clear that I was. A security officer greeted me and ran my bag through an X-ray machine. I then passed through a metal detector into a small lobby with three receptionist windows and a large poster with the same keywords that hung above Camila in the Metro North office: effi-ciency, accuracy, courtesy, knowledge, and seamlessness.

One of the upper managers, or "deputies," from the office es-corted me to a larger room where roughly seventy-five WTW workers were divided up into cubicles large enough to include one-on-one meetings with participants.[8] I soon learned that this flat distribution of labor was, however, a bit misleading when considering the opera-tional hierarchy of GAIN.

There are, in fact, different "levels" of workfare programming. The largest level at GAIN is the most basic one. The workers I shad-owed usually called it "regular flow" or simply "the floor," and it is sequentially divided by two major unit types: intake and approval. Intake workers primarily handle onboarding and appraisal assign-ments before handing their cases off to approval-side workers for longer-term service. Some cases, however, are diverted up to more case-intensive units. The next level is "specialized supportive services." This is still workfare, but employment is framed as a more distant goal separated by surmountable "barriers" in mental health, substance use, and domestic violence. Finally, above this in terms of programming intensity, there is a smaller set of workers assigned to "family stabilization" units, which include all the same referrals as specialized supportive services plus some for children's programming (e.g., counseling and tutoring). It also includes a targeted program called Linkages, which helps synchronize GAIN requirements with those imposed by the county's primary family-policing agency, the Department of Children and Family Services. As one worker described it to me, family stabilization is like specialized supportive services "on steroids." START has a similar, though more rudimentary, structure that separates casework not only based on the sequential distinction between intake and approval but also on the intensity of intervention—though it lacks any family stabilization efforts. START workers further from "the floor" nonetheless offer more specialized attention to a fewer number of cases.

While there are important differences between WTW workers depending where they are stationed in this complex division of labor, much of their job is the same. Those on the floor have more cases, and they are more likely to directly emphasize employment than those assigned to more specialized case management, but all GAIN and START WTW workers are essentially charged with authorizing, observing, and incentivizing their participants' welfare-to-work activities. A key part of their job is to get participants to partake in program-legible hours so that they can remain eligible for cash aid, whether it be for CalWORKs (for those in GAIN) or General Relief (for those in START). Legible hours may include formal employment or structured job searching. But while getting their subjects to work may be the ultimate objective, it need not be the immediate objective if there are "barriers" to handle first.

Tracy, a Black GAIN worker in her mid-thirties, is stationed in a specialized supportive services unit. There, she works cases handed to her from the floor.[9] In turn, she primarily works to refer these clients to mental health, domestic violence, or substance abuse treatments. Several of her participants also take part in various education programs to meet their activity hours. At any given time, Tracy holds about seventy specialized supportive services cases, the vast majority of which are for those completing their workfare activity hours with programs focused on teaching, healing, or stabilizing participants for the sake of their employability.[10]

One sunny January morning, I stepped into Tracy's world. Once inside, I moved a chair to the side of the desk so that I could see both Tracy and her computer screen, which she kindly angled a bit for me to get a better view. Tracy, a five-year veteran WTW worker, is quiet but very generous in explaining how her job works.

One of the first things Tracy showed me was a thick binder with what must have been hundreds of documents detailing the contact information and eligibility criteria for DPSS contracted programs throughout the county. Despite its size, Tracy told me, "There's never enough providers." She quickly qualified this statement to note that there are never enough providers that match her clients' needs. Tracy can easily find contracted substance abuse programs, for example, but sometimes they're far away from her participants or have inconvenient hours. Likewise, she does not have trouble connecting participants to general domestic violence (DV) services, but they do not always provide the kinds of interventions her clients want (e.g., domestic violence *housing*).

For the most part though, there is a lot of mystery to the structured activities Tracy and her peers link their participants to. She described the programs as "black boxes" and somewhat embarrassingly admitted that she didn't know exactly what specific interventions are being made within most of the organizations she pipelines her clients to. Her insights are largely limited to program flyers and the occasional insights provided by her participants. Tracy's task is to push people into black box activities for the sake of changing them.[11]

I watched as she made some phone calls, typed some emails, and completed some paperwork at her cubicle. First, she called Hannah, one of her DV participants. Per Hannah's current welfare-to-work contract, she is required to see a contracted DV counselor three hours a week.[12] The rest of her GAIN activity hours are to be spent on full-time community college coursework. It was the school hours that concerned Tracy on this particular day. She called Hannah after receiving, from a CalWORKs counselor at the community college, a new course schedule and requested major change.

"I know you took twelve credits last semester and struggled," Tracy said over the phone. "You feel comfortable doing twenty-two credits? . . . I don't want you to get overwhelmed." Tracy was worried Hannah was planning to take too many classes. Her tone struck me as authentically caring and encouraging. She spoke more as a kind coach than a cold bureaucrat. After advising Hannah to drop a couple of classes, Tracy then asked about the request to change majors. She explained, "I want you to graduate and move to the next level, to a four-year institution." Hannah confirmed her intended major change and explained how her community college counselor supported the shift. Tracy said the major change was fine, but it required a new welfare-to-work contract. She ended the call by telling Hannah about a $500 ancillary payment she could give her for schoolbooks.

After Tracy hung up the phone, she immediately began some paperwork. She added information about Hannah's school activity under the employment services tab on the California Statewide Automated Welfare System (CalSAWS). She then printed a new welfare-to-work contract. She highlighted the sections that needed to be signed by Hannah and then dropped it in the mail.[13] Tracy then processed ancillary funds for internet support—$20 a month to be added to Hannah's electronic benefit transfer (EBT) card—since her activity qualifies for this aid. Next, she emailed the CalWORKs counselor at the community college. She noted that Hannah's new major has been approved, but she expressed concern that so many major changes would affect time to graduate. Finally, Tracy emailed her supervisor. She explained to me that because of the complexity of this case, it must be sent to a supervisor and then the supervisor must send it to a deputy for authorization.

Before moving on to the next case, Tracy took a quick restroom break. Upon her return, she noticed my furious notetaking. Like many of the workers I shadowed, she seemed amused by my interests in her routine work processes. She asked with some levity and surprise, "This stuff doesn't bore you?" I assured her I found her work fascinating. And as a student of the labor process, I was neither lying nor exaggerating. I was happy to witness Tracy's particular world of work—a world where she helps maintain a stretched and frayed safety net made not only of referrals to employment programs but also to schools, health care, and more.

Extending Olivia

Tracy admitted that WTW work can be a bit mundane. However, she also noted that it can be taxing. The job "takes a toll," she told me. "I can't help but get emotionally invested in participants."[14] She assured me that her concern for Hannah and the other participants she aided under my gaze was genuine, and given the interactions I observed, I believed her. I also believe that she finds much of her work to be rewarding.

This was evident to me when I watched Tracy work an "extender" case. Extenders are for special GAIN cases on the welfare assembly line; they are for clients who are conditionally permitted to participate in the program and receive cash aid even though they "timed out" of CalWORKs.[15] Remember, CalWORKs is a *Temporary* Assistance for Needy Families program. The federal government limits these benefits to sixty months for parents (but not children).[16] However, extenders can be given to CalWORKs parents under special circumstances.

As Tracy explained to me, extenders are given to people "who timed out but need mental health, domestic violence, or substance abuse [services]" in order to receive a full CalWORKs check. Materializing an extender keeps the adult case on the assembly line when it would otherwise have been diverted off. Without an extender, the participant can only receive cash aid for their children.

In this particular case, the extender request is from Olivia, a midtwenties mother of one who was referred to specialized supportive services from the GAIN floor. As Olivia approached the end of her CalWORKs clock, this other WTW worker informed her of the extender policy. Neither Tracy nor I knew the exact details of this conversation, but per their notes posted on CalSAWS the worker referred Oliva's case up from the floor to specialized supportive services so that she could request an extender for domestic violence services.

I watched and listened to Tracy as she called Olivia. "I see you're requesting domestic violence services," said Tracy after a brief greeting. "You have timed out of CalWORKs," she continued. "Once you get in domestic violence services, you'll get benefits." Because all domestic violence cases require an in-office signature (for reasons of privacy and security), Tracy noted, "We have to bring you in here first and sign a contract before you get services." She then explained to her participant that before this errand she would need to complete a forty-five-or-so-minute interview over the phone.

Olivia agreed to do the interview then and there. Tracy opened an OCAT—the Online CalWORKs Appraisal Tool—screen in CalSAWS and began the interview. After stating some of the pre-question descriptions and disclaimers, many of which she seemed to know by heart, Tracy asked the questions listed on the OCAT tab and entered Olivia's responses into the computer.

I captured the appraisal interview from beside Tracy, by listening to her end of the conversation and watching what she input on the computer:

"Do you identify as a female?" Yes.

"I see you have one child." Yes.

"Do you need a childcare referral?" Yes.

"Are you currently working?" No.

"Have you worked a job that's provided a paystub?" Yes.

"If offered a job interview tomorrow, would you have clothes for the interview?" Yes.

"What about ID and Social Security card? Would you be able to bring that to an interview?" Yes.

Tracy was fairly robotic in both tone and content at the beginning of the call. However, after many more standardized yes/no and short-response questions, the interview became more conversational. Her tone softened a bit when she asked Oliva why she did not currently hold a job. Tracy seemed to sympathize with the participant's struggle to find decent-paying work. "Any restaurant or retail experience?" she asked, going off script a bit. Oliva said no and then stated that she was interested in a career in finance or a related field. Tracy recommended Oliva look into business programs.

But school enrollment won't help with activating an extender. So Tracy moved on and shifted her attention to questions of domestic violence and health. She pulled out some standardized screening forms to organize the process. As expected, Oliva confirmed her need for domestic violence services. And while she did not indicate any substance abuse treatment needs, she did score a few points on the mental health evaluation form—mostly because she reported feeling sad and nervous in the past thirty days. It wasn't enough to warrant a mandatory referral to the Department of Mental Health (DMH), but it was enough to offer a voluntary referral.

"Ok," Tracy said as the interview came to a close. "So, you can go forward with a domestic violence or a mental health extender. You can also get both services . . . . You tell me what's easiest." The conversation then shifted away from programming substance and toward issues of convenience. Tracy wanted to know which referral would be the most practical for Olivia. She explained that a domestic-violence service referral requires an in-person visit to the office for a contract signing and an initial visit to the service provider. The mental health referral requires two appointments via DMH, but it is possible that both can be completed remotely over the phone.

Despite being initially referred to specialized supportive services from the GAIN floor for a domestic violence extender, Oliva ended her appraisal interview with a plan to extend her CalWORKs clock via mental health services. Per policy, Tracy did not need to refer Olivia to DMH. The mental health screening score simply necessitated a voluntary referral offer. However, Tracy, in her search for her participant's path of least resistance, compared referrals and gave Olivia the choice to self-sort into domestic violence or mental health treatment. By the end of the interview, the question of greatest importance was not which service better matched Olivia's primary problem or "employment barrier." Instead, Tracy searched for the referral that was "easiest" for Olivia at that particular moment in her life.[17]

Problem Solving

Frontline work at DPSS has long involved at least some employees referring their clients to various providers across the delegated and discontinuous welfare state. Beyond testing means, a significant minority of workers have been tasked with alleviating a multitude of sufferings, or "problems," with referral-based "solutions." The following quote comes from a DPSS manual printed as social workers were becoming increasingly rare following the emergence of eligibility workers: "The Social Worker's job can be viewed, in part, as a function of matching a problem with a solution. The problems experienced by service clientele vary widely, and the social worker cannot be expected to personally solve all such problems . . . . Therefore, when the social worker and client cannot solve such problems alone, the social worker can refer the client to (or match the client with) a particular community resource."[18]

Welfare workers, be they social workers in in the mid-century or WTW workers today, have long had the function of "matching" problems with solutions via referrals.[19] At least at DPSS, they have never been direct providers of services. Instead, they have long confronted suffering with referral sheets—and now screens. So, what has changed in the past half century? Much can be said about transformations in the methods of matching. Referrals have become more standardized via screening forms, procedure trees, computerized appraisal tools, and so on. More on that in a bit.

But standardization is just part of the story. The problems and solutions have also shifted with the rise of workfare. The kinds of suffering seen as worthy of program referrals is now more narrowly and explicitly recognized as "barriers to employment," a broad pathology covering individualized deficiencies in knowledge, health, and domestic life. While the provision of means-tested assistance has long been coupled with efforts to promote self-sufficiency and personal responsibility, this intensified in the 1980s as county welfare departments throughout California became more explicitly committed to pushing their recipients deeper into the world of work.[20] Indeed, go-to remedies for a series of problems are now also more specifically oriented toward labor market participation and readiness. Formal referrals for education, mental health treatments, shelter aid, and so on have certainly become more numerous via the rise of GAIN and START, but they have also been explicitly geared toward teaching, medicating, or stabilizing subjects for the sake of their employability. This, in turn, is officially pursued under welfare-to-work programming for the sake of funneling people off means-tested assistance and into an elusive existence of self-sufficiency and personal responsibility.[21]

WTW workers like Tracy are, in short, heavily constrained by not only the solutions they can offer but also the kinds of problems they can intervene in. As welfare-to-work case handlers, they are given a referral toolkit designed specifically to mitigate "barriers to employment." On this portion of the welfare assembly line, the instruments in this kit are the primary tools they have at their disposal.

Even so, this does not mean she cannot exercise any discretion at all. Tracy may need to update an employment services tab on her computer and print workfare-oriented contracts when making most of her referrals, but she has some latitude to rethink the problems and solutions she's matching. Sure, Tracy grilled Hannah and Olivia about their labor market prospects, but she seemed more concerned with assuring they remained minimally compliant with GAIN so that they could continue to receive cash aid. She may have been limited by rules and tools, but her "matching" job still allowed her to "work with" participants.

Not everyone I shadowed worked referrals this way. Consistent with the policy as written, and in contrast to Tracy, some WTW workers I shadowed were more preoccupied with employment barriers as the primary and most immediate problem of concern. Others complained about the "lax" COVID rules and said part of the toolbox of solutions must include more negative sanctions in addition to referrals. For the most part, however, I was exposed to workstyles and perspectives like Tracy's. Rather than find cubicles manned with stern champions of work-first programming, I generally encountered workers interested in helping their clients stay afloat on CalWORKs and General Relief until the state inevitably reduced their benefits.

Referralfare

To be clear, workfare is alive and well in Los Angeles. While roughly 38 percent of adults on CalWORKs are excused from participating in GAIN due to medical reasons, parenting very young children, or a handful of other situations, most do participate in the welfare-to-work program.[22] In January 2020, before "COVID good cause" policies temporarily paused sanctions and expanded exemptions, GAIN workers registered 31 percent of program enrollees in activities of employment, job club, structured job searches, and the like.[23]

However, many participants are also engaged in alternative and supplemental activities. During that same month, GAIN workers enrolled approximately 11 percent of their subjects in GED classes, vocational programs, college programs, and related educational activities.[24] They connected roughly the same number to mental health and substance abuse services.[25] GAIN workers also referred about 11 percent of participants to domestic violence services. These work-alternative activities may not fully cover a participant's programming activity hours (up to thirty hours for single parents), and they are certainly not exclusionary. My time in GAIN offices and my conversations with WTW workers nonetheless suggest that referring and registering these alternatives is a crucial part of the job. And while I do not have comparable data for START, my fieldwork suggests these workers are even more likely to refer their subjects to these work alternatives because these mostly single, and often homeless, participants are seen as suffering from more intense employment barriers. Added together, WTW workers in the welfare agency I studied help maintain a complex web of programming referrals that involves not only workfare proper but also schoolfare, medfare, and housefare.

TABLE 3 Workfare alternatives and supplements

	Schoolfare	Medfare	Housefare
Ends	Employability	Employability	Employability
Means	Learn	Heal	Stabilize
Examples	Employment skills classes, GED prep, college credit, vocational training	Mental health treatment, substance use disorder programming, medical exemption	Temporary housing assistance, childcare, domestic violence counseling

Table 3 details some of the core similarities and differences between these workfare alternatives and supplements. They all share the official end of employment. The ultimate objective is to connect participants to activities like GED prep, substance use disorder programming, and temporary housing assistance so that they can, in turn, become more employable. The assumed means of doing so, however, are distinct. Schoolfare activities mandate that participants learn; medfare activities mandate that participants heal; and housefare activities mandate that participants stabilize—all for the sake of employability. As such, referrals to these kinds of activities do a lot to enable workfare, especially on paper. Most are literally printed on welfare-to-work contracts. But in practice, these referrals can also serve as temporary safety valves for WTW workers to provide some momentary relief from labor market tyranny.

This is not to suggest that welfare workers in GAIN and START only write program referrals, but it is a central part of their jobs. It is the primary way they make active subjects of the workfare state—that is, clients who participate in formally recognized welfare-to-work activities. Of course, these workers also famously warn and sanction their participants per federal and state regulations, first with warning letters and then with aid cutoffs.[26]

However, we can't really understand these punitive mechanisms without recognizing the importance of extradepartmental referrals. Sanctions are slapped on noncomplaint participants, usually those who have not undertaken a referred activity like a GED class or a mental health treatment.

It's not just the sticks that are linked to referrals. So too are the carrots. WTW workers are equipped to give small forms of ancillary aid to support their participants' referred activities. They can, for example, give petty funds for bus passes, textbooks, and other resources to support activity compliance. Referrals to extradepartmental programs are not everything, but they are critical to understanding frontline labor in mandated workfare programs like GAIN and START.

Where eligibility workers see customers, WTW workers *make participants*. Making participants entails more than turning welfare recipients into "cases" in either GAIN or START. It means mandating and guiding subjects into particular activities beyond the welfare office—not just into work but into classrooms, clinics, and more. This is an essential feature of the welfare assembly line.

Schoolfare

Welfare workers in Los Angeles have long been referring their cash aid recipients—first those on AFDC and then later those on CalWORKs and General Relief—to classrooms. In the 1960s and 1970s, frontline workers referred or directed many clients to adult and remedial education centers.[27] However, it was not until GAIN in the 1980s and START (formerly GROW) in the 1990s that schoolfare was really solidified in Los Angeles.[28]

Since their inception, GAIN and START have equipped WTW workers with the tools to refer participants to various education and training programs administered by the Los Angeles County Office of

Education (LACOE).[29] As the nation's largest regional educational agency, LACOE is mostly known for the services it provides K–12 students across the county's fragmented school districts. However, for WTW workers, LACOE is a common place to refer adult participants to. A LACOE referral is but another "box to check"—or at least a box to seriously consider checking—on essentially all cases.[30]

The boundaries between workfare and schoolfare are often fuzzy. When WTW workers make a referral to LACOE—usually with a single phone call and follow-up email—it is often for job-readiness classes that lead not to a degree or certification but instead to the expectation that clients will initiate a job search. GAIN workers, for example, refer many of their participants to LACOE for job club. This month-long class offers lessons in resume building, interview strategies, and the like. Such programming focuses primarily on teaching labor market skills.

Schoolfare, however, involves more than just job club courses. GAIN and START workers also write referrals to LACOE for adult basic education services, high school equivalency programs, English-as-a-second-language courses, and lifestyle classes.[31] They also refer participants to this same agency for short-term skills training so they can become employable as security officers, nursing assistants, logistic technicians, and so on. Some courses focus broadly on office occupations. WTW workers are also trained to see and count specific kinds of education as legitimate program activities. In this regard, participants can do a kind of "reverse referral" into schoolfare by enrolling in approved postsecondary schooling and then submitting documentation to have it count toward program hours.[32]

In promoting its GAIN operations, the LACOE website states that they seek to "serve local businesses and employers" by connecting them with employable welfare recipients.[33] External evaluations of the program have also noted how job club instructors ask participants to treat the class "like a job" and to get "into the habit of coming to job club on time and dressed appropriately" so that they are better prepared for the "world of work."[34] Even the more school-like activities such as the GED prep courses, vocational programs, and college credits are broadly justified under a workfare logic. School is not referred or recognized for its own sake; it's always promoted as a path from welfare to work.

Indeed, the point of schoolfare is to turn participants—who are disproportionally poor mothers and disproportionately Black and brown women—into students so that they may then be turned into self-sufficient workers. As educational expert Vanessa Sheared notes, recent welfare reforms in the United States have come with "a growing sentiment to assist women 'get off' welfare by providing them with educational opportunities that lead to 'work,'" and more specifically work in the formal economy.[35]

Maybe it was because I was a university professor poking my head around the offices, but that was certainly a sentiment I confronted during my fieldwork. The majority of the GAIN and START workers I met told me they valued education and preferred to guide their participants toward some kind of schooling—be it in LACOE, a community college, or a state university. They certainly saw differences in the quality of their schoolfare referrals. WTW workers were generally less optimistic about job club than they were about other programs at LACOE. Regardless, they mostly framed schooling as a relatively promising way to change their subjects into more self-sufficient worker-citizens. It was at least typically seen as a more promising activity to list on welfare-to-work contracts than simple job searching.

Medfare

WTW workers funnel many of their participants not just into classrooms but also clinics. They work within a broader field of interventions in which the boundaries between social services and health care have become especially blurred.[36] As cash aid became stingier, more poor people turned to the doctor's office for disability claims, the emergency department for nonmedical aid, health bureaucracies for housing vouchers, and other medical organizations for social services. At the same time, welfare agencies like DPSS have increased their focus on medicalized forms of assistance. This is evident in the district offices where far more Medi-Cal cases are processed than CalFresh, CalWORKs, or General Relief cases.

In the GAIN and START cubicles, much is done to produce a kind of medfare. WTW workers direct their participants into health-oriented programs that are used for potentially excusing or substituting workfare activity hours. Workers typically initiate this funneling by making referrals to those with more power to define a person as ill, disabled, or disordered. In essence, they identify participants as *potentially* needing medial exemption or aid and then refer them to those with more medical expertise to cast an official judgement.

START workers, for example, usually begin their welfare-to-work assessments by asking their participants if they have any health issues that limit their employability. If a participant articulates even a general concern, workers are instructed to give them a physical health assessment form for them to take to a Medi-Cal-accepting clinic of their choice. The form is a sort of standardized doctor's note to be completed by a primary care provider and returned directly to the GAIN office. The frontside includes checklists for various medical problems and medically legible disabilities (e.g., stroke, cancer, total deafness). The backside asks more pressing questions about whether or not the participant's medical condition "prevents full-time sedentary work" or whether there are limitations to lifting or frequent standing and walking. GAIN workers similarly direct potentially sick and disabled participants to clinics to confirm their inability or limited ability to work. But where exemption paperwork tends to focus on pathologies of "physical health," documentation leading to the substitution of standard workfare activity hours tends to emphasize "mental health" and "substance use disorders."

This is particularly apparent in GAIN. Because CalWORKs is a state- and federally funded program that is audited more regularly than General Relief, the tracking of weekly activity hours is especially important. GAIN workers utilize a two-sided screening form to determine whether their participants can or must be referred to a clinic for a more thorough evaluation. Workers ask participants if they have, in the past thirty days, felt debilitatingly nervous, frightened, or "down in the dumps" and whether or not they have had trouble sleeping, eating, or focusing. They also ask about thoughts of harming themselves and other people and whether the participant has "heard or seen things other people don't see or hear." Workers then calculate a score based on the answers to determine whether a more in-depth clinical assessment via DMH is mandated. Should a DMH worker deem it appropriate or necessary, the participant is then referred to a public or contracted mental health clinic.[37]

On the same form, workers then ask their participants five questions about frequency of alcohol consumption, prescription drug abuse, and injections "for non-medical purposes." Another score is then calculated to determine whether a substance use disorder screening is required via a treatment contractor, many of whom are subcontracted by the Los Angeles County Department of Public Health.[38] If and once a referred assessment concludes with a recommendation for mental health or substance use disorder programming, WTW workers are then tasked with tracking their participants' attendance in treatment.

Like schoolfare, the general point of medfare, at least on paper, is to fix subjects so that they may become employable and eventually ineligible for cash assistance. Both the classroom and the clinic are seen as temporary stops on a straight and narrow road off welfare. Referrals to these spaces are formally justified in the name of changing people from "dependent" to "self-sufficient." As one mental health services flyer that START workers frequently give their participants states, "Counseling can also help you remove barriers keeping you from self-sufficiency and employment." Likewise, a nonprofit contracted by DPSS to provide mental health and substance abuse treatment to GAIN participants offers services "targeted to help each client achieve an optimal level of functioning, with a focus on self-reliance and a successful transition into stable employment."[39]

This is not to say that WTW workers are fully convinced their medfare referrals are good. Some, like Emilia, a fifty-one-year-old Latina WTW worker in the Monterey Park GAIN office, worry that DPSS medical exemptions and substitutions encourage malingering.[40] She told me between making a few phone calls in her cubicle, "We're not empowering them . . . . We're incentivizing them to be sick. It's cool to be sick." A more general sentiment I encountered among workers, however, concerned the suspected inadequacy of the mysterious programs they were referring their participants to. Lori, a forty-six-year-old white WTW worker in the same office, told me she was concerned the mental health programs clients were referred to after a DMH assessment were focused more on work than on wellness. That was certainly the impression she got from her participants who enrolled in these programs.

Housefare

What I am calling *housefare* covers a range of interventions focused on the domestic life of participants, or lack thereof. Often, housefare entails referrals to paltry forms of aid to cover temporary or permanent shelter costs. However, it can also involve referrals to services that seek to supplement or shape relations in the home via childcare, domestic violence counseling, and more. Either way, the point of housefare is to stabilize a participant's household conditions so that they are enabled to work or at least participate in schoolfare or medfare activities.[41]

GAIN workers, for example, often make simple and largely informal referrals to specialized "homeless eligibility workers" in the district offices. They do this by giving participants the phone number for DPSS homeless specialists and by handing (or mailing) fact sheets and paper applications for a series of meager shelter benefits limited to those receiving CalWORKs. The most popular of these is a state-funded aid program that gives $85 a day (for a maximum of sixteen cumulative days) for a family of four to stay in a hotel.[42] There is then a supplemental county program for participants to access fourteen additional days of "hotel money" after they have exhausted the state program.[43] GAIN workers can also refer their clients to these DPSS homeless workers for eviction prevention funds, moving assistance, and short-term rental subsidies.[44] Meanwhile, START workers can help connect their participants to rental subsidies of up to $475 a month for an individual ($950 for a couple), but this requires participants to dedicate nearly half of their General Relief grant ($100) to rent.[45] They can also provide them with a $500 once-in-a-lifetime move-in assistance grant.[46] Drops in the bucket to say the least.

All these forms of aid come with explicit behavioral expectations. Those in the GAIN program who are offered temporary housing assistance (e.g., "hotel money") must actively seek permanent shelter. Meanwhile, those offered permanent shelter assistance (e.g., eviction prevention) are mandated to work full time or participate in schoolfare or medfare activities.[47] And getting the paltry rental or move-in assistance tied to General Relief assumes participants are compliant with the START program.

Housefare can also take the form of referrals to programs focused on the relational dynamics of the home. These, too, ultimately aim to augment a broader, if highly symbolic, mission to change people from welfare dependent to self-sufficient. Like aid for shelter costs, this kind of housefare aims to enable participants' engagement in approved welfare-to-work activities.

Consider a few examples. GAIN workers can refer clients to one of a dozen childcare referral agencies contracted by the California Department of Education. Such a "referral for a referral" is designed to connect participants with a licensed childcare provider.[48] Beyond this, GAIN workers can connect their participants to "license-exempt child care" resources so that more informal forms of care, like that provided by a "friend, family member, or neighbor" can be compensated.[49] They can also refer clients to a series of contracted domestic violence services including specialized counseling, domestic violence shelters, parenting classes, legal aid, and more.[50] Referrals for many of these programs are handled by GAIN workers in specialized supportive services or family stabilization units where casework is more "intense."

As with educational and medical referrals, those for various forms of domestic assistance are not particularly new at DPSS. Before GAIN and START, DPSS maintained a referral book that included services for housing aid, marriage counseling, day care centers, and the like.[51] The rise in workfare programming expanded and transformed these kinds of referrals into what I am calling housefare. These referrals are not only more common and more standardized; they are also more explicitly connected to a broader mission to push the poor off welfare and deeper into the "world of work."

Proletarianizing the Program Brokers

Wrench in the Works

At end of the century, DPSS managers were proudly articulating a vision of welfare consistent with Clinton-era reforms: "The new social contract between the welfare system and participants represents a fundamental break with the past. Until now, the welfare system's primary mission was to determine eligibility and deliver benefits in the correct amount and in a timely manner.... The new mission of the welfare system is to help families become economically self-sufficient by providing services and enforcing the requirement that participants avail themselves of those services.... The Department of Public Social Services (DPSS) must transform itself into a service-delivery organization that motivates and empowers participants."[52]

This was indeed a new way to understand welfare offices in Los Angeles, but it did not emerge out of thin air. By the mid-1980s, DPSS was a relatively well-greased people-processing machine. Social workers had largely been purged from the payroll. And, once Children and Family Services became a separate department in 1984, the agency became an even more specialized bureaucracy for issuing, maintaining, and, of course, denying benefits. Sure, this was still a time of casework, and the vocabulary of customer service had yet to be integrated into the department discourse; but it was in the aftermath of this reorganization that DPSS looked most like a place explicitly designed to process people. There was a kind of ritualistic simplicity if you were a client: take a number, have a seat, wait your turn. A worker on the welfare assembly line would eventually call you and would then render you legible as either "eligible" or "ineligible" of aid.

But then, in 1985, California lawmakers passed the GAIN Bill, which tasked county governments with integrating more people-changing efforts into their welfare offices.[53] It was no longer enough to distribute aid quickly and accurately. Welfare offices needed to also turn the poor into self-sufficient worker-citizens. These spaces were to become less like welfare bureaucracies and more like "a cross between a temporary employment agency and a therapist's office."[54] That, at least, was the mythology of welfare reform.[55]

GAIN was not a surprise for those who were paying attention. County governments had been toying around with smaller workfare initiatives since the early 1970s, and before that the postwar welfare state had long emphasized some work-oriented welfare interventions.[56] Much of this was made possible through a series of federal waivers that allowed local welfare agencies to condition AFDC payments on job-search and employment-readiness programming for able-bodied parents.[57] Such amendments were especially appealing to politicians who wanted to enforce the moral principles of work over cash assistance while also tightening the budget—that, at least, was the general sentiment shared by Republican governor George Deukmejian and, a bit reluctantly, by the Democratic state legislature at the time.[58] The logic was relatively simple: If welfare offices could transform their subjects from "welfare dependents" into "self-sufficient citizens," then this would increase state legitimacy while decreasing state budgets.[59]

The state-wide GAIN plan was most explicitly inspired by the San Diego Workfare Pilot Program.[60] That particular program was implemented in direct response to the so-called taxpayer revolt of 1978 mentioned in the introduction. San Diego County Board of Supervisor Paul Eckert testified before the Assembly of Human Resource Committee in Sacramento and made these motivations crystal clear:

> The time immediately following the passage of Proposition 13 in 1978 was a period of financial crisis for counties. For the first time, supervisors such as myself were forced to make budgetary decisions that placed the funding of state-mandated programs such as Aid to Families with Dependent Children ahead of strictly county services such as road maintenance and expensive capital improvement projects such as jail construction. . . . The board began to critically re-examine its philosophical approach to public assistance programs. What we found was a system aimed at accommodating as

many recipients as possible with maximum speed and efficiency. We then recognized that we had lost sight of a more fundamental concern, that of assisting welfare recipients to break away from their dependency on welfare.[61]

Eckert and his peers reasoned that they could save money and also remoralize welfare by pushing recipients off the dole and further into low-wage labor.[62] Their demonstration study randomly assigned recipients to job search workshops and mandated work.[63] The workshops covered resume and interview strategies and supplied recipients with job listings and a telephone book to cold call potential employers, while the mandated work experience assigned recipients to three months of work with a public or private nonprofit organization.[64] The proponents of workfare clung to evidence that the program increased formal employment and earnings among AFDC mothers, but they tended to downplay the fact that these women "didn't make enough money to go off welfare," nor were the increased earnings enough to significantly reduce benefit payments.[65]

Nonetheless, a huge wrench was thrown in the works. GAIN became state policy in 1986, and counties were expected to convert their welfare offices into people-changing bureaucracies within a couple years. Accurate and efficient people-processing would no longer cut it. Workfare was imagined to be a kind of budgetary and legitimacy safety valve that would help siphon people off benefits.

But, as Governor Deukmejian would later bemoan in the press, GAIN was not launched as a "true 'workfare' program."[66] As part of a legislative compromise, the program included a heavy emphasis on schoolfare (e.g., basic, vocational, and higher education) and, to a much lesser extent, medfare (especially medical exemptions from participation) and housefare (e.g., childcare subsidies).[67] And this only became more intense when AFDC was replaced with CalWORKs, as one county planning document from 1997 makes clear: "The range of welfare-to-work services will be far broader than ever before, including substance abuse treatment, mental health services, domestic violence counseling, and other services to help participants overcome their barriers to employment."[68] An intensifying challenge for welfare administrators was to connect recipients not only to job-related services but also to services that were meant to teach, cure, and stabilize them so that they could, in theory, become more employable.

This necessitated a different kind of welfare worker. The employee would need to not only monitor and sanction workfare participants but also broker referrals to a range of contracted programs stretched across a fragmented safety net. This worker would also need to be funded with stretched resources, since GAIN was effectively a welfare austerity program. In other words, neither eligibility workers nor social workers would do.

Narrowing Discretion

Shortly after the GAIN Bill passed in Sacramento, managers at DPSS began working on their Los Angeles–specific plan for the program. Agency leadership simultaneously considered two basic models for staffing: one emphasizing insourced discretion and one emphasizing outsourced indiscretion. The former would add a new job to the county payroll, while the latter would contract case management services out to a third party. For the latter to work, however, county administrators needed to convince state officials that such workers would have "no discretion" and instead would be executing procedures established by DPSS.

For their in-house option, management imagined a "journeyman level classification," which they labeled "GAIN Specialist."[69] Such specialists would have relatively high levels of discretion and would "utilize casework skills and make independent judgements for the purpose of developing reliance and self-sufficiency among the GAIN participants."[70] In addition to interacting with potential employers, these specialists were meant to interact with educators, childcare providers, and health care workers. And, as was the case with the workers I shadowed more than three decades later, it was assumed that these specialists would wield both carrots and sticks in the form of ancillary payments and sanctions. However, adding GAIN Specialists to the county payroll soon receded to a backup plan.

Privatization was more appetizing to management and the conservative majority Board of Supervisors. They were understandably reluctant to integrate a people-changing initiative into an already strained but generally effective people-processing machine.[71] They were also curious: If GAIN policy so heavily assumed the provision of program contracts, then why couldn't DPSS contract the execution of frontline case management as well? This would save money by reducing labor costs.[72]

DPSS Director Eddy Tanaka requested the California Department of Social Services to provide details on exactly what could be contracted. The response from above was clear: Due to both federal regulations and California policy, the state could only delegate to its own officials or agents (e.g., county governments) "the authority to exercise administrative discretion."[73] Bureaucrats in Sacramento argued that job training, education services, substance abuse programing, childcare, and the like could (and arguably should) be contracted out to nonprofit and for-profit entities. However, core GAIN work like registration, appraisals, referrals, sanctions, ancillaries, exemptions, and the regulation of welfare-to-work contracts could not be outsourced because they required the exercise of significant discretion over welfare benefits.

The reaction in Los Angeles might best be described as a blending of malicious compliance and legal creativity. Tanaka and the Board of Supervisors reasoned that if the problem was discretion, then perhaps they could eliminate it. They figured DPSS could de-sign a case management contract with protocols so detailed that frontline WTW workers would have no autonomy over determining appraisals, referrals, sanctions, and so on.[74] They marched forward with this logic and soon reviewed proposals submitted by four organizations.

In late 1988, Maximus, a for-profit management consulting firm based in Virginia with zero experience with welfare services, won a $7.8 million-a-year contract.[75] Maximus would still need to employ WTW workers to handle GAIN cases, but these workers would, ac-cording to Tanaka and colleagues, "not perform any discretionary duties."[76] The labor process would, at least on paper, be overdeter-mined by one of two forces: strict protocols from above and partici-pant choice from below.[77]

The plan was for DPSS to design a welfare assembly line specific to the GAIN program and then have Maximus actually run the thing across five offices throughout the county.[78] To help standardize pro-cedure and assure easy monitoring of the line, the county contracted with a software company to develop a new computer program, fittingly called GEARS (GAIN Employment Activity Reporting System).[79] The "computerization of GAIN" was done to automate case tracking, streamline document generation, and minimize "worker involvement."[80]

And, as if imagining that the WTW workers could themselves be a bit like computers, DPSS managers developed a series of codes and commands to structure the kinds of interventions these new welfare workers would perform. They constructed dozens of procedure trees for GAIN workers to follow.[81] One tree, for example, guided workers, step by step, on how to execute a participant appraisal and determine possible exemptions before developing a welfare-to-work contract. Another guided workers in the referral process, detailing how to implement job-service, educational-service, and training-service referrals before ushering participants into a ninety-day job search activity if unemployment continues.[82] One of the more complex trees advised workers about how to handle noncompliant participants, carefully detailing the temporal ordering of sanctions and the rules for determining whether any violations might be accepted under "good cause" provisions.[83] Again, the hope was to eliminate as much worker discretion as possible to justify the legality of outsourcing. The designs of these trees were only to be modified by DPSS officials since it was in their *design*—not their execution—that management argued discretion was at play.

But no computer program or collection of procedures trees could prevent critics from questioning the Maximus contract. The union, frustrated that GAIN funding did not translate into more good county jobs, argued that this privatization violated the law because discretion could never be fully eliminated from welfare work.[84] A similar sentiment was articulated in Sacramento. "It's case management," noted one state bureaucrat in a joint oversight committee meeting at the time. "It's hard for me to conceive of case management being anything but discretionary, particularly in the GAIN program where you're counseling, advising clients how to change their lives significantly."[85] Meanwhile, welfare rights activists argued the contract was bad for the poor and only served to make Maximus rich.[86] Indeed, it was estimated that the contract would essentially pay the top executive at Maximus $238 an hour and his second in command $204 an hour ($653 and $560 in 2025 dollars), effectively making them the highest-paid government "employees" in the state.[87]

However, it was the state legislature and the Deukmejian Administration that provided the most significant challenge to what was to become the first major privatization of frontline welfare services in the United States.[88] They deemed the contract illegal—again on the basis of irreducible frontline discretion—and "retaliated by limiting the county's funding."[89] DPSS was preparing to enact their backup option of employing public GAIN Specialists. But, in one of his final acts as president, Ronald Reagan, who had strong network ties to Maximus, provided the necessary federal authorization for the contract, setting a new precedent for the privatization of WTW programming across the nation.[90]

That was not the end of the drama in Los Angeles. The initial contract with Maximus expired after three years. By that time, the political composition of the Board of Supervisors shifted from the right to the center and the contract was not renewed.[91] The backup plan of adding county-employed GAIN Specialists, now titled "GAIN services workers," became the primary strategy.[92] But the earlier privatization had done a lot to narrow discretion. The assembly line machinery—including the GEARS computer program and the procedure trees—moved into dedicated GAIN offices run by DPSS. Then, in 2000, after another round of fierce debates over welfare contracting, a split Board of Supervisors allowed Maximus to again "provide complete-non-discretionary case management services for the Department's GAIN welfare-to-work program" in the San Fernando and Antelope Valleys.[93] This time, Maximus outbid Lockheed Martin, a defense contractor that had, in the wake of the Cold War, shifted some of its focus toward privatized welfare operations.[94]

This mixed system is still in play today.[95] GAIN workers come in two general species: county and private. DPSS administrators insist that today they save 21 percent by contracting GAIN operations in the San Fernando and Antelope valleys, a savings they credit to the cheaper labor outsourced by Maximus.[96] As noted in chapter 2, the latter is characterized by more precarity, lower compensation, and higher-intensity workloads, but both are defined by highly standardized labor processes. The WTW assembly line, now also implemented in workfare programing for General Relief recipients, is in full effect. While GEARS has been eclipsed with CalSAWS and the printed procedure trees have been absorbed into boxes and drop-down menus in the OCAT tab, the spirit of proletarianized policy work remains. But to what end?

Painful Avenues into Nowhere

Less than two years after the GAIN Bill was signed into law, the Coalition of California Welfare Rights Organizations in Sacramento nicknamed the program PAIN: painful avenues into nowhere.[97] While hyperbolic, the subsequent history of California workfare suggests there are good reasons to embrace the acronym. The addition of WTW workers, contracted or not, has done little to seriously challenge poverty; but it has done a lot to impose additional burdens and sanctions on a highly politicized minority of poor Americans: recipients of cash assistance. The GAIN labor process has mostly integrated the symbols and rituals of a people-changing bureaucracy into a people processing one. While this may add value in the form of increased state legitimacy, it does little to nothing to extend the life chances of participants.

A major evaluation was published nearly ten years after GAIN became state law.[98] Researchers from a third-party research institute conducted a random-assignment experimental study in six counties, including Los Angeles, where subjects were either mandated to participate in GAIN (treatment) or precluded from the program (control). While the study found that GAIN increased the employment rate, the effects were modest: 65 percent among the treatment group versus 60 percent for the control group. And the increased earnings for the GAIN participants were very low: roughly $50 more a month over a five-year period.[99] This was coupled with roughly a $25 monthly reduction in welfare payments, mostly due a systematic shedding of GAIN participants from the dole in years three, four, and five.[100]

The findings were even more bleak in Los Angeles. While GAIN increased the employment rate by 5 percentage points there as well

(49 percent among the treatment vs. 44 percent among the control), there was no statistically significant increase in earnings. Adding insult to injury, there was a $23-a-month reduction in cash assistance.[101] So much for lifting families out of poverty!

Still, state officials found hope in one county: Riverside. There, the GAIN program increased the employment rate by roughly 10 percentage points (72 percent among the treatment vs. 62 percent among the control). As Peck notes, Riverside GAIN was "distinctive in its exhaustive emphasis on placing welfare recipients in a private-sector job—any job—as quickly as possible."[102] This strategy contrasted to the more schoolfare focus of Los Angeles County at the time, but it too included a handful of supplemental services (e.g., childcare).[103] The key difference was that Riverside focused on quick employment before remedial education referrals and the like. It also did not focus its GAIN interventions on their poorest and most vulnerable clients like Los Angeles and the other counties in the study. Even so, Riverside GAIN did little to challenge poverty. The increased employment translated into nearly $85 a month in employment earnings and a $45-a-month reduction in AFDC payments.[104] Netting $40 more a month ($84 in 2025 dollars) is not insignificant when you're poor, but it does little to combat overall hardship.

The program was nonetheless deemed a "success" because a) the AFDC savings were larger than the program costs (material benefit); and b) it enforced work and the imagery of self-sufficiency (symbolic benefit).[105] Riverside came into the national spotlight just as the federal government was considering how to replace AFDC with TANF. This led to what Peck calls a "Riversidization" of welfare departments across the US in the subsequent years. But it was in California where Riverside GAIN seemed to have its greatest impact. On the ten-year anniversary of the GAIN Bill, the California legislature incorporated mandatory upfront job searches, extended stays in job clubs, and more features of Riverside GAIN into the state model.[106] Where San Diego furnished a key model for statewide workfare, Riverside intensified its focus on employment-first programming. This did not eliminate schoolfare, medfare, or housefare but rather acted as a solid reminder that such services should always be directed toward what matters most: putting cash aid recipients to work.

Under 1996 welfare reform, AFDC and GAIN were replaced with CalWORKs. The policy set out to "end welfare as an entitlement and put people to work" as well as "ensure that taxpayers are protected from those who fail to live up to their end of the agreement or those who defraud the system."[107] CalWORKs reaffirmed a county obligation to administer welfare-to-work programming. Such programming no longer needs to be called GAIN throughout the state. That is obviously the case in Los Angeles, but most other counties have opted to rebrand their workfare programs and their employees. In Oakland, for example, the welfare-to-work program for CalWORKs recipients are worked not by GAIN workers but by "employment counselors" inside "Self-Sufficiency Centers" run by the Alameda County Social Services Agency.[108] But the work is effectively the same: augmenting workfare with schoolfare, medfare, and housefare. Whether in Oakland or Los Angeles, CalWORKs maintains a Riverside-style approach focused on pushing participants toward low-wage employment via referrals to a range of third-party services. For most participants, these are still "painful avenues into nowhere."[109]

Despite these patterns, the Los Angeles County government has remained committed to the workfare fantasy. In 1999, the Board of Supervisors launched GROW (General Relief Opportunities for Work) to put extremely poor nonparents to work.[110] In summer 2023 this program was rebranded START (which, again, is an acronym for Skills and Training to Achieve Readiness for Tomorrow).[111] Regardless of the name, the program is heavily modeled on GAIN and involves a similar kind of cubicle work. The hourly expectation for participation is lower for this sister program at twenty hours per week, but it also linked with lower amounts of aid. Those who are compliant with (or exempt from) START receive a pathetic $221 a month.

The tragedy is that programs like GAIN and START are staffed by many well-intentioned people. While there are certainly some jaded and even punitively oriented WTW workers, my fieldwork and interviews suggest that there are more workers who have an authentic desire to alleviate the suffering of their participants. These workers, even at Maximus, tend to hold a relative calling concerned with aiding the poor. But this is a calling denied and twisted by larger policy directives imposed from above. These employees still have to work within the tight constraints of standardized appraisals and black box referrals. And while they have some carrots (e.g., ancillary payments), they are limited in how much they can distribute, and they are also expected to wield sticks (e.g., sanctions). They can only eliminate the pain of workfare to a very limited extent.

And, like the eligibility workers, the WTW workers are stretched thin. They may not be as proletarianized, given that they possess caseloads and are expected to "get to know" their clients more. But they still clock into a welfare assembly line that gives them only a bit more discretion than eligibility workers have in determining how to handle their clients.

Mechanized Social Work

In the previous chapter, I argued that social work effectively died in the Los Angeles welfare office. It was buried under an assembly line designed for accurate and efficient means testing. Welfare has become McDonaldized with respect to not only its frontline labor but also its discourse of customer service.

The rise of welfare-to-work programming has complicated the people-processing objectives of contemporary welfare. No one enters a McDonald's to be transformed; they enter to be conveniently served and momentarily appeased. Workfare programs like GAIN called forth a different kind of welfare worker focused not only on promoting and policing client employment but also brokering a range of auxiliary programs.

County supervisors and welfare managers were pressured by the state legislature to integrate an intensive case-based social work into the welfare assembly line. What emerged, however, was not the professionalized, problem-solving social work of the mid-century welfare office but instead a highly mechanized version of social work. Bureaucratic engineers retooled social work in two major ways. First, they centered both the problems and the solutions on highly individualized concerns of employment and self-sufficiency. Second, they dramatically narrowed the discretionary power of these new welfare workers.

But while the labor of workfare programming today may take the form of mechanized social work, it is important to remember that *workers* like Tracy are not robots. The retooled system is, relative to eligibility work, an intensive form of case management, but it is highly standardized and focused on a work-first mission. This constrains frontline labor in important ways, but some worker autonomy is still exercised. I was surprised that so many of the workers I met were generally less convinced by the formal objectives of workfare and were more committed to helping their participants stay afloat with ancillaries, extenders, and exemptions.

It is in these kinds of activities—not the sanctions or the cold imposition of employment expectations—that these workers find the greatest sense of meaning and purpose in their labor. And, relative to the lower pay and less autonomy of eligibility work, WTW work is widely understood to be the better job. It's just too constrained to be social work, traditionally understood.

Taken together, this and the previous chapter suggest that there are two interconnected sublines of production in Los Angeles welfare offices—one for eligibility workers to "see customers" and one for WTW workers to "make participants." The evidence suggests both kinds of workers have been proletarianized and stretched thin under pressures to produce a customer service state on the one hand and a workfare state on the other. The next two chapters provide some more explicit comparisons the eligibility workers and WTW workers, first by focusing on issues of disciplinary power and second on issues of connective labor. Both will serve to complicate but also sharpen an analysis of proletarianized public servants in the suffering city.

5 Disciplining the Line

Writing about DPSS in the immediate years following 1996 welfare reform, social scientists Alejandra Marchevsky and Jeanne Theoharis characterize the district offices like this: "Today, a person who wants to apply for public assistance in L.A. County must visit an Eligibility Office. In these prison-like structures, visitors pass through metal detectors and past armed security guards on their way to the clerk who is cloistered behind a Plexiglas window. There they must wait for hours in a crowded waiting room before being seen by an Eligibility Worker. From an administrative standpoint, these offices have been redesigned away from social work to run like a well-oiled assembly line."[1]

Indeed, like the securitization of schools, hospitals, and more during the late twentieth century, welfare offices have become more prison-like, and this has been coupled with an emphasis on intensifying work on the frontlines.[2] For DPSS specifically, the punitive turn in welfare occurred not simply with the rise of workfare programs and their sanctions but also in response to distinct local anxieties over urban unrest. Management became increasingly concerned in the early 1990s about "client-on-employee violence" involving "weapons, drugs, and gang-related activities" even though such incidents were rare overall.[3] Facing scrutiny from elected officials and the local media, DPSS managers also felt an increased obligation to find and expel cheating recipients even though—again—such offenses were rare in the grand scheme of things.[4] It was under these conditions that managers increased spending not only on safety glass and metal detectors but also on a "secret computer system designed to prevent fraud" and a now-defunct fingerprint system for tracking recipients.[5]

The possibility of punishment became ever present in the twenty-first-century DPSS offices. I never entered one, for example, that did not clearly display the mugshots of those recently convicted of welfare cheating. Published by the Welfare Fraud Prevention and Investigations Section, these posters shame and warn. They include descriptions of the crime—usually involving some deception about one's earnings or family composition. The posters also detail the amount of funds defrauded from each program, the specific sentencing, and the office that initiated the fraud investigation. For example, a Metro North customer who apparently defrauded CalWORKs of $1,750 and CalFresh of $1,705 via "unreported earnings" was "sentenced to 3 YEARS SUMMARY PROBATION, 75 COMMUNITY SERVICE DAYS, [and was required to] make FULL RESTITUTION in the amount of $3,455.00 and pay a $150.00 FINE." These details were posted under the photo of the customer-turned-criminal's frowning face, amidst a collage of other mugshots. "YOUR FRAUD REFERRALS DO MAKE A DIFFERENCE," state these posters, which were affixed to every welfare office lobby and breakroom I entered during my fieldwork.

But it is not just the clients who are subject to investigation and punishment. Workers on the welfare assembly line are also penalized, albeit in less public and humiliating ways. While digging in the archives I encountered a number of incidents of workers being punished by managers with terminations, suspensions, and more. One employee in a South Los Angeles office in 1993 was suspended without pay for "discourteous behavior," and more specifically for failing to pay a couple of parking tickets issued by in-office security.[6] In a more extreme case the next year in Compton, two workers were arrested for fraudulent benefit issuance and theft of over $10,000 in food stamps.[7] This was the result of a "sting operation" coordinated by DPSS managers and the Sheriff's Department.

We should be careful, however, not to reduce the welfare assembly line to mere despotism and coercion. The kinds of incidents noted above are real and noteworthy, but they are also generally rare. Most clients are not referred for fraud, and fewer are punished for it. And even if sanctions are frequent in workfare programs during tight labor markets, it is important to remember that most who receive benefits from bureaucracies like DPSS are not enrolled in welfare-to-work programs like GAIN or START to begin with. Likewise, most workers at DPSS are not suspended, fired, or arrested. Such incidents make for spicy archival material, but they are even rarer than the punishment of clients. Punitive action is, in other words, present and often spectacular. But it is also uncommon. Most clients pass through metal detectors—and most workers clock in and out of their shifts—without being punished.

Rather than see welfare offices in the suffering city as narrowly punitive, we should see them as broadly *disciplinary*. The difference is important. Where punishment is generally repressive (e.g., severance of aid and termination of employment), discipline is generally productive (e.g., yielding self-serving clients and efficient workers). Discipline certainly includes punishment, but it also includes rewards—a combination of sticks and carrots but usually more of the latter. Indeed, clients and workers alike return to the welfare offices not because they are subject to punishment but because they seek livelihood in the form of benefits or paychecks. Threats of negative sanctions may keep them "in line," but other mechanisms of disciplinary power render them as largely self-regulating recipients and workers.

In this chapter, I argue that a theory of disciplinary power is essential for understanding the welfare assembly line and the proletarianized public servants it assumes. While it is important to recognize eligibility workers and WTW workers as frontline exercisers of disciplinary power, it is also essential that we see them as subject to this same general power, albeit in different ways. The eligibility workers tend to be subject to more explicit techniques of disciplinary power than the WTW workers, but the former tend to expose their subjects to fewer disciplinary techniques than the latter. In other words, while eligibility workers are subject to more disciplinary techniques than WTW workers, customers (i.e., clients of eligibility workers) are subject to fewer disciplinary techniques than participants (i.e., clients of WTW workers). The defusal of disciplinary power is unevenly hierarchical with some significant variation depending not just on which *side* of the desk one finds oneself on the assembly line but also on which *kind* of desk one works at.

Disciplinary Power in the Welfare Office

Michel Foucault's *Discipline and Punish* offers an analysis of prisons, not welfare offices.[8] But in it we find a general theory of disciplinary power that other social scientists have used to make sense of social assistance regimes.[9] Joe Soss, Richard Fording, and Sanford Schram's aptly titled *Disciplining the Poor*, published more than three decades after Foucault's masterpiece, is arguably the best example.[10] Drawing on a case study of welfare-to-work programming in Florida, the authors repeatedly turn to Foucault to understand welfare offices as sites of "productive power where particular mentalities of rule and modes of self-discipline are fostered."[11]

But what exactly is disciplinary power, and why is it productive and not repressive? In the simplest terms, it is a power exercised to make individuals. As Foucault puts it, discipline "is the specific technique of a power that regards individuals both as objects and as instruments of its exercise."[12] He also writes, "The individual is no doubt the fictious atom of an 'ideological' representation of society; but he is also a reality fabricated by this specific technology of power that I have called 'discipline.'"[13]

Not to be confused with basic exercises of punishment, discipline more typically involves the distribution of rewards and punishments for the sake of fostering the generative capacities of inmates in prisons, students in schools, patients in hospitals, workers on assembly lines, and so on. The point is not simply to make "docile bodies," as it is sometimes said, but also to forge knowable, useful, and self-regulating subjects.[14]

Theorizing the specific mechanics of this power, Foucault writes, "The success of disciplinary power derives no doubt from the use of simple instruments; hierarchical observation, normalizing judgement and their combination in a procedure that is specific to it, the examination."[15] Put more plainly, disciplinary power involves surveillance, judgement, and the combination of these things in rituals of examination.

With respect to hierarchical observation, Foucault argues that the exercise of disciplinary power is enabled by architectures and procedures that make populations more seeable and knowable.[16] Prisons, for example, are designed to make prisoners visible to guards. But Foucault also gives other examples: schools are designed to make students visible to teachers; hospitals are designed to make patients visible to nurses; and factories are designed to make workers visible to supervisors. Hierarchical observation is made possible by a pyramidal system of gazes, meaning that even the observers are exposed to observation (e.g., wardens watching guards, principals watching teachers, doctors watching nurses, and upper managers watching supervisors).

Normalizing judgement, the second instrument of disciplinary power identified by Foucault, "compares, differentiates, hierar-

chizes, homogenizes, excludes."[17] Differentiation and homogeniza-
tion, at least at first appearances, seem like contradictory ends. My
interpretation is that disciplinary subjects can be homogenized
within particular categories that are graded both internally and externally. There may, for example, be a stark division between passa-
ble and unpassable students, but both categories can have their own
rankings (e.g., passing students with A, B, and C grades and failing
students with D and F grades). Regardless, Foucault is quite clear
that "the power of normalization imposes homogeneity;" "but," he
goes on, "it individualizes by making it possible to measure gaps, to
determine levels, to fix specialties and to render the differences useful by fitting them one to another."[18]

The final instrument, examination, is simply the combination of
hierarchical observation and normalizing judgement. From school
tests to medical assessments and from performance evaluations to
eligibility-determination calculations, examinations combine surveillance with normalization. Such techniques do not brainwash a
uniform mass. Instead, they produce individuals and more specifically self-governing subjects who not only regulate their own behavior but who also resist disciplinary power.

Turning to the welfare office specifically, Soss and colleagues help
us understand how workers exercise disciplinary power in their interactions with clients. They focus on welfare-to-work programming for
TANF recipients. In Los Angeles this is called GAIN, but in Florida it's
called Welfare Transition (WT). The workers in WT are employed by
contracted organizations, like the minority of GAIN workers in the
San Fernando and Antelope valleys. These workers closely monitor
their participants within structures of *hierarchical observation*. As in
California, these Florida workers rely on computers to see and know
their subjects—their addresses, their incomes, the members of their
households, and, of course, the times they spend on mandated and
approved activities. They cast *normalizing judgement* by evaluating

subjects according to their adherence to welfare-to-work contracts. WT workers also do the kinds of referralfare work detailed in chapter 4, and this, too, requires a kind of normalizing judgement to classify participants as "in need" of schoolfare, medfare, and housefare interventions. As with their counterparts in GAIN, they routinely *examine* their subjects, constantly updating their case files with marks of in/ compliance and with records of sanctions. Such workers discipline their recipients in an effort to transform them into more "responsible worker-citizen(s)."[19] Soss and his coauthors label this overarching strategy for responsibilizing poor individuals accomplished through disciplinary power, "neoliberal paternalism."[20]

Despite its title, *Disciplining the Poor* does not just focus on the disciplining of workfare participants. The authors study "how discipline operates on 'both sides of the desk.'"[21] They convincingly argue that we cannot understand the governance of the poor without also considering the governance of frontline welfare workers. The neoliberal paternalistic turn in poverty governance that took place in the late twentieth century—most dramatically through programs like GAIN in Los Angeles in the 1980s and eventually across the nation in the 1990s—did not mean such workers were simply recruited to exercise more discipline. They themselves were also subject to a more intensive version of this power under the guise of efficiency, quality assurance, and other market-oriented performance measures.

And this continues to be the case today. As with the poor, the point of disciplining workers from above is not simply to coerce their labor but to produce "subjective understandings, perceptions, and choices at the front lines."[22] This is accomplished, albeit always incompletely and with the possibility of resistance, through hierarchical observation, normalizing judgement, and examination exercised by managers. Local welfare administrators, facing their own pressures from state and federal governments, attempt to foster a sense of personal responsibility among frontline workers while also narrowing and directing their discretionary field.[23]

Soss and his coauthors, inspired in large part by the work of Celeste Watkins-Hayes in Massachusetts, show how this disciplinary turn on both sides of the desk was deeply racialized and gendered.[24] Disciplinary power exercised upon welfare recipients in the United States intensified as more women of color accessed public benefits following the welfare rights movements of the 1960s and 1970s. And while we should not confuse coincidence for conspiracy, extant theory suggests it is no accident that disciplinary power intensified on the other side of the desk as more workers of color, and Black women in particular, became employed in welfare offices.[25]

There are nonetheless limits to the analysis offered in *Disciplining the Poor*. The authors write about "welfare recipients" in general, but they really focus on TANF recipients and link them historically to AFDC and other means-tested cash assistance programs that targeted poor parents. However, cash-aided parents make up a minority of clients who find themselves in large welfare bureaucracies like DPSS. Far more people contact offices like these for health insurance, food stamps, and other programs where aid is not limited to parents. Likewise, Soss and colleagues focus on "frontline workers" within welfare-to-work programs. But they too are a specific minority. Most people employed on the frontline of welfare offices help administer other programs and do work that better approximates people processing than people changing. Put another way, Soss and his coauthors concentrate on WTW workers rather than eligibility workers, but there are six times more of the latter than the former at DPSS.[26] It is, therefore, hard to carry their models over to one of the largest local social service bureaucracies in the United States when most of DPSS's clients and most of its workers are not accounted for.

TABLE 4 Administrative and paternalistic discipline

	Administrative	Paternalistic
Objective	People processing	People changing
Emphasis	Eligibility workers > customers	Participants > WTW workers
Priority	Worker efficiency	Client self-sufficiency

To help extend the analysis, I examine the labor process on the welfare assembly line to reconstruct a theory of disciplinary power. I consider the significance of disciplinary power not just for WTW workers and their "participants" but also for eligibility workers and their "customers." Thus, I don't just consider both sides of the desk; I also consider the *different kinds of desks* on the welfare assembly line. Disciplinary power, I argue, looks different across the sublines of the customer service state and the workfare state.

Table 4 conceptualizes and compares two forms of disciplinary power, which I label *administrative* and *paternalistic*. While both rely on similar techniques for fostering responsible subjects by way of hierarchical observation, normalizing judgement, and examination, they come with distinct objectives and emphases. Administrative discipline helps advance a people-processing mission by focusing on the labor of eligibility workers first and the lives of customers second. In contrast, paternalistic discipline helps advance a people-changing mission by focusing on the lives of participants first and the labor of WTW workers second. While both administrative and paternalistic discipline can be identified at essentially all desks where workers confront clients, the former seeks to promote worker efficiency and best complements people-processing activities, and the latter seeks to promote client self-sufficiency and best complements people-changing activities.

The People-Processing Desk

Carmen and Her Customers

Carmen, a Latina eligibility worker at South Central, has been employed by DPSS for over twenty years—basically her entire adult life. I met her in a South Central office and watched as she worked task after task in a second-floor cubicle. She doesn't work in a call center, but like many of the district office eligibility workers I shadowed, she spent much of her time talking to customers on the phone. And, whenever I saw her at her desk, she almost always sported a headset. During my fieldwork, Carmen most frequently worked a specific stream of calls for CalWORKs and CalFresh customers who need to complete eligibility status reports in order to maintain benefits.[27]

Carmen does this work within a system of hierarchical observation. While she rarely meets customers face-to-face, Carmen's job mandates that she "see" them. She does so with phone calls and digital records, both of which provide windows into the private lives of customers. She observes them in and through an organizational hierarchy where both the quantity and quality of visibility tend to vary according to one's vertical positioning.

And while her vision from inside her cubicle of those below is hazy and incomplete, Carmen can always see her customers better than they can see her. To callers, Carmen is a voice and a title. She's not their caseworker; instead she is the relatively anonymous task-worker who happened to answer the phone. In contrast, Carmen is equipped with specific tools with which to see her customers.

I watched, for example, as Carmen closely reviewed a CalFresh customer's most recent paystub on her screen. It was for $1,200 gross pay for eighty hours of work at $15 an hour. I also watched as she asked another customer some fairly detailed questions about the cost of rent and utilities and how those expenses were shared among the adults in the household. And while she was on the phone with one

CalWORKs customer, I watched as she reviewed bank statements the customer submitted earlier through DPSS's mobile app.[28]

But hierarchical observation is a necessary—not a sufficient—condition of responsibilization. It is one technique of disciplinary power. Instruments of visibility do not fully determine *how* someone will be seen. Most notably, these tools do not automatically provide frameworks for what monitored actors should be doing or how they should be evaluated, rewarded, or punished.

Another technique is critical: normalizing judgement. This, above all, places individuals into a "field of comparison."[29] Observation is not typically done for its own sake. Instead, observers see to scrutinize and to determine intervention. In short, they see to normalize. This does not, however, suggest the regulation of a simple dichotomy between normal and abnormal. Instead, normalizing judgement, as a way to peer through the lenses of hierarchical observation, functions primarily to separate and differentiate cases.

We can identify some of this judgement in the casual statements of workers. "I want to be sympathetic, but sometimes I just don't believe them," Carmen told me between calls. Comments like this, which were relatively common among the eligibility workers I met, illustrate the importance of judgements of normality. These workers are often on the lookout for a specific kind of moral shortcoming among their customers: *deception*. It is common to doubt the authenticity of customers' stories, and Carmen admitted she finds a kind of thrill in identifying the rare instance of fraudulent paperwork. She and other workers also complained quite frequently about another sin among their customers: *negligence*. She grumbled about customers who lost their paperwork, missed important deadlines, and otherwise failed to "stay on top of things." Carmen largely spoke about deservingness in terms of which customers were ostensibly truthful and diligent—in a word, responsible.

She is charged with both seeing and judging her customers with an *eligibility gaze*. As noted in chapter 3, eligibility workers not only render subjects legible; they render them judgable. Carmen's work leads to a determination of who is eligible and ineligible. Both categories, but especially the eligibility one, also come with their own internal gradations (e.g., eligibility for a specific quality and quantity of aid). As an eligibility worker mostly focused on recertification tasks, Carmen sees her customers in order to assess whether they still qualify for their aid and whether or not any adjustments should be made. She helps situate them in a field of comparison less in reference to other specific cases and more in reference to general standards of eligibility.

In short, Carmen examines her customers. She combines hierarchical observation with normalizing judgement to make and maintain "cases" that are divided into a series of tasks worked by multiple eligibility workers. While Carmen is not a caseworker with an assigned caseload, her labor still centers on specific cases situated in a field of documentation.[30] That field exists most obviously in a digital form—in CalSAWS. Such examination seeks to render not only individualized cases, but also responsibilized ones.

Carmen and Her Managers

Hierarchical observation, normalizing judgement, and examination are not solely imposed on clients. Workers like Carmen are also exposed to these techniques. They, too, are monitored and measured but within different fields of comparison. Pressures from above conspire to make them into individuals—just not of the same bureaucratic type as clients are made. Instead, management seeks to discipline people like Carmen into responsible frontline workers.

Carmen is examined according to a close *managerial gaze*.[31] She may not be very visible to her customers, but she—and more specifically her *work*—is highly visible to her managers. She is situated in an open cubicle that makes her hands, screen, and paperwork generally observable to anyone who walks by. But this physical exposure is less significant than the digital exposure that constitutes hierarchical observation in the office. Just as Carmen can see her customers through screens, so too can her proximate and distal managers see her.

Through programs like CalSAWS, Current, and Cisco Finesse, Carmen's managers can see what tasks she is working on as well as how long she has been handling a given task. And just as her customers submit applications and related forms for her to scrutinize, she prepares and sends her work up to supervisors for them to evaluate. Any adjustments Carmen makes to a customer's food stamps, for example, must first be delivered to and approved by her immediate manager. This is an evaluation less of customers' eligibility and more of the eligibility workers' labor—to make sure the *t*'s are crossed and the *i*'s are dotted.

In many respects, Carmen is more visible to her managers than her customers are to her. This runs somewhat counter to what Foucault would have us expect. The primary subjects of the district offices and call centers—those seeking and receiving benefits—are certainly visible, but not as much as those who perform the labor of this surveillance. Carmen is watched more intensely than she watches her customers. While it is certainly true that she knows more intimate information about her customers than her supervisors know about her, the fact remains that Carmen is more intimately observed by management.[32] From a distance, Carmen knows a lot about her customers' money, romantic partners, and so on. Beyond what's gleaned from casual conversations between tasks and in the break rooms, supervisors do not typically know such private details about their workers. They nonetheless observe and scrutinize the work life of their subordinates very closely.

As another eligibility worker I shadowed put it, there is "no escape" from the close monitoring of frontline labor by supervisors. Even when they work from home—an opportunity that expanded during the pandemic but has continued to grow since the offices reopened to in-person customers in 2021—Carmen and other welfare workers are made visible to supervisors via the other programs they access on their county-issued laptops.[33] Digital task timers, autogenerated work logs, and so on keep eligibility work perpetually visible. Supervisors are also in frequent contact with these remote workers via phone and email. Sometimes the supervisors even observe their in-office workers from home via a digital telescope of sorts.

"There's so much micromanaging," Carmen told me in the limited privacy of her cubicle. "It's overwhelming." I wondered if her words had some kind of conjuring power, because soon enough an email notification appeared on her screen. It was from her supervisor, Jenny.

On this particular day Jenny was working from home. Carmen insisted that Jenny's being home didn't really matter since she primarily supervises and communicates through the computer anyway. One of Carmen's biggest pet peeves is Jenny emailing requests and questions from across the room when she could just walk over and talk to workers directly. When Jenny's home, Carmen is less annoyed about receiving an email notification from her.

Still, the news is rarely good. In this case, Jenny emailed Carmen to send back some paperwork. A "send back" usually involves a request to correct a minor error in a previously completed task. Carmen had indeed submitted some inconsistent forms, and this prompted Jenny to send a one-line email asking her to resolve the problem. Apparently, one page Carmen submitted mentioned a customer's $100 weekly recycling income while another page did not. I watched as she quickly made the correction and resent the paperwork to Jenny for authorization. Just as eligibility workers scrutinize their customers' documents and look for errors, so too do the supervisors scrutinize their workers' documents. Each is judged by those above them according to particular norms—be they norms of aid eligibility or norms of productive quality.

The supervisor's judgement of frontline labor, however, does not end there. Jenny also focuses on the quantity of Carmen's production. More specifically, she focuses on the speed of task completion. If Carmen is classified as "idle" on her task-management program for more than fifteen minutes, she risks getting an email from Jenny asking for updates on her workflow.[34]

Why fifteen minutes? Because the idle status is often correctly assumed to be false or at least significantly misleading. Recertification tasks can require additional protocol searching, emailing, and more, which escape the eye of the department's computer surveillance. A couple of supervisors I spoke to said they understood this and assumed most of the so-called idle time was spent working. They nonetheless expect this system status to be minimized for the sake of efficient task completion. Supervisors also know the program is visible to deputies above them as well as the generally mysterious managers in the "line operations" office at headquarters. While it is unclear at street level how often deputies bother to look at the system from their four-walled offices, supervisors nonetheless feel pressure to assure tasks are being completed in a timely fashion by the workers in their cubicle units.

Later in the shift, Carmen received another email from Jenny. Again, I wondered if Carmen had some kind of magical ability to turn words into reality. She was at least accurately forecasting her interactions with management. Jenny sent an email asking why Carmen had been listed as idle for more than fifteen minutes. Carmen had paused to massage her hand and take a few sips of water during her shift, and she was slowing down her normal routine a bit to talk to the nosy ethnographer in her cubicle. However, she was never really idle during the time Jenny was inquiring about. Carmen simply forgot to feed her most recent call into Current, the task-bank DPSS was utilizing at the time (see chapter 3). She quickly noted this in an email to Jenny, who never responded. Carmen certainly seemed annoyed by the exchange, but she also felt a bit vindicated since it was more "proof" of the micromanaging she had been describing to me. "They [management] want back-to-back from us," she would later tell me. "We're supposed to respond to calls all the time."

While eligibility workers watch out for deception and negligence, their supervisors watch out for errors and idleness. The former corresponds to an eligibility gaze, and the latter corresponds to a managerial gaze.

Administrative Discipline

Disciplinary power is exercised on both sides of Carmen's desk. Her work helps maintain the poor as what sociologist Javier Auyero calls "patients of the state," the generally docile subjects of long and uncertain queues.[35] She imposes an eligibility gaze across her screen and phone not only to see who qualifies for aid but also to help normalize those who are eligible for benefits into responsible consumers of public benefits. Carmen may be in the business of processing rather than changing people, but her taskwork helps maintain customers as both knowable and accountable.

That said, disciplinary power is more explicitly exercised *on* Carmen than *by* her. She is subject to a more intense managerial gaze than she subjects others to an eligibility one. This is not to suggest that she is more oppressed than her clients are. As Patricia Hill Collins reminds us, there are differences between disciplinary and structural domains of power, even though they tend to interlock and harm common populations in a capitalist, racist, and sexist society.[36] Carmen may be in a privileged position relative to those she serves, but within the microcosm of the welfare office, she is more a target than an exerciser of disciplinary techniques. The managers of people-processing labor focus much of their attention on the productivity of their workers.[37]

I label this style, or emphasis, of disciplinary power *administrative*. While disciplinary power may be generally diffused, in this case it is organized in such a manner that it focuses on frontline labor first and their clients second. The general point of administrative discipline on the welfare assembly line is to promote the efficient processing of people. While this model necessitates a particular kind of clientele—engaged customers—they are, in many respects, secondary to the primary subjects of disciplinary power in this context: frontline welfare workers.

This efficient processing of people is accomplished by focusing disciplinary technologies on eligibility workers so that they can work faster and more accurately. Disciplinary power, however, works a bit differently in the workfare programs, which I cover next.

The People-Changing Desk

Rosa and Her Participants

While Carmen plugs away on eligibility-determination tasks in South Central, Rosa works on general-flow START cases in the San Gabriel Valley. Like Carmen, Rosa is a Latina DPSS worker who has been employed with the agency for over two decades. The conditions of their labor look remarkably similar, at least at first blush. Both spend a majority of their time inside cubicles. Like Carmen, the eligibility worker, Rosa, the WTW worker, watches her clients and records their personal details in CalSAWS. Rosa even sports an identical headset and communicates with most of her subjects by phone. Both of these workers are also monitored and observed by unit supervisors who are in turn watched by deputies and other higher-up managers who are observed by county, state, and federal auditors.

Like Carmen, Rosa sees her clients more than they can see her. However, Rosa's job necessitates that she sees even more of them than Carmen does. I watched as she worked a handful of her five hundred or so active welfare-to-work cases. Unlike Carmen who receives phones calls, Rosa and the other START and GAIN workers I shadowed spent much of their time calling their subjects. Before making any call, however, Carmen told me she always reviews files on CalSAWS to "learn the case" a bit. She sees what is known (and unknown) about the individual's work, education, and health histories. Rosa also considers her subjects' housing records to see if they may qualify for some paltry housing assistance specific to General Relief recipients. Her job, as she put it to me, is to "usher them out of welfare" by facilitating their participation in the START program.

Where eligibility workers like Carmen impose an *eligibility gaze*, WTW workers like Rosa impose a *participatory gaze*. They examine cases according to different dichotomies and gradients. Rather than see a split between eligible and ineligible, they see one between compliant and noncompliant. And then, within the normal category of compliant, they see another dichotomy between exempt and nonexempt, each with their own internal variations (e.g., "mental health exemption"). Rosa examines her cases to see who should participate in welfare-to-work programming and what activities they should participate in specifically. This necessitates that they know more about their subjects than what eligibility workers know about theirs.

I watched and listened as Rosa ran some intake procedures for Tiffany, a mid-twenties General Relief recipient who had recently started receiving the $221-a-month cash grant. Like Carmen, Rosa asked lots of questions about personal circumstances. She did not, however, pry into details of income, property, household composition, and so on. Instead, she asked questions like these: "You working now?" "Any felonies?" "Any psychological problems?" "What kind of career you want?" Rosa focused on what Tiffany is actually doing, what she is capable of doing, and what she should be doing.

Through her questioning, Rosa learned that Tiffany, who works one day a week babysitting a family member for $120 a month, did not complete high school. "You should consider a GED program," Rosa said before telling Tiffany about the ancillary aid she can offer to help support such an effort (e.g., money for transportation and books). If not a GED program, Rosa explained that Tiffany would likely need to do some job search activities to remain compliant with START requirements. However, because this was just an initial conversation to inform Tiffany of what is generally expected of her as a participant, Rosa did not yet refer her to any specific program. Before ending the call, Rosa scheduled another appointment with Tiffany a month from then. She explained to Tiffany that at this future meeting she would need to refer her to either some education or employment services. Rosa's examination of Tiffany would continue then.

Between calls, I learned a bit more about Rosa's general perceptions of participants. While Carmen warned me of deception and negligence among her customers, Rosa warned me of different sins: *dependency* and *laziness*. "You got to understand that our clients are like elementary-age intelligent," Rosa told me before alerting me of START participants who would languish on General Relief if it weren't for time limits and work requirements. She said, "I love people and love helping them," but she missed her sticks: the workfare sanctions that were paused during the pandemic. For her, sanctions—which included not just the termination of benefits but also warning letters and mandated meetings—were important tools for motivating otherwise lethargic subjects into participation. "They need little ways to learn responsibility," she told me when I asked about the utility of START sanctions.

Indeed, there is not just a qualitative difference between an eligibility gaze and a participatory gaze. The clients of START and GAIN are evaluated by frontline workers according to more norms and more gradations. At the risk of sounding like a broken record, they are more carefully evaluated with respect to work history, educational level, medical need, and so on. In many respects, this difference between people processing and people changing is to be expected. Efforts to change people, even if mostly symbolic, should require more disciplinary power, which should entail not only more surveillance but also more normalizing judgements.

Rosa and Her Managers

Like Carmen, Rosa is rendered visible by her superiors. But the latter is exposed to a relatively *distant managerial gaze*. Indeed, this gaze is not as intense for WTW workers as it is for eligibility workers. Rosa and her peers are certainly expected to be accurate and efficient. But they are afforded more autonomy and less supervisory scrutiny in the labor process. Where eligibility workers are closely monitored, WTW workers are met with cursory scans.

Consider something as simple as a standard fifteen-minute break, which both eligibility workers and WTW workers are given twice a shift. Rosa took a nearly thirty-minute break when I was with her. No one that I was aware of ever questioned her about this. Indeed, nobody seemed to be watching. I noticed other WTW workers stretch the fifteen-minute rule during my fieldwork as well. In contrast, Carmen was held to a stricter standard. A tardy return from a break, she and other eligibility workers told me, would effectively guarantee a question from a supervisor. Rosa and other WTW workers were not so closely monitored. WTW workers are certainly expected to work efficiently, especially since most of them hold caseloads in the several hundreds, but they are just not so intensely watched by those above them.

Some leeway in breaks is one thing; autonomy in the practical dimensions of the labor process is another. As mentioned in chapter 4, WTW workers do not have much discretion, especially when compared to the social workers that were more common in the agency before the rise of workfare programming. Decision trees, scripted interview questions, a limited kit of black box referrals, and more dramatically limit their discretion. However, relative to their eligibility worker counterparts, they have significantly more autonomy over their labor and from their managers.

Shortly after Rosa updated Tiffany's file, she turned her attention to Ella, a woman who was just reenrolled in General Relief benefits. After playing a bit of phone tag, Rosa successfully reached her new participant and asked many of the same questions she posed to Tiffany. Rosa was pleased to learn that Ella, a thirty-or-so-year-old woman, was currently enrolled in a local community college with aspirations of transferring to a four-year university and obtaining an art degree. She was also happy that Ella was already receiving mental health services. "I see, I see," Rosa said as she nodded her head and jotted notes. "Good for you." After a short pause in the conversation, Rosa told Ella she would call her back in a couple minutes.

When she hung up the phone, Rosa told me she wanted the participant to stay involved in her current education and medical programming. She explained to me, however, that making these activities comport with START requirements would be difficult. For one thing, Ella was only enrolled in six credits, but START generally requires seven to count as legitimate welfare-to-work hours. Thinking out loud, she said to me that the best option would probably be either a medical exemption or a medical referral. I nodded as if I knew what she was talking about.

"Follow me," she said abruptly. A determined Rosa, trailed by a confused ethnographer, walked two cubicle aisles over to her supervisor's desk. We met supervisor Jim, a white man whose exceptionally tall height is noticeable even when he sits. Unlike Jenny, a mysterious manager who communicated with Carmen over email, Jim was a permanent fixture in this office. We stepped into Jim's relatively spacious cubicle. Rosa summarized Ella's situation and asked for Jim's advice. Rosa did not ask Jim if an exemption was appropriate. She also did not ask Jim to make a decision. This was simply an impromptu meeting to clarify and rank Rosa's options.

Rosa asked Jim which exemption route sounded best to him. One option was to do a mental health screening and then refer her to the Department of Mental Health (DMH) for further evaluation (and likely programming). Another option was to send Ella a form, which would allow her current clinician to do the assessment and recommend an exemption. Jim said that if he were Rosa, he'd follow the second path for logistical reasons, but he made it clear that the decision was ultimately Rosa's.

Jim then offered some unsolicited advice, picking up on one of the details Rosa shared about Ella's case. He recommended Rosa "ask about that art degree," arguing that art school was not a "viable" activity that would "lead to a good job." Rosa acknowledged Jim's opinion but did not commit to actually bringing this up with Ella.

When we returned to her cubicle and were no longer in Jim's earshot, Rosa told me that she simply disagreed with him on this point. She explained that such an activity is probably good for Ella in more ways than just expanding job opportunities. Plus, she noted, "It shouldn't matter, if she gets an exemption anyway."[38]

After confirming that both paths—a medfare referral and a medical exemption—were reasonable, Rosa called Ella back on the phone. She ultimately let the participant make the decision. Ella decided to initiate paperwork for both a referral and an exemption "just in case," and this meant an increased runaround on both sides of the desk. However, Rosa didn't seem to mind. She completed a mental health screening over the phone for the DMH referral and then prepared a form and some instructions for Ella's current clinician to fill out in the event that Ella preferred an exemption.

Supervisors certainly examine the labor of WTW workers, but they do so far less than they do with eligibility workers. While county WTW workers complained of micromanaging, rigid protocols, and the like, they all seemed to recognize and appreciate their relative autonomy. They recognized their autonomy in large part because they had all been eligibility workers before being promoted to GAIN or START. And while not all eligibility workers aspire to be WTW workers, all the county-employed WTW workers I met told me they preferred their current job over means testing. Most emphasized the pay bump as a key motivation to move into GAIN or START, while others suggested it provided more meaningful work with clients. All seemed to agree, however, that the increased autonomy was a significant justification for the move. Managers may demand a lot from WTW workers, but at least they do not breathe so heavily down their necks.

Paternalistic Discipline

Again, disciplinary power is exercised on both sides of the desk. Clients and workers across the welfare assembly line are subject to hierarchical observation, normalizing judgement, and examination. However, this discipline varies in significant ways depending on the kind of desk these clients and workers find themselves at. Where disciplinary technologies tend to focus on labor at people-processing desks, they tend to focus on clients at people-changing desks.

The managerial gaze imposed on Rosa was less intense than the one imposed on Carmen. Both were watched and judged by management, but Rosa was watched and judged less. She was examined according to fewer norms and gradations. Meanwhile, the participatory gaze that Rosa imposed on her clients was more intense than the legibility gaze Carmen imposed on hers. Rosa's participants were examined in a deeper way as their life histories, present circumstances, and stated aspirations were more thoroughly scrutinized.

I identify this disciplinary power as *paternalistic*. The general point of paternalistic discipline, as sociologist Anthony DiMario notes, is to change people by constricting their freedom *"for their own good."*[39] Such efforts may indeed rely on faulty assumptions about dependency and on misguided promises of the labor market, but the state is at least nominally focused on transforming welfare-to-work participants into self-sufficient worker-citizens.

Extant scholarship suggests this is largely a transformation on paper, but significant energy is directed toward such an end nonetheless.[40] This is accomplished by focusing disciplinary technologies on the participants of such programs. WTW workers are certainly disciplined, and often in the name of administrative efficiency like the eligibility workers, but they are less closely examined in the labor process. Indeed, like a parent, they are entrusted by state authority to discipline their subjects with carrots and sticks.

"You Are Responsible for Your Own Actions"

While talk is cheap and taped paper is even cheaper, I hold that we can learn a lot about welfare offices by reading the writing on the walls. From the "Quality Standards" sign that appeared in chapters 3 and 4 to the mugshots mentioned at the beginning of this chapter, the messages are often too bold to ignore. Many of these texts seem to shout at the customers and participants passing by and are frequently posted in both English and Spanish. "Save Time . . . GO ONLINE," yells one sign in the lobby at the San Gabriel district office in El Monte. "EBT Cardholders BEWARE!" screams another. "It is critical to protect both your identity and your EBT card's information in order to prevent your benefits from being stolen." And on the walls around the GAIN and START cubicles, there are plenty of "ENROLL TODAY!"

signs for nine-month medical assistant training classes and related short-term education programs. Not even the bathrooms are safe, as I learned when I stepped into the men's room for customers in the Metro North district office: "GENTLEMEN PLEASE DO NOT PEE ON THE FLOOR!!! THANK YOU FOR YOUR COOPERATION."

The spaces reserved for workers are also filled with signs. The walls in most office breakrooms, for example, hold flat-screen monitors that cycle through digital bulletins and announcements. These include signs to remind workers of shifting protocol and procedure, tips for ergonomic stretches, and instructions on how to anonymously report employees suspected of EBT fraud. And, consistent with the internal labor state and internal labor market themes mentioned in chapter 2, there are signs detailing the labor union activities and county job openings.

One printed message in El Monte is especially blunt. It reads, "YOU are RESPONSIBLE for your own actions," and it is hung high above a tackboard listing flyers for GED courses, criminal record expungement, job training, and other services for START.[41] While the sign is clearly intended for workfare participants, it is posted in a space mostly occupied by DPSS employees. In fact, as far as I could tell during my fieldwork, the nearby tackboard is largely used by START workers whenever they need to collect information for a program referral.

With this in mind, I can't help but think this sign is also speaking a bit to the WTW workers. It is certainly hung high enough to see over the walls of many cubicles. Perhaps it was hung there in part to remind workers of START's mission to foster accountability among their subjects. Or perhaps it was posted as a more general message for the time—a cliché, some might say, in what has been called the age of responsibility.[42]

Either way, the responsibility banner is a more than fitting sign for the welfare assembly line as I experienced it. Beyond the explicit emphasis on personal responsibility in workfare programs like START and GAIN, the district office workers largely assumed that their customers were accountable and generally capable of handling the runaround, completing errands, turning in paperwork, navigating hotlines and websites, and so on. At the same time, managers generally expected both eligibility workers and WTW workers to responsibly pace their work, minimize errors, reduce their idleness, and creatively solve problems. And where WTW workers are held personally accountable for their caseloads, eligibility workers confront even more stressful expectations regarding responsibility. Under the taskwork regime, they are expected to correct all mistakes on the cases they touch, even if they concern different tasks entirely. Shandra, who we met in chapter 2, reflected on how she was recently "talked to" by quality control workers. "So, the way it's set up is if you're the last person to touch a case, whether you're right or wrong, it's on you, period." Workers like her may not be punished much, but they are frequently "corrected" and "taught" in an effort to maintain both efficiency and accuracy.

Responsible subjects do not appear out of nowhere. They must be fabricated, and cheap banners won't do the trick. Neither will simple repression. Responsible subjects are yielded through particular techniques for fostering self-regulation and a generalized sense of accountability. A theory of disciplinary power, reconstructed to account for differences not only between labor and clientele but also between the people-processing and people-changing desks, helps explain how responsibilization is made and maintained. Foucault's classic concepts of hierarchical observation, normalizing judgement, and the examination prove to be particularly useful starting points for unpacking how such power is variably exercised on the welfare assembly line.[43]

I concur with Soss, Fording, and Schram that disciplinary power is exercised on "both sides of the desk."[44] I also agree this generally takes a paternalistic form in welfare-to-work initiatives. But most of DPSS's offices—not to mention most of its clients and workers—are not focused on such people-changing objectives. Even under post-1996 welfare policy, these efforts are secondary to the people-processing aims. And people-processing necessitates a disciplinary power that tends to be less paternalistic and more administrative. Each form of disciplinary power targets "both sides of the desk" unequally, with paternalistic discipline emphasizing clients over workers and administrative discipline emphasizing the reverse. Administrative and paternalistic discipline help forge responsible workers and clients, but to different extents and degrees. Where paternalistic discipline primarily seeks to promote client self-sufficiency, administrative discipline primarily seeks to promote worker productivity. This unevenness helps generate two kinds of proletarianized public servants in the DPSS policy factory, one for the faster conveyor belts of means testing and one for the slower conveyor belts of program brokering.

6   Dis/Connected

Like students adorning their lockers, many of the welfare workers I shadowed beautified their cubicles. They covered their florescent-lit spaces with family photos, bobble heads, and, quite often, Disneyland souvenirs.

One cubicle in a district office caught my eye every time I walked past it. An eligibility worker hung two signs side by side. In isolation they were banal, but together they were bewildering. One was a wooden sign that read, "I thought I wanted a career. Turns out I just wanted paychecks." It's the sort of thing you might see on sale next to novelty coffee mugs with related office-humor zingers. The other was a poster from a recent SEIU Local 721 rally, and it read, "WE ARE THE ♥ OF LA COUNTY'S SAFETY NET."

The first sign expresses, and maybe exaggerates, a sentiment I heard repeatedly during my fieldwork and interviews. Welfare work is, at its core, something done for pay. Like essentially all work under capitalism, such labor is largely, though perhaps not solely, done out of necessity. Most working-age adults must sell their labor power— that is, their capacity to work—to employers for a wage. The paycheck, a primary means of subsistence and livelihood under capitalism, is no doubt a reason to repeatedly show up to the same cubicle.

But if the first sign evokes the material assumptions of Karl Marx, the second evokes the integrative assumptions of Émile Durkheim.[1] As noted in chapter 2, the eligibility workers and WTW workers I shadowed often expressed a sense that their labor, while highly specialized, contributes to some larger collective good. As the self-proclaimed "heart" of the Los Angeles safety net, these workers often described themselves to me as not only an integral but also a caring force committed to a mission. These paradoxical sentiments speak, at least in part, to the contradictory relations that welfare workers enter into with their clientele, the living subjects of their work.

In many respects, these relations are present but generally *disconnective*. They are increasingly alienating, to borrow another popular concept from Marx. According to Marx, wage laborers under capitalism are "alienated" or "estranged" not only from each other, but also from the products of their labor. As Marx puts it, the "*alienation* of the worker in his product means not only that his labour becomes an object, an *external* existence, but that it exists *outside* him, independently, as something alien to him, and that it becomes a power of its own confronting him; it means that the life which he has conferred on the object confronts him as something hostile and alien."[2] While Marx imagined producer-product alienation to occur between living labor and inanimate objects, we can apply it to frontline governance workers who objectify their labor into living subjects likes "recipients," "patients," "inmates," and so on. This objectification may not be as totalizing or involve as much passivity as those who work on nonhuman materials, but most frontline public servants nonetheless create and confront "cases" that are external and alien to them. Decreased in-person interactions, furnished in part by the introduction of new technologies (e.g., hotlines and mobile apps) and a greater division of labor (e.g., separation of intake-side and approval-side activities), expands the social distance between workers and clients. A fair amount of distrust and suspicion from both parties also helps maintain a general sense of detachment.

That said, these relations are still necessary and can still be reasonably framed as *connective*. In contrast to Marx, Durkheim might push us to see the relations between frontline governance workers and their clients as less alienating and more integrative. These relations can foster an integration of dissimilarity based complementary difference, or what he calls "organic solidarity."[3] For Durkheim, integration and connectivity are generally to be expected even within modern societies where people may *seem* to be detached from one another. In his words, "Individuals are *linked* to one another who would otherwise be independent; instead of developing separately, they concert their efforts. They are *connected to one another* and the links between them not only function in the brief moments when they engage in an exchange of service, but extend considerably beyond."[4] This solidarity of dissimilarity, like all solidarity, assumes some degree of empathy or recognition of the other. As Durkheim puts it, "There can certainly never be solidarity between ourselves and another person unless the image of the other person is united with our own."[5]

With these tensions in mind, we can see how worker-client relations in the welfare office may foster not only apathy and struggle but also empathy and solidarity. Workers often seek out connections with their clientele and they do so variably across the assembly lines for eligibility work and WTW work. Where the disconnections are usually justified as "part of the job," the connections are usually touted as part of what makes the work "more than a job."

This chapter examines the dis/connections between proletarianized public servants and clients—an intensifying contradiction of work on the welfare assembly line. I show how eligibility workers and WTW workers variably engage in what sociologist Allison Pugh has recently dubbed "connective labor."[6] This labor involves workers "creating and sharing an emotional recognition of another person, through a process of 'seeing' or reflecting them, in order to create value."[7] She gives several examples, including the work done by physicians, teachers, counselors, and other occupations that are also of interest to scholars of frontline public services more generally.

I argue that connective labor is both constrained and enabled on the welfare assembly line. Building on the insights from the previous chapter, we can see how worker-client connectivity is systematically discouraged under administrative discipline, while worker-client connectivity is more systematically directed under paternalistic discipline. Put another way, while people-processing activities (more common among eligibility workers) tend to suppress connective labor, people-changing activities (more common among WTW workers) tend to standardize it. Both eligibility and WTW work, however, ultimately involve a contradictory mixture of connection and disconnection. This, in turn, structures the opportunities for workers to advocate for their subjects.

Dis/Connections with Customers

Vanessa and Jordan

Vanessa is an eligibility worker specializing in General Relief intake processing at the South Central office. She's a Latina woman in her early-thirties, and, like many of the employees I met at DPSS, she worked in customer service before she started a career in welfare. In her case, she worked as a bank teller. Vanessa is quick to tell me that eligibility work is significantly better not only because the hours are more stable and the pay is higher but also because the labor is intrinsically more valuable. Issuing checks to the poor is, Vanessa insisted, simply more rewarding than depositing them for the bank, and working for a safety net organization is better than working at a for-profit firm. Her current job involves more paperwork and has her interacting with fewer people in person, but she is nonetheless confident that it fosters more meaningful connections with so-called customers. She must get to know the typical General Relief applicant in a more intimate sense than the typical bank patron. And, at least relative to her days as a teller, she must see her current customers as something closer to ends in themselves.

This does not mean, however, that Vanessa is deeply connected to those applying for the meager $221-a-month cash assistance offered through General Relief. She speaks to most of her customers only once through short and heavily scripted intake interviews during which she verifies identity and asks about income, property, ability to work, family status, and more. These are often conducted over the phone, but when I shadowed her no one answered for their scheduled interviews. This was not very surprising. General Relief applicants, who must generally make less than $221 a month, have less than $100 in cash, and own less than $2,000 in personal property, are notoriously difficult to reach. They rarely have dependable phone numbers, let alone permanent mailing addresses. Often, the best bet for conversation occurs when these individuals show up to the office. That was certainly the case when I shadowed Vanessa. Her first contact of the morning was a walk-in applicant.

A worker from the lobby requested someone from Vanessa's unit to conduct a General Relief screening and interview downstairs. I followed Vanessa from her cubicle on the second story down to the main floor. We walked to the "booths," which, at least in the South Central office, reminded me of fixtures for an inmate visitation center. In contrast to the interview cubicles I encountered in the other district offices, many of these had permanent glass dividers that separate eligibility workers from their clients. Vanessa told me that she always uses these particular booths for General Relief applicants. "You want the glass for this population," she said, suggesting that she does not want to get too close to the applicant we have not even seen yet.

Unlike the archetypical CalWORKs applicant, the archetypical General Relief applicant is assumed among workers to be more destitute, masculine, and isolated. As another worker once put it, these are the "Skid Row types" who are ineligible for CalWORKs because they do not have children in their custody. Many workers understood General Relief applicants to be dirtier and more dangerous, and Vanessa was not the only worker I met who preferred to meet them behind a glass shield.

I sat next to her on the staff side of the booth as she picked up the phone on the desk and instructed the applicant over the intercom. "Jordan Cook, please enter door two. Jordan Cook, door two." I heard her voice echo through the lobby, which was separated from us by a brick wall and heavy metal doors.

Jordan, a Black man roughly the same age as Vanessa, entered through door two and Vanessa waved him over to our booth. She introduced me as a researcher, and Jordan and I exchanged a quick nod across the glass. After a few introductory questions, Vanessa learned that Jordan had a minor daughter in his custody. It was possible that the lobby worker who checked him in assumed he was not a parent and funneled him toward General Relief.

Vanessa quickly explained to Jordan that because of his parental status, he was not eligible for this aid but that he could and should apply for CalWORKs. "Can you help me with that?" asked Jordan. "No," said Vanessa. "That's a different worker." She did not provide many instructions on how to apply for CalWORKs, nor did she note that it pays more than General Relief. She seemed eager to end the conversation and return to the list of General Relief intake tasks that awaited her upstairs.

Jordan rubbed his forehead, took a deep breath, and then asked, "What about food stamps?" "No," she responded with an indifferent tone and a stone face. "Another worker is assigned for that interview, but I can check you in with her." Vanessa, while technically equipped with the skills to process CalFresh applications, is not permitted by her supervisor to handle them unless they're coupled with General Relief applications.

The best she could do was quickly deny General Relief and redirect Jordan to different workers on the assembly line. Her task—the determination of eligibility for a particular form of cash aid— was complete. She simply had nothing else of consequence to offer Jordan since he was not eligible for the kind of aid her unit focused on.

She dismissed a dejected and discouraged Jordan back to the lobby. He seemed less angry than confused. But more than anything, he seemed exhausted from the long wait and runaround that seemed to come with a visit to the welfare office.

I followed Vanessa back to her cubicle upstairs. A seemingly bottomless pile of General Relief intake tasks awaited her. I never saw Jordan again, and it's likely that she never did either.

Vanessa was not unique in her approach. I witnessed numerous face-to-face transactions in the district offices that might best be described as cold or at most lukewarm. Even when aid was approved, the in-person interactions I observed between eligibility workers and their customers in these spaces were often quick, mundane, and completed with minimal visible emotion beyond the obvious frustrations of the clients.

While Vanessa may indeed find this work to be more meaningful than processing bank transactions, I could not help but think her current appointment involved customer encounters that were more similar than different to what I might experience at a bank. If anything, my encounters with tellers feels significantly warmer: at least I'm met with smiles and cheerful greetings, even if they are forced and phony. As we might expect from an office so closely approximating a people-processing bureaucracy, Vanessa's encounter with Jordan was somewhat hurried and fairly frigid.

This certainly does not mean all encounters between eligibility workers and their customers are cold. For example, in chapter 3 we saw that Camila and Kayla both found ways to connect with their customers and "share the runaround." There are nonetheless strong organizational pressures that severely limit opportunities for connective labor.

Discouraging Connectivity

Impersonal interactions between eligibility workers and their clients are not new, especially not in South Central. These workers have long been accused of being cold, apathetic, and often inconsiderate toward the living subjects of their labor. During increased civil society building after the Watts rebellion in the mid-1960s, community organizers chastised welfare workers who largely "[didn't] understand and [didn't] care" about their clients and who held "punitive and contemptuous attitudes."[8]

The problem, however, was apparently broader than South Central. Department administrators a half century ago confronted a slow but steady agency-wide increase in the "number of complaints from the public regarding public discourtesy," and internal documents suggest that eligibility workers in particular were central to this problem.[9] Today, the issue apparently continues, although complaints do not so much come in the mail; they take the form of poor customer service reviews posted online. Some have turned to Yelp.com, a popular site for consumer-citizens to evaluate not only restaurants but also public bureaucracies like housing authority offices and sheriff stations. There, many have vented about "rude," "hostile," "terrible," "horrible," "mean," "disrespectful," and "dismissive" eligibility workers.[10]

In the 1970s, management reasoned that the problem of discourtesy was due largely to 1) workers' poor coping skills with "high pressure situations" and 2) weak rapport between workers and an increasingly racially diverse clientele.[11] Their response to both of these issues was basically to retrain frontline labor.

The staff development division made a training video on how, among other things, "to break the bad news to a client" and how to remain courteous "under pressure."[12] They also designed staff awareness trainings not only on the "culture of poverty" but also on "minority cultures."[13] This, it was assumed, would make eligibility workers more empathetic, or at least more sympathetic. Trainers aimed to warm eligibility workers' chilled perceptions of their diverse clientele by teaching the workers about their particular worldviews. As an added bonus, employee trainers screened the 1971 short film *Bill Cosby on Prejudice* in an effort to make frontline staff more aware of their own biases.[14] Management assumed they could enable workers through cultural competency trainings to better connect with clientele. Perhaps unsurprisingly, I found no evidence in the archives that any of these trainings actually worked to increase rapport, promote courtesy, or reduce formal complaints.

In fact, the forces of worker-client alienation seemed to only intensify as caseloads increased much faster than the number of eligibility workers. Opportunities for meaningful connections with clients were almost certainly doomed to fail—even if (and that's a big if) they marginally improved through awareness trainings—due to the dramatic increase in the client-to-worker ratio. Eligibility work moved closer and closer to the pure form of a people-processing bureaucracy. One eligibility worker in 1991 described the scenario like this: "There used to be a time when I enjoyed my job. But I can't get satisfaction out of it anymore. Because we really don't help anyone. We just push them through the door until they come back again."[15]

Then came federal welfare reform in 1996 and the local fallout and transformations in 1997 and 1998. In addition to multiplying workfare programs like GAIN across the nation, federal changes inspired many structural and symbolic changes within the district offices. Among these was a shift in labels and institutional discourse. As noted in chapter 3, those who entered the district office were now to be called "customers" instead of "recipients."

For the district offices, and eventually the new call centers, this focus justified management's shift from promoting connectivity on paper to all but explicitly discouraging it. Connectivity may be important for worker-client relations traditionally understood, but if those clients are *customers*, then it need not be, as counterintuitive as that may sound. For DPSS, "good customer service" carries forward the cultural repertoire of courtesy, but it also integrates and prioritizes a new frame: convenience. We can think of this as efficiency from the imagined standpoint of the customer.

Consider, for example, how Antonia Jiménez, one of the recent directors of DPSS, put it:

> I'm always thinking about how to improve the way we deliver services to our customers. If I were in that person's shoes, how would I want to be treated? Why do we have to do it this way? Is there a better way? . . . For instance, the people we serve are working families—they don't have the time to drive an hour to get services or spend hours in our office applying for benefits. I looked at that system and said, "We need to make it simpler for our customers." We shouldn't be making it difficult for customers to get service; we need to simplify the process to better serve our customers. In LA, customers can now apply to renew their benefits without having to fill out paperwork or come into our offices.[16]

Where management in the 1970s attempted to make cultural interventions into the front lines for the sake of better "courtesy," management in the twenty-first century has focused more on shifting procedures for the sake of better "customer service." Today, things like rapport are just not as significant as things like simplicity in the Los Angeles welfare office. In fact, managers candidly look for ways to reduce contact between eligibility workers and their subjects. While reductions may be largely motivated by efforts to reduce operational costs, they are, at least explicitly, justified as something basically good for *the customer*—the new welfare subject who is assumed to be primarily interested in convenience.

Indeed, the efforts to reduce contact, and thus the opportunities for connectivity, predate the COVID-19 pandemic and even Jiménez's specific interventions. Shortly before she was the director, the department boasted in a report that their 2014–2016 strategic plan was explicitly focused on advancing technologies that "greatly reduced [the] need for customers to go a DPSS facility."[17] Key to this effort was an increased emphasis on online applications, call centers, and a mobile app. Opportunities for contact may have increased, but these moments of contact are assumed to involve low levels of connective labor.

The most powerful strategy for discouraging connectivity between workers and clients in the district office, however, seems to come in the form of taskwork. This way of organizing work, as Virginia Eubanks notes in her account of welfare automation in Indiana, assumes a "severing" of worker-client bonds.[18] By breaking up cases into a series of discrete tasks, managers have explicitly fueled a disconnection between employees and customers. This is not an accident or collateral damage. It is an explicit goal. Taskwork is assumed, among other things, to make the process more convenient for customers because they are no longer tethered to specific caseworkers. Multiple eligibility workers, especially those now working in the call center and storefront-like conditions detailed in chapter 3, can presumably answer their questions.

It is important to note, however, that disconnection through task-work did not emerge unchallenged. In a public statement published just before management effectively killed off casework for the majority of eligibility workers, the union wrote that "the new work system would turn the county's social services administration into an assembly line and eliminate the time and space frontline professionals have to build trust with their clients."[19] These organizers voiced a defense of the connective labor that is enabled under casework, or what they and their contract phrased as "client-based" labor. They argued that casework has enabled eligibility workers to "provide clients the personal attention they need to be connected to all services to which they are entitled in a timely, courteous, and thorough manner."[20] In contrast, they said, taskwork "forces clients through a rushed and increasing impersonal process."[21]

It is within this larger organizational history that Vanessa encounters Jordan. She labors under conditions that explicitly discourage connectivity. Vanessa is tasked with reviewing Jordan's eligibility for a specific cash-aid program, executing a determination, and moving on to the next intake-related task. She is only able to get to know her customers in a very narrow sense. And for her, it is probably best if these short in-person encounters with this particular client population—stereotypically men without shelter—occur through a glass barrier.

Dis/Connections with Participants

Sofia and Wendy

Worker-client interactions look a bit different in the GAIN offices where labor focuses more on program brokering than on means testing. And, in light of what we learned in the previous chapters, we know these spaces at least ostensibly fall closer under the category of people-changing bureaucracies. While the district offices focus more on determining eligibility for aid, the GAIN offices seek to promote transitions off welfare. They attempt to do this by promoting the controlling image of self-sufficiency against that of dependency.[22] These efforts may be futile and littered with problematic assumptions, but they are nonetheless real. GAIN workers are tasked with promoting transitions from welfare to work not by changing the labor market but by changing clients. They attempt to fix their participants so that they are more employable. Whether they succeed is somewhat beside the point. It is the effort far more than the outcome that structures the interactions between workers and clients in the GAIN offices.

One morning, while in the South Los Angeles GAIN office, I shadowed Sofia. She is a Latina worker like Vanessa but is about ten years older. She also has more experience in the department, having worked for several years as an eligibility worker in a district office before she became a GAIN worker a half decade ago. Just as Vanessa described eligibility work as more meaningful than bank telling, Sofia described WTW work as more meaningful than eligibility work. Like most of the GAIN workers I met, she emphasized that her job necessitates stronger connections with clients.

WTW work requires employees to "get to know" their program participants in a deeper sense. While Sofia spends a lot of time on the phone talking to clients like Vanessa does, she is required to ask more intimate questions so as to better link people to employment or, more commonly, to schoolfare, medfare, and housefare programs. I sat with her as she asked incoming participants questions like "How would you describe the relationship with the other parent and your child?," "Has a partner ever damaged your property?," and "How often do you consume alcohol?" I also listened as she used an assessment script to ask participants if they had any "physical or mental health problems" and how often they felt "nervous," "exhausted," "motivated," "scared," and so on. While the questions are just as standardized, the topics addressed in the GAIN offices (as well as in the START program) are generally more intimate than those addressed in the district offices.

And, as demonstrated in the previous chapter, the work done in GAIN offices is also more case based than task based. Sofia, in particular, had 133 active cases when I shadowed her. All were CalWORKs customers in the nearby South Los Angeles and Long Beach neighborhoods who had been mandated to participate in GAIN.

One of her cases was Wendy, a Black woman roughly forty-five years of age. Sofia has spoken to Wendy multiple times during the last couple of years, both in person and over the phone. In addition to connecting her to a range of services, Sofia helped excuse Wendy from mandatory program "activity" obligations when she and her children were evicted from their apartment. By placing her case on "homeless good cause" status, Sofia temporarily reduced Wendy's pressure to participate in job training, GED prep, therapy, and other welfare-to-work activities. She also referred Wendy to a special unit of "homeless eligibility workers," who were at least able to grant her some additional, albeit very small, amounts of cash aid via the state's CalWORKs Homeless Assistance program (approximately $1,400 total). Reflecting on this, Sofia told me, "Participants just have to talk to us and explain their situation. . . . Communication is key."

I sat with Sofia in her cubicle as she worked on Wendy's case. While the participant was still homeless, Sofia needed to remove her from the good cause exemption. That was because Wendy was in the midst of getting a job at an in-home-care company and she was urgently requesting clothing and transportation ancillaries. Sofia told Wendy to visit her in the office and she'd get her squared away.

Before Wendy arrived, Sofia called the participant's new employer to confirm she had actually been hired. She then prepared a "welfare-to-work contract," which had to be signed before ancillaries could be issued. The contract stipulates that Wendy must work or participate in GAIN-approved activities for at least thirty hours a week to continue to receive CalWORKs for herself (her children are covered regardless). After she printed the contract, Sofia turned her attention to the ancillary paperwork in the few minutes before Wendy was scheduled to arrive. Wendy reported that she needed scrubs. I watched as Sofia printed a search result for scrubs from the Walmart website to include in an $80 ancillary request for two shirts and two pairs of pants. She double-checked with her supervisor a few cubicles down the hall to confirm that this was the most she could offer.

The transportation ancillary was not so straightforward. Normally, she would calculate transportation from the participant's residence to their place of employment. If the distance were more than two hours by bus (according to an online trip planner) she would be awarded "mileage" or "gas" (roughly fifty cents per mile). Wendy, however, was homeless. Sofia had to use a welfare office address for the calculation.

Making matters even trickier, the destination address entered had to be the office for the caregiver company, but that was not actually where Wendy would be reporting for work. She would be dispatched to multiple homes throughout the week. "That's driving while working," Sofia told me in a frustrated tone. "We can't help with that." All Sofia could do was grant funds for a slightly more expensive bus pass than what she was technically eligible for ($110 instead of $65 for gas). This gave Wendy a few extra dollars in ancillary funds, but it did little to ease Sofia's discontent.

The frustration with cases like this, as Sofia and other GAIN workers told me, comes not only from having limited tools and resources to help people. It also comes from constantly confronting rules and regulations that explicitly contradict the welfare-to-work objective, let alone the more benevolent mission to aid poor families. This is a frustration that tends to weigh heavier on WTW workers like

Sofia than on eligibility workers like Vanessa. But there's not much time to dwell while on the welfare assembly line. The best Sofia or any GAIN worker can do for these kinds of cases is quickly guide them through a complex and contradictory system to assure that they are at least given *something*. On occasion, they can shake a few extra crumbs loose.

By the time Wendy arrived for her appointment, Sofia had the welfare-to-work contract printed and ready to sign. We met the participant in a mostly vacant waiting room, where she stood up slowly from her seat and limped in our direction. "Are you ok?" Sofia asked with a soft and concerning voice. "Oh yeah," Wendy responded in pain. "I just have this pinched nerve." "Oh, I'm sorry," said Sofia, before she introduced me and we walked to the meeting room.

The space where Sofia met Wendy reminded me of a classroom. It was a large, open room with roughly a half-dozen desks where workers could meet participants. A clerk sat at the front, like a classroom proctor, ready to help the WTW workers with printing, escorting participants, and more.

Sofia explained the contract to Wendy and noted that she must work thirty hours a week to maintain compliance with GAIN. She also explained that receipts would be needed for the clothing ancillary (to avoid an over-issuance penalty) but not for the transportation ancillary, suggesting that the latter would be like "extra cash." Wendy liked hearing this. "Oh, thank you!" she said with some levity in her voice. "No problem," said Sofia, "I'm sorry we couldn't do more."

While signing the contract, Wendy asked about jobs at DPSS. She heard a rumor that one of the district offices had been converted to a call center and that they were hiring GAIN participants. Sofia confirmed the rumor but noted that hiring is through the county's Transitional Subsidized Employment (TSE) program, a nine-month activity for workfare participants that *may* lead to permanent employment. Wendy stressed that this sounded much better than the job she had recently secured, and Sofia agreed. If the TSE appointment became a permanent position, Wendy would likely earn more money, have better benefits, and do work that was less physically demanding.

However, after some additional case review, Sofia determined that Wendy did not have enough time on her CalWORKs clock to participate in this activity. The TSE program administrators would make exceptions for those with at least six months remaining, but Wendy only had three months left. Again, Sofia confronted a rule that prevented her from assisting her client in a manner she found appropriate.

Wendy seemed disappointed, but she also seemed accustomed to a bombardment of bad news and setbacks. She was at least relieved to learn that in three months she would only lose her own cash aid. Wendy's children would remain covered so long as they were in her custody. And, while the ancillaries were paltry, she said she was glad to get some extra funds to help with clothing and transportation.

We said our goodbyes and a clerk walked Wendy back to the main entrance of the building. After scanning and processing the newly signed contract, Sofia sent a request to her supervisor to "rush" the ancillaries to Wendy today. Before turning her attention to her next appointment, Sofia told me that Wendy was a "good case" and that she seemed "really interested in working. . . . They [other clients] are usually not very eager to work." For this reason, Sofia was especially frustrated that she could not help more. I was struck by how little "deservingness" could actually benefit participants like her.

When compared to the interaction between Vanessa and Jordan, the one between Sofia and Wendy was warm. Sofia seemed to take on a bit of Wendy's stress and problems. In contrast, Vanessa seemed relatively disinterested in, if not apathetic to, Jordan's suffering. Sofia seemed to empathize, or at least sympathize, with Wendy.

But just as we should not overgeneralize Vanessa and Jordan's encounter, we should not overgeneralize Sofia and Wendy's. I certainly met GAIN and START workers who did not connect so deeply with their participants. Still, connective labor is something generally enabled and directed in welfare-to-work programming.

Directing Connectivity

As already demonstrated, DPSS presents itself not only as a people-processing bureaucracy but also as a people-changing bureaucracy.[23] The department aims, under the command and legitimacy of state and federal regulations, to transform welfare customers into self-sufficient worker-citizens. We cannot ignore that a significant minority of department operations explicitly orient frontline staff toward developing, regulating, and commodifying labor power near the bottom of a complex urban hierarchy.

Indeed, programs like GAIN and START are manifestly focused on *transforming* cash aid customers into ex-customers via formal employment. START, for example, is said to be a program that "provides employment and training services to help employable General Relief (GR) customers obtain jobs and eliminate the need for GR benefits."[24] Likewise, GAIN is a "welfare-to-work program for customers who are receiving CalWORKs" that is focused on promoting "self-sufficiency and independence."[25]

We should not write such statements off as "just talk." While there is no convincing evidence that such programs seriously challenge systemic poverty, there is evidence that these interventions do in fact increase low-wage, high-precarity employment for many subjects.[26]

As noted in chapter 3, workfare initiatives in the 1980s threw a huge wrench into the people-processing machinery of post–civil rights welfare offices. Local agencies like DPSS were suddenly tasked with focusing on a new subject: the *participant*, the client exposed to—and almost always mandated to partake in—specialized people-changing programming. By the time Clinton-era welfare reforms in

1996 cemented welfare-to-work programming across the nation, DPSS was ready to double down on the mission of workfare and its auxiliary focus on schoolfare, medfare, and housefare.

In 1997, Phil Ansell, a longtime DPSS manager, summarized the approach to the press: "While [meeting] with participants, workers will be expected to promote the message of welfare-to-work and relate to them in a way that is empowering. In the past, welfare has viewed recipients as essentially passive vessels, expected to follow certain rules and then we do things for them. We now must help them take control of their lives, motivate them to create a belief that their lives can be better."[27]

Such a shift necessitated the mechanized social work detailed previously. The demand for connectivity increased as a people-changing mission was mixed into a people-processing bureaucracy. A subset of workers, be they employed in house or through a contracted organization like Maximus, were tasked—at least on paper—with transforming recipients. At the same time, efforts to rationalize that labor and to integrate it into the welfare assembly line also intensified. Assessments, referrals, sanctions, and more became highly systematized in the form of procedure trees, drop-down menus, and so on. Thus, while management attempted to systematically discourage connectivity in people-processing operations, they attempted to systematically direct it in people-changing operations.

Connective Labor on the Welfare Assembly Line

Michael Lipsky's *Street-Level Bureaucracy* gives us reason to suspect that welfare labor is variably "alienated."[28] He juxtaposes alienation with "altruism" and, more specifically, with client-focused "advocacy."[29] Lipsky acknowledges that social workers, cops, teachers, nurses, and other so-called street-level bureaucrats may authentically advocate for their clients, but he is clear that such acts are relatively rare and often ineffective. This is because advocacy is largely incompatible with bureaucratic power, a social force that seeks to maximize efficiency, standardization, and control at the expense of customized treatment. With this in mind, we may assume that WTW workers are at least slightly less alienated (and thus slightly more altruistic) than eligibility workers because their labor is a bit more discretionary. That would be generally consistent with the comparisons made across the previous chapters.

Such a framework, however, can only get us so far. For one thing, Lipsky largely dismisses advocacy and altruism as institutional mythology. Frontline workers in his estimation are basically disconnected and estranged from the subjects of their work. Lipsky fails to consider how connectivity between workers and clients, even if very limited, may constitute an essential and durable component of policy execution. In other words, he risks overemphasizing alienation and provides few tools for explaining why something like worker-client solidarity might emerge through the labor process. And, in separating alienation from advocacy, he does not consider how the two can exist simultaneously not only within the same organization or shift but within the same productive practice.

I argue that connective labor is a common yet undertheorized feature of frontline public service work, even when the conditions of that work severely limit workers' control and afford them only narrow and superficial discretion. Unlike Lipsky, Pugh pushes us to consider how workers are tasked with witnessing and conveying their clients' emotional truths in order to execute their work.[30] Through a process she labels "colliding intensification," the need for connective labor has increased under contemporary capitalism as have efforts to rationalize that labor. This allows us to see, among many other things, how the labor of advocacy can be alienating by way of its systematization.

Managers at the agency systematically *discourage connectivity* between eligibility workers and their customers and systematically *di-*

rect connectivity between WTW workers and their participants. The organization of task-based eligibility work in the district offices and call centers enables but does not guarantee relatively cold exchanges between workers and their clients. Things, however, are a bit different in GAIN and START units where managers demand caseworkers to "get to know" their clients more intimately, albeit in a heavily scripted and constrained way. WTW workers dig a bit deeper into their clients' histories, aspirations, and burdens, and this enables, but does not guarantee, relatively warm exchanges between workers and clients. While worker-client connectivity is like a sticky substance that managers aim to rid from people-processing procedures, it is a malleable substance they aim to mold in people-changing procedures.

It may be the case that disconnection and alienation are the best descriptions for the typical worker-client relation among proletarianized public servants, but we should not write off connectivity and altruism as just institutional mythology. At the same time, we should be careful not to overemphasize the significance of something like connective labor within agencies like DPSS. We should understand dis/connection as a basic contradiction of the welfare assembly line.

Conclusion

Like Los Angeles generally, welfare offices in this county are best narrated using themes of sunshine and noir. On the one hand, these are spaces for issuing aid to over a third of Angelenos. In no way is this a postwelfare city; there is much to be protected in the name of alleviating suffering. DPSS distributes aid to over four million people, with its largest programs being Medi-Cal (3.5 million) and CalFresh (1.6 million).[1] Cash assistance remains small, covering less than a half million residents across CalWORKs (279,000) and General Relief (123,000), but it's not nothing.[2] On the other hand, such aid is notoriously stingy and obtaining it can come with the hefty price of runarounds, mandated service participation, abrupt terminations of assistance, and more. Those seeking aid from DPSS have to jump through many hoops mandated by federal and state law to obtain these paltry amounts of assistance. Such moment-to-moment inefficiencies are embedded in a system that has improved efficiency in a fundamental way: by increasing the client-to-worker ratio.

The Welfare Assembly Line offers unique insights into these contradictory spaces by examining the frontline workers that make and maintain them. More specifically, this book examines their labor process and how it has changed over the past six decades. I argue that welfare work in the agency has been increasingly proletarianized, with workers losing significant control over not only the products but also the processes of their labor. They have been stationed on two major sublines of mass policy production, one for yielding a customer service state and another for yielding a workfare state. And while the latter comes with more worker autonomy, both are heavily standardized, efficiency-oriented, and disciplined. Their managers are structurally incentivized by the dual pressures of austerity and legal demand to increase productivity and extract more labor effort. The welfare assembly line, with its instruments of automation and structured divisions of labor, is what has allowed the agency to expand the reach of benefits and services with limited staffing resources.

But again, we must not narrate this entirely as noir. I never visited an office illuminated only with fluorescent bulbs. The California sun almost always snuck through the windows. Workers were not entirely alienated or immiserated. Many were quick to remind me how grateful they were for their good county jobs in a labor market filled with insecure and vocationally unfulfilling positions. Even some of the most routinized aspects of their work were framed optimistically. And while the customer service and workfare conveyor belts no doubt push clientele rapidly through (and often off) the assembly line, workers do find opportunities to "work with" clientele they find especially deserving of their limited attention.

All of this motivates and is the consequence of theoretical reconstruction. First, a close analysis of the welfare assembly line revealed significant anomalies in light of street-level bureaucracy theory. I did not encounter frontline people processors or people changers exercising wide discretion. I instead met workers with narrow discretion. And what discretion remains is increasingly exercised over more superficial rather than more substantial matters of policy execution. The historical record shows this was an intentional design of productivity and quality control by management.

A general theory of the labor process helped me rethink frontline welfare workers as *proletarianized public servants*. Again, these workers are best characterized not by their discretion but by their lack of control over the labor process. This is, however, not a simple story of deskilling or alienation. Among other things, I had to wrestle with the fact that workers across both the customer service and the workfare state production lines were generally committed to their jobs. At the same time, we had to contend with the fact that automation has not simply reduced these workers to mere appendages of machines. Even when management tries to explicitly reduce discretion to zero with things like scripted interviews, benefit calculators, and procedure trees, workers find ways to preserve and exercise their autonomy on the assembly line.

Two additional theories—one on disciplinary power and another on connective labor—helped me further unpack variations in this autonomy. The former was reconstructed to account for differences in administrative and paternalistic discipline and helped clarify how not only the clients but also the workers are responsibilized on the welfare assembly line. The latter challenged a simplistic theory of alienation and was reconstructed to consider how welfare workers are variably dis/connected with their clients depending on their assembly line position.

But thus far I have skirted some important questions, namely: What should be done about the welfare assembly line? Should we leave it alone and accept it as a normal feature of bureaucratic progress, especially amidst increased pressures to run government like a business? Should we abolish it? Should we return to a more traditional era of social work in which, at least on paper, efficiency is secondary to effectiveness? Should we completely reimagine what such effectiveness even means in the contemporary welfare state? What about working toward a new era in which welfare departments, with assembly lines or not, are obsolete?

My answer to these questions rests on three primary assumptions. First, I assume that so long as capitalism—interlocked with racism and sexism—persists, there will be racialized and gendered poverty that the state must govern. Whether it be by aiding, punishing, or even neglecting relatively poor populations, state responses to poverty will continue to be exercised in contradictory ways. I think universal program proposals like Medicare for All, a universal basic income, and even food stamps for everyone are definitely worth investing in and would do a lot to relieve suffering, but such massive reforms will not eliminate relative poverty in a society in which amassing wealth depends on the exploitation of dominated and marginalized populations. There will always be a need for the state to regulate poor populations under capitalism, whether to reproduce their labor power, neutralize social unrest, express state legitimacy, or simply alleviate their suffering for its own sake.[3] Second, I assume that such regulation, no matter how automated, will depend on frontline public services labor. Whether they be welfare workers, police officers, emergency department nurses, or some other frontline laborers in a devolved, delegated, and discontinuous state, such workers will continue to make and remake the state daily. And just as I think poverty persists so long as capitalism does, so too do I assume that frontline public servants will continue to be necessary for governing the poor. Automation will continue, and artificial intelligence may very well thin out many jobs in the welfare state, but there will still be human labor on the front lines—even if that labor is stationed behind a screen or a phone. Third, I assume such governance is more socially just when it prioritizes aid and assistance (rather than coercion and punishment) and when it is robust (rather than frail). So-called Gov-Tech vendors like the Change and Innovation Agency are at least right about one thing: There is a "capacity crisis" in welfare agencies.[4] But rather than innovate methods that squeeze more paltry aid out of a thinned workforce, we should abate austerity and dispel the myth that there are not enough resources to radically aid the poor. Redirecting resources from prisons, jails, and police toward welfare programs that are more generous and less punitive is a promising blueprint for reducing the suffering that concentrates toward the bottom of the social hierarchy.[5] But that is not nearly enough. A significantly expanded safety net will require dramatic income and wealth redistribution. If we can't eat the rich, we should certainly tax the hell out of them.

None of this justifies an abolition of the welfare assembly line. The best way forward, short of dismantling capitalism, is to continuously reform the mass production of welfare distribution so that it is better for both clients and workers. I do think benefits should be distributed quickly, accurately, and conveniently for aid recipients, and the McDonaldization of welfare has done a lot to rationalize this process in the district offices and call centers. But we must also recognize that doing so efficiently tends to come at the price of intensified working conditions on the frontlines. Investments in the welfare state should therefore come with increased expansions and protections of good government jobs. And while I believe welfare offices should offer more than just benefit payments, we should be leery of a mechanized social work powered by a workfare logic. Strengthening referral ties between welfare workers and a fragmented network of medicine, education, childcare, and even potential employers makes sense, but this should be done for the sake of reducing suffering generally not mandating employment specifically.

A few broad changes come to mind. First, we can reduce, if not outright eliminate, eligibility requirements and administrative burdens for a range of programs. This would increase cases and expand the provision of aid. And while it would increase the workload and would necessitate hiring more welfare workers, it would ideally reduce the work required for any individual case. In fact, it would likely motivate the elimination of some means-testing jobs on the assembly line. Rather than trim overall staffing and reduce good government jobs, this can and should motivate reassignment to alternative positions. And, no, more welfare-to-work programs is not the answer.

This leads me to another point. We should redirect interventions away from missions of self-sufficiency and toward missions of self-determination.[6] Where the former seeks to siphon people off public assistance, the latter, as I imagine it, would expand people's capabilities through public assistance. We should abolish workfare as well as the schoolfare, medfare, and housefare programs that are narrowly focused on increasing employability for its own sake (or for the sake of thinning the recipient list and protecting the budget). Such initiatives heavily constrain and often discourage welfare workers who see their own ability to alleviate poverty severely limited by welfare-to-work missions.

We should also seriously consider curtailing the taskwork model in favor of a less proletarianized casework model. As several union members noted in my conversations with them at a rally outside a Board of Supervisors meeting in September 2024, this would strengthen worker-client connections (assuming caseloads were contained) and could reduce managerial incentives to micromanage staff (assuming casework widened and deepened worker discretion). Such a shift would surely slow the assembly line down, but a slower pace could be countered with more hiring and reduced administrative burdens. With this recommendation I do not mean to suggest that casework is perfect or that there is no space for call centers or even some task-based operations in welfare departments. As one top manager reminded me, "People on straight Medi-Cal don't really want or need a caseworker. They just want health insurance." This is a fair point. It's also worth noting that a handful of the employees I met who were hired after the massive shift toward taskwork in 2021 said they had no real interest in doing casework. But the taskwork model should nonetheless be approached cautiously and sparingly if the goals are effectiveness (not just efficiency) and quality of work (not just quantity of work). Collective bargaining, as well as insights from welfare recipients and advocates, should be central to these decisions.

Temporary reactions to the COVID-19 pandemic should give us hope that some of these changes are possible. In response to increased economic insecurity, as well as efforts to maintain social distancing, there were significant reductions to the administrative burdens for all of DPSS's major programs. Among other things, clients were not expected to visit offices, provide "wet signatures," or do as many lengthy runarounds. This reduced the labor of legibility, of "seeing customers," since there was less paperwork. And while workfare persisted, lax pandemic rules, including a broad COVID good cause exemption, momentarily turned GAIN and START from mandated workfare programs to voluntary programs for ancillaries and referrals. Sure, the resources remained paltry and did little to advance the self-determination of clients, but the pandemic rules provided some temporary relief from the misleading project of self-sufficiency.[7] COVID also rapidly expanded a workplace benefit almost universally praised by labor: the massive expansion of remote work opportunities. These changes provided clear evidence that the welfare assembly line is a malleable technology that can be modified to improve wellbeing for both clients and workers. But, with the exception of remote work, many of these benefits have waned.

Achieving more permanent improvements requires far more than the political will of local welfare administrators. As noted in the introduction, department managers are tasked with organizing frontline labor to materialize policy according to strict guidelines set by the state and federal governments. Neither the director of DPSS, nor the County Board of Supervisors they report to, can do much of anything to tweak means testing or program brokering expectations.

They are legally commanded to run assembly lines for the customer service and workfare states with limited staffing budgets. And while state governments have more authority than municipalities and counties to adjust such conditions, much of this ultimately depends on federal regulations for Medicaid (for Medi-Cal), TANF (for CalWORKs), and SNAP (for CalFresh).

My hope is that this book will encourage you to consider the importance of local welfare workers in these discussions and many like them. Expanding an assembly line focused on the mass and fast distribution of assistance may be just, but we should not forget the workers that enable such distribution. Their lives also depend on the line, not for public benefits but for a paycheck and a sense of meaningful labor.

I also hope this book contributes to a larger conversation about work in America. Frontline public sector employment, of which public benefits bureaucracies are just one component, has long remained a secure niche for populations historically marginalized in the private sector. This case study suggests that there is still much to celebrate here, even in an era where public bureaucracies are increasingly managed like private businesses. However, it also suggests that scholars and citizens concerned about the world of work should be mindful of the structural transformations in so-called good government jobs. Paying attention to shifts in the public sector labor market is an important part of this, but it is not enough. We must also examine and critique transformations in the frontline labor process. Doing so not only helps us see how policy is materialized but also reveals how frontline workers are increasingly—though never entirely—disempowered through automation, standardization, and divisions of labor. It may very well be the proletarianized public servant rather than the street-level bureaucrat whose work most defines this sector in the twenty-first century.

APPENDIX

Notes on Data and Method

In many ways this project began two years before my interaction with Deputy Diaz recounted in chapter 1. After hearing then DPSS director Antonia Jiménez proudly speak about the "customer service" orientation of her department at a local conference on prisoner reentry in 2019, I emailed her to see if I could shadow frontline workers. Again, I was heavily inspired by the work of Michael Lipsky, Celeste Watkins-Hayes, and others.[1] I pitched the project as an exploratory study on frontline public service work. To my delight, she quickly forwarded my request to a unit of administrators focused specifically on research partnerships.

I worked with these administrators to craft a proposal for shadowing workers across a range of units and offices. We agreed that shadowing fifty workers throughout five offices would be a good starting point. I requested offices in South Los Angeles (where I worked at the time), the San Gabriel Valley (where I lived at the time), and downtown. My hope was to capture a diversity of workers and clients, and this is also why I requested to observe both district office and welfare-to-work operations. The administrators and I agreed that it would make the most sense logistically for their unit to contact deputies at these offices and then have them identify workers who would be willing to have an outside observer shadow them for at least half of a shift.

But before I could actually enter these offices as a researcher, I had to clear a series of hurdles. I struggled a bit to get the project approved by the Institutional Review Board (IRB) at the University of Southern California (my employer at the time). While it was easy enough to structure protocols of informed consent and confidentiality for the workers, or "primary subjects," I was intending to shadow, it took me a couple of proposal submissions and phone calls with IRB officials to convince them to allow a "waiver of consent" for all "secondary subjects" (including clients, supervisors, and fellow workers that my so-called primary subjects would interact with during observations).

Once my proposal received the necessary blessing from IRB, I then had to make the project legible according to DPSS's protocols for outside research. This required, among other things, approval from the labor union. Key to this was assuring that I would not print the real names of workers and that managers would not mandate participation in the study. I also needed to develop a memorandum of agreement (MOA). The MOA replicated many of the details in the IRB protocols, but it was distinct in one major regard: It established a research relationship not between DPSS and myself but between DPSS and my employer. My eventual move from the University of Southern California to Boston College in 2022 made this particularly complicated for reasons I do not understand. All I know is that this required some nerve-racking assistance from "county counsel" behind the scenes.

However, the biggest impediment to the project was neither IRB nor the MOA. It was the COVID-19 pandemic. I cleared the hurdles noted above just weeks before DPSS offices shut down and the vast majority of workers were mandated to work from home. Some employees stayed in offices to collect paper applications handed to them from masked clientele outside. I was understandably forbidden from beginning my observations. So I waited. And waited. The offices eventually opened up again with smaller numbers of in-person workers who were not only masked but also fever-checked upon entry. Administrators once again understandably determined that I was inessential to operations and delayed my entry until fall 2021.

In November of that year, I began observations in welfare offices. Per the MOA, I had approval to shadow fifty workers across five offices: the South Central District Office in Watts, the San Gabriel Valley District Office in El Monte, the Metro North District Office in West Lake, the GAIN Region V South County Main Office in an unincorporated area just south of Compton, and the GAIN Region III San Gabriel Valley Main Office in Monterey Park. Due to concerns over the spread of the omicron variant of COVID, four workers cancelled their observation sessions, leaving me with a sample of forty-six.

I was not given much choice or provided many insights into how workers were selected for the shadow observations. Administrators from headquarters simply sent me a schedule of workers to shadow and the contact information for the deputies I should check in with upon my arrival. A couple of the workers I shadowed told me they were "voluntold" to sign up by office managers despite the fact that the MOA clearly framed participation as consensual. Most, however,

TABLE A1 Shadow observation demographics

	Total (n = 46)	Eligibility workers (n = 27)	WTW workers (n = 19)
Age (mean)	42	40	44
Female (%)	80	78	84
BA degree or higher (%)	74	63	89
White (%)	7	7	5
Black (%)	13	19	5
Latino (%)	56	48	68
Asian (%)	22	22	21
Middle Eastern (%)	2	4	0

said they were invited by their supervisors or deputies but were given the option to say no. In fact, I met a few workers in the office who later admitted that they turned down the study invitation because they did not quite understand what it was for. I also met some who said they were frustrated they were not invited to participate, and one such worker speculated it was because management did not want me speaking with disgruntled employees. The deputies and supervisors I spoke to about this, however, insisted they simply wanted to attach me to workers in a way that was most convenient and least disruptive to the workflow. One thing was made clear to me across all the offices I studied: deputies wanted to spread the burden of my observations across multiple units.

Table A1 summarizes some basic demographic information for the forty-six workers I shadowed. Of these employees, twenty-seven were eligibility workers and nineteen were WTW workers (either for GAIN or START). Those I shadowed were mostly women, college graduates, and Latino (including those who identified as Hispanic or Chicano). Of course, for the reasons mentioned above, this is not a representative sample. As noted in chapter 2, official employment records from the county suggest that in the fourth quarter of 2022, frontline DPSS staff was 79 percent female, 19 percent white, 18 percent Black, 45 percent Latino, and 18 percent Asian.

I began each observation session by introducing myself as a sociologist interested in frontline welfare work. I always made it a point to say study participation was voluntary and that I would not print workers' real names. I also noted that I would not record confidential information about their clients and asked that they simply introduce me to others as someone who was shadowing their work for the day. I also promised I would not share my field notes with management. With the exception of the four scheduled workers who canceled observations due to concerns over omicron, all of those I met at this stage agreed to participate.

The workers I shadowed were very kind and seemed genuinely happy that someone was studying *them* and not just the clients or welfare policy in the abstract. Some treated the observations like a kind of pseudo-training, narrating each step of their work. Others simply went to work and relied on me to ask specific questions as needed. Almost all of these workers invited me to sit beside them so that I could see their computer screens. With the exception of a couple of workers who put their calls on speaker at a low volume, I usually could not hear what clients were saying on the other end of the phone. This was obviously not a problem when I shadowed workers during their in-person encounters, but several conversations were in Spanish and other languages I do not know. Being able to see workers' screens—including the answers they entered in response to client interviews—helped me follow conversations. And workers were always willing to answer quick questions I had about their client encounters immediately after.

I jotted handwritten notes while in the field. I, of course, couldn't write *everything* down, and there were in fact many things I was forbidden from recording. I did not jot any identifying information about clients—whose names, dates of birth, addresses, Social Security numbers, and more were often visible to me. But given that this was a theory-driven case study on the *labor process*, I was not interested in such information. My focus was on the practices of workers—what they did, at what speeds, and so on. I spoke to them and jotted down what they told me regarding their work, but these encounters were not interviews. The focus of my hand-written recordings was firstly on worker practices and secondly on worker perceptions. I then used these jottings to type more detailed field notes, and I always did so within twenty-four hours of completing an observation. Because I was forbidden from using an audio recorder in the field, all quotes from fieldwork conversations are paraphrased.

Each observation session was limited to a half of a shift (approximately four to five hours depending on the worker's lunch break). I had hoped to shadow them for longer, but administrators understandably wanted to limit my presence. As one deputy kindly explained, any outside observer tends to "slow things down." At one point in my fieldwork, administrators from headquarters attempted to limit my observation sessions to one hour each, but I was able to successfully argue against this. Administrators from headquarters told me half shifts where the best I could get. The welfare assembly line, as I came to understand it, required fast hands and minds undistracted by nosy sociologists. And per the MOA, my objective was to minimize my obtrusiveness in the offices.

While some workers jokingly said I was "like a fly on the wall," that was obviously not the case. In addition to asking lots of clarifying questions about the labor process, and slowing that process down as a result, many seemed to see me as a curious figure in the cubicles: a six-foot-tall white guy sitting alongside a labor force made mostly of women of color. Workers frequently reminded me that, because of my age (I was thirty-four at the time), I did not "look like a professor," but I was no doubt an outsider. Other employees would occasionally pop their heads into the cubicles I was observing to ask who I was and what I was doing there. I was sometimes met with relief: "Oh, thank God," said one worker after hearing I was an academic. "I thought you were with CIA"—Change and Innovation Agency, the software vendor that sold DPSS the Current program, mentioned in chapter 3.

I have no doubt that my presence in the field exerted influence on the very object I was studying: the labor process. On one occasion, a worker told me that her supervisor instructed her to show me the "interesting stuff" and, much to her delight, she was temporarily removed from a mundane assignment of manually fixing a list of system-generated errors in CalSAWS. Likewise, another worker— again much to her delight—was told not to answer calls on the "redetermination line" as initially planned and instead to do some lobby work so that I could *see* worker-client interactions. One worker told me that she believed one of the women I was shadowing was "showing off," "doesn't usually work that hard," and isn't usually "that nice to customers."

Such messaging may have seriously distressed a researcher committed to a positivist vision of science, but I am no such researcher. I am a reflexive scientist and assume the ripples I produced in the field were not only inevitable but insightful. I was a *participant observer*.[2] I may not have done much to help those I shadowed with their work, but I participated in the social life of the welfare office, at least temporarily.

This participation led me into spaces beyond the cubicles and lobbies. I frequently spoke to other workers in breakrooms, hallways, and parking lots. A handful invited me on in-office walks to stretch our legs and meet other workers during breaks. I often wandered the offices alone and collected (or photographed) flyers, pamphlets, and other artifacts. Several deputies and supervisors kindly invited me into their offices and cubicles to chat informally about DPSS programs, my study, and more. I was even granted access to a couple of staff meetings and training sessions. While administrators at headquarters seemed especially nervous about me slowing the welfare assembly line, I generally felt welcomed by both labor and management in the five offices I observed.

I would, however, be lying if I said I was satisfied with the amount of fieldwork I completed at DPSS. I never assumed six months of fieldwork would be enough. But, in my initial conversations with administrators, I realized ethnography was a foreign concept and asking for something like continuous or years-long access wouldn't fly. I figured I could ask for a relatively small sample of fifty workers across five offices and then request more later, after building rapport. I had used this strategy in previous projects—one studying a prison in Oregon over the course of a year, and another studying a fleet of ambulances in California over two years.[3]

This approach, however, did not work for the studied welfare department. As I inched toward my final observations at Metro North, I requested to do additional fieldwork, either at one of the offices I had previously observed or at a new one. Administrators from headquarters told me that the MOA did not allow this.

A few months later, I moved to New England. From there, I submitted an amendment to the MOA and requested the opportunity to conduct interviews and supplemental observations in department meetings and workshops. This request was, however, denied without reason. And when I explicitly asked for one, I received none—just a note that the "decision is final."

I turned lemons into lemonade. The refusal to conduct additional fieldwork motivated me to enter the archives. Indeed, I had no intention of historically embedding my case until I was iced out of the field.[4] When an archivist handed me my first box containing DPSS manuals and letters from the early 1970s, I assumed I would simply use this material to supplement the observations. But I soon fell in love with archival research. It was like finding lost puzzle pieces scattered in the backs of libraries and museums. Examining artifacts from the past helped me make sense of the present.

Table A2 summarizes the archival material I examined for this book, arranged in the order in which I encountered them. I mostly relied on the Online Archive of California (OAC), a resource that catalogues archival material maintained by over three hundred libraries, museums, historical societies, and other institutions throughout the state, to identify relevant collections.[5] It was by searching for material on DPSS that I discovered that the University of Southern California held thirty-nine boxes of records for this agency spanning from 1949 to 1999 (bulk 1970-1980). For weeks after my fieldwork, I pored over these materials, which mostly contained memos and letters (e.g., usually between managers), protocols and plans, meeting agendas and minutes, reports (both internally and externally

TABLE A2 Archival material

Collection	Years	Location	Kinds of material
LA County DPSS Records	1948–1999 (bulk 1970–1980)	University of Southern California Libraries Special Collections	Memos/letters Protocols/plans Agendas/minutes Reports News/bulletins Client forms Training materials
Papers of Alicia Escalante	1961–2001 (bulk 1960s–1980s)	University of California, Santa Barbara, Department of Special Research Collections	Memos/letters Agendas/minutes Reports Client forms Training materials
Collection of Kenneth Hahn	1954–1993	Huntington Library, Manuscript Collections	Memos/letters Protocols/plans Reports
California Social Welfare Archives, Miscellaneous Publications	1946–1990s	University of Southern California Libraries Special Collections	Reports Agendas/Minutes Protocols/Plans
Yvonne Brathwaite Burke Papers	1959–1980 (bulk 1966–1980)	University of Southern California Libraries Special Collections	Memos/letters Protocols/plans Reports Client forms
Papers of Edmund D. Edelman	1953–1994 (bulk 1974–1994)	Huntington Library, Manuscript Collections	Memos/letters Protocols/plans Reports Motions
Gloria Molina Papers	1964–2014 (bulk 1991–2005)	Huntington Library, Manuscript Collections	Memos/letters Protocols/plans Reports Motions
California State Assembly of Human Services Committee Records	1976–2006	California State Archives	Memos/letters Protocols/plans Reports Client forms

(*continued*)

Collection	Years	Location	Kinds of material
Carl Washington Papers	1979–2002	California State Archives	Protocols/plans Reports Client forms
California State Senate Industrial Relations Committee Records	1972–2000	California State Archives	Memos/letters Protocols/plans Reports News/bulletins
Los Angeles County Federation of Labor Collection	1860–2018	California State University, Northridge, Special Collections and Archives	Memos/letters Reports News/bulletins
SEIU Local 535 Records	1967–2007 (bulk 1967–2000)	Walter P. Reuther Library, Wayne State University	Memos/letters Reports News/bulletins

Note: I did not visit the Alicia Escalante Papers in person. I requested a scan of five folders remotely.

authored), news and bulletins (including departmental newsletters), client forms (e.g., applications, flyers, and pamphlets), and staff training materials. After I moved to New England, I used OAC to track and triage other relevant materials scattered throughout other collections. I traveled to Los Angeles, Pasadena, Sacramento, and Northridge to examine similar DPSS-related documents tucked away in various collections for state and county organizations (e.g., California State Assembly of Human Services Committee Records) and individuals (e.g., Papers of Edmund D. Edelman). I also made a trip to Detroit to examine some records of SEIU Local 535, the first union to represent DPSS workers.

As with my fieldwork, my archival work focused on the frontline labor process at DPSS. My goal was not to narrate a general history of the department but rather to "isolate bits and pieces of the archive to make sense of sociological cases and build sociological arguments."[6] With the exception of the DPSS records, in which I effectively browsed every box and opened almost every folder, I examined material organized into broad topics concerning staffing, management, workload, union communications, human resources, training, budget, department newsletters, policy implementation, technology, protocol changes, and anything else that seemed potentially insightful for a study of the labor process. I cast a wide net and asked the archivists to pull many boxes. I would then browse these materials looking for pertinent information in light of my theory-driven case study. Like an ethnographer, I also jotted notes while in the archives, and I frequently used these to expand into larger narratives from home. However, I mostly assembled archival material by scanning relevant documents as PDF images on my iPad. On two occasions, I paid to have entire folders scanned and emailed to me by archivists (one folder in the Kenneth Hahn Collection and five folders in the Alicia Escalante Papers). What initially started as an effort to supplement the participant observations quickly grew into a corpus of scanned documents much larger than my field notes.

I soon realized, however, that there were important voices missing or marginalized in the archival material I reviewed: the voices of workers. Even the union materials I examined fell short as they mostly included documents authored by union organizers. And while the fieldwork put me in conversation with workers, my time spent in their cubicles was mostly focused on the actual practice of labor. I concentrated by and large on what workers were *doing* on the welfare assembly line. I needed to *talk* with workers.

Knowing DPSS administrators were unwilling to help me set up interviews, I pursued these independently. I received IRB approval, under a different set of protocols detached from the MOA, to recruit and interview current and former "welfare workers" in Los Angeles. And because these interviews were to be conducted during workers' personal time and not while they were on the clock, I did not need to receive a site permission form or any other kind of administrative authorization from DPSS. This also meant, however, that I could not invite interview participants through their work emails or phone numbers (which would have been almost impossible to identify without the assistance of administrators anyway). To help increase participation, I offered $50 gift cards to Target or Amazon to all interview participants.

I first attempted to recruit interview participants through social media. Facebook, Instagram, and Twitter all proved to be dead ends, mostly because I couldn't find many people who indicated they worked at DPSS on these platforms. The few that did list DPSS as an employer did not respond to my messages. I also did not have much luck recruiting participants on Reddit. I direct messaged a number of users on the threads mentioned in chapter 2, but I only recruited one participant this way. And, when I posted a study invitation on one of these threads, I was inundated with scammers looking to score a gift card. I had somewhat better luck on LinkedIn and was able to recruit nine interview participants after sending out fifty-one invitations to all the active users I could find who listed DPSS eligibility worker or DPSS GAIN/START service worker as a current or former job (three kindly refused to participate, and the rest never responded even after multiple follow-up requests). I also recruited five students who were enrolled in the California State University Northridge (CSUN) Master of Public Administration Program where I knew some DPSS workers were enrolled in a special degree program for county employees. Faculty in that program kindly forwarded a study flyer to their students. The remaining forty-five interview participants were all recruited by word-of-mouth. I asked everyone I interviewed to pass my cell phone number or email address to any current or former employees or supervisors who might be interested in participating. This was also how I was able to recruit workers currently employed in the privatized GAIN offices in the San Fernando and Antelope valleys.

Table A3 summarizes some basic demographics of the sixty individuals I interviewed (across a total of eighty-seven interviews). All interviews were with current or former employees of DPSS or Maximus, the for-profit company contracted to run GAIN in the San Fernando and Antelope valleys. As with those I observed, the majority of those I interviewed were women. Most were Latino and most also held a bachelor's degree or higher. It is worth noting that three of the five individuals who identified as white (8 percent of those interviewed) made it a point to also tell me they were Armenian. Because interviews focused on a range of experiences during these individuals' tenure at DPSS, they cannot be easily categorized by the position of the interviewee. Almost everyone had some experience as an eligibility worker, including those who were promoted to WTW work or management. A quarter of those I spoke to had some experience working for Maximus, but many had since been hired by DPSS. I was only able to formally interview five managers, including a former director of DPSS, two eligibility supervisors, a county GAIN supervisor, and a Maximus GAIN supervisor.

Interviews averaged forty-four minutes in length and were all conducted remotely on the phone (and a couple times on Zoom). Several interview sessions were squeezed into workers' lunch breaks and lasted between thirty and forty-five minutes, while most other sessions lasted closer to an hour and sometimes longer. As noted in the introduction, the point of these interviews was not to survey this nonrandom sample but to a) better understand processes identified in the fieldwork and archives and b) better account for the perceptions (rather than just the practices) of workers. As such, I did not ask each interviewee the same questions nor did I focus all our conversations on the same themes. Sometimes I fo-

TABLE A3 Interview demographics (n = 60)	
Age (mean)	37
Female (%)	82
BA degree or higher (%)	80
White (%)	8
Black (%)	22
Latino (%)	67
Asian (%)	2
Middle Eastern (%)	2
Eligibility worker experience (%)	93
WTW worker experience (%)	27
Management experience (%)	8
Maximus experience (%)	25

cused on biography (e.g., "How did you get into this line of work?") and other times I asked about recent work experiences (e.g., "Can you walk me through your shift today?"), perceptions of the job (e.g., "What do you find most rewarding about the job? What do you find most challenging?"), relations on the shop floor (e.g., "Can you tell me about your relationship with your supervisor?"), and so on. The most insightful responses were gained, however, through my specific questions about work procedure. Interviewees frequently chuckled at my nitty-gritty questions about CalSAWS and related tools. Veteran workers were especially amused by my questions about expired protocols and computer programs. I also used the interviews as an opportunity to run some of my analysis ideas by workers. Every interview was audio recorded and transcribed.

These interviews proved to be immensely valuable. They not only offered new insights into workers' perceptions; they helped clarify questions that emerged during the writing of this book. This is why I conducted twenty-seven follow-up interviews with subjects I believed could answer particular questions. I am also grateful to a couple of interview participants who kindly kept me updated with protocol changes, union actions, and more via text message.

In addition to the office observations, archival research, and interviews, this book also relies on a range supplemental materials. These include observations of two major welfare management conferences in 2023 and 2024 (California Welfare Directors Association [CWDA] meetings in Anaheim and San Diego, respectively), the *Los Angeles Times* and other news archives, public datasets maintained by the county and state, multiple California Public Records Acts requests, and interviews and informal conversations with a handful of other actors (e.g., an employee at the Los Angeles County Office of Education GAIN Division, other county workers at a labor rally in 2024, and several software vendors I met at the CWDA meetings).

All of this research, as noted in the introduction, was done in service of a theory-driven case study.[7] As my mentor Michael Burawoy taught me, the point of social science is neither to "test" theory nor to "discover" it; rather, the point is to *reconstruct theory* in light of empirical anomalies. *The Welfare Assembly Line* is the product of such an effort.

Notes

For locations of archival holdings, see table A2.

Introduction

1. Davis 1990: 18.

2. Consider the opening line for one news report in the *New York Post*: "Authorities in California have ceded prime real estate on the Venice Beach boardwalk to a rotting cast of vagrants—a microcosm of the insanity plaguing the Golden State amidst its spiraling homeless crisis" (Hernandez and Sedacca 2023).

3. Out of the nearly three thousand counties spread across the US, Los Angeles ranks among the top 3 percent of counties with high inequality between top income earners and the masses (Sommeiller, Price, and Wazeter 2016).

4. According to Menendian and Gambhir (2021), Los Angeles, Long Beach, and Santa Ana, CA, comprised the sixth most segregated metropolitan statistical area in 2019. Per a report by the University of Southern California Program for Environment and Regional Equity (2017), wages for white residents are relatively high even when accounting for inequalities in credentialing. That same report notes, "College-educated women of color with a BA degree or higher earn $11 an hour less than their White male counterparts" (USC Program for Environmental and Region Equity 2017: 5).

5. Addams 1911; Du Bois 1899; Engels (1845) 1892.

6. This rate is for the first quarter of 2023 as captured by the California Poverty Measure (Bohn et al. 2023). This particular measure accounts for place-specific cost of living and a range of safety net supports ignored by the official poverty measure (Stanford Center on Poverty and Inequality 2021). The latter

puts the estimated poverty rate for Los Angeles County in 2022 per the American Community Survey at 13.7 percent, a bit higher than the national rate of 12.5 percent. Consistent with national trends, official poverty in the county is slightly feminized with 55 percent of the officially poor in the county being women and girls. Official poverty in the county is also racially patterned with white and Asian rates hovering around 11 percent while the Latino poverty rate is 16 percent and the Black poverty rate is 20 percent (Stanford Center on Poverty and Inequality 2021). But official poverty can be exceptionally misleading. As sociologist David Brady (2021) notes, this measure "is irredeemably flawed, unreliable, and deeply problematic. It was devised in the 1960s based on an estimate of an emergency food budget in the 1950s, and has not been updated to reflect subsequent dramatic changes in a family's needs."

7. Lytle Hernández 2017.

8. Wacquant 2009: 52, 146.

9. DeVerteuil 2015.

10. For a crash course in the sociology of poverty governance, read the following books in this order: *Regulating the Poor* (Piven and Cloward 1971), *Punishing the Poor* (Wacquant 2009), *Disciplining the Poor* (Soss, Fording, and Schram 2011), and *Redistributing the Poor* (Lara-Millán 2021). While there is no consensus in this literature on whether such governance functions primarily to reproduce labor power, neutralize social unrest, express state legitimacy, or simply reduce suffering for its own sake, these authors and many who have extended and reconstructed their theories tend to agree that it helps maintain the poor as "both marginal and central to the social order" (Soss, Fording, and Schram 2011: 1; see also Seim and DiMario 2023). My point is that the *maintenance* of poverty necessitates aid that may be superficial but is often broad. We do not live in a post-welfare era as much as an era of thinned, yet often wide, welfare.

11. Brady 2009: 6–7.

12. Bohn et al. 2023.

13. Based on a January 2025 statistical report published by DPSS (Los Angeles County Department of Public Social Services 2025).

14. Los Angeles County Department of Public Social Services 2025. The report does not include comparable calculation for Medi-Cal benefits. The average benefit amount for General Relief is reported to be $209.01, but this benefit is mostly standardized as $221 (more on this in chapter 3).

15. For more on the tax credits and the "fiscalization" of poverty governance, see McCabe 2018 and Halpern-Meekin et al. 2015. For more on disability pay-

ments and how they increased following 1996 welfare reform, see Hansen et al. 2014. For more on the medicalization of poverty governance, especially in Los Angeles, see Seim and DiMario 2023.

16. Beckett and Western 2001; Comfort 2015.

17. Halpern-Meekin et al. 2015.

18. Hansen, Bourgois, and Drucker 2014.

19. Seim 2020: 6–7.

20. The total number of Aid to Children with Dependent Children (AFDC) recipients peaked nationally in 1994 at 14.2 million (Office of Family Assistance 2019). That same year, Medicaid covered 34.2 million low-income individuals and food stamps covered 27.5 million (Kaiser Family Foundation 1996; United States Department of Agriculture 2024).

21. McDonnell 2020: 1.

22. Weber 1978: 973. It is also worth noting that there are varieties of bureaucracy, even within capitalism, with some bureaucracies being more authoritative and vertical and some being more representative and horizontal. Sociologist Alvin Gouldner (1954), in reconstructing Weber's theory, identified the following "patterns" of bureaucracy: punishment-centered bureaucracy (what we might describe as relatively authoritarian), representative bureaucracy (what we might describe as relatively democratic), and mock bureaucracy (in which the rules are explicit but generally not obeyed) (see also Talking About Organizations Podcast 2021; Meyers 2022: 229–30).

23. Herd and Moynihan 2019.

24. Baldassare et al. 2000.

25. Baldassare et al. 2000.

26. Davis 1990: 180. In an endnote Davis (1990: 215) said, "This, I believe, was how the now defunct *Los Angeles Herald-Examiner* once headlined the tax revolt."

27. In the immediate aftermath of Proposition 13, the state "bailed out" local governments (Taylor 2018; Terrell 1981). As Baldassare et al. (2000: 1) note, "A series of legislative acts, in response to Proposition 13 and its political aftermath, has placed the state government in the dominant role of allocating revenues to the cities, counties, school districts, and other governmental entities that are responsible for providing local services to residents."

28. According to an election day poll conducted by the *Los Angeles Times* and Channel 2 News, 69 percent of those who voted for Prop 13 "thought welfare should be cut, if necessary, to lower property taxes" (Scott 1978). Likewise, social

scientists David Sears and Jack Citrin (1982: 48–49) found that many Californians at the time wanted increased spending on a variety of services (e.g., schools, streets, police, and public transportation) but not on "welfare."

29. Chief Executive Office of Los Angeles County 2023.

30. Chief Executive Office of Los Angeles County 2024.

31. At the "Fiscal Essentials 101" and "Fiscal Essentials 102" workshops I attended in October 2023 at the California Welfare Directors' Association conference in Anaheim, it was repeatedly emphasized that staffing was the largest expense county welfare departments had to control. A similar point was iterated by DPSS director Keith Comrie in 1978 when he was interviewed by the *Los Angeles Times* (Scott 1978).

32. Lara-Millán 2021. See also Eubanks 2018. Whereas Lara-Millán focuses on poverty redistribution (e.g., shuffling clients between organizations) and Eubanks on increased automation in poverty governance (e.g., digital case management systems), this book explores another outcome that tends to couple redistribution and automation: intensified proletarianization of frontline public service labor.

33. SEIU 721 2021b.

34. Eubanks (2018) observed a similar resistance to factory-like conditions in welfare offices in Indiana.

35. Author's calculations for 2017 (last year with reliable data) (Los Angeles County Auditor-Controller 2023).

36. Los Angeles County Auditor-Controller 2023.

37. I borrow the language of "people processing" and "people changing" from Hasenfeld (1972; 2010). More on this in chapter 1.

38. Lipsky 1980.

39. Berstein 1978.

40. "Welfare Caseloads Increase in August, 1980," 1980, Yvonne Brathwaite Burke Papers, Box 86, Folder 3; Los Angeles County Department of Public Social Services 2024a. See chapter 3 for details.

41. To be clear, there is some mixture of these terms across eligibility work and WTW work. Eligibility workers frequently use the term "participant" or "PT" to describe their clients, and WTW workers occasionally use the term "customer" to describe their clients. Official documents also use these terms interchangeably across both occupations. However, the "customer" title is more common in eligibility work and is historically linked to that occupation in DPSS. Likewise, the "participant" title is more common in WTW work and is historically linked to that occupation in the department.

Chapter 1. The Policy Factory

1. Lipsky 1980.

2. As Burawoy (2009: 43) reminds us, "We begin with our favorite theory but seek not confirmations but refutations that inspire us to deepen that theory. Instead of discovering grounded theory, we elaborate existing theory." See also Levenson and Seim 2024.

3. Lipsky 1980: 13.

4. Lipsky 1980: 13.

5. Lipsky 1980: 60.

6. Lipsky 1980: xv.

7. Lipsky 1980: 180–2.

8. Lipsky 1980: 180–2.

9. Lipsky 1980: 180–2.

10. Lipsky 1980: 14, emphasis added.

11. I thought I had cleverly invented this term in the field. I jotted it in my notes only to later discover that others have used this phrase to describe the computerization of frontline services (Bovens and Zouridis 2002), the increased interaction between citizens and "e-government" via the internet (Landsbergen 2004), and the emergence of "data discretion" among street-level bureaucrats navigating and manipulating datasets in their day-to-day work (Gordon et al. 2024). I use the term to describe the shifting platform of work—from the physical street to the digital screen. I'm partial to political scientist Aurélien Buffat's (2015: 152) definition: "In a screen-level bureaucracy, new technologies support case assessment. Human intervention occurs only partially. Limited discretion exists."

12. Lipsky 1980: 13.

13. Eubanks 2018.

14. See also Dubois (2010) 2016, especially the forward by Steven Maynard-Moody.

15. Provided by an unnamed administrator via email when I was soliciting departmental feedback on an earlier version of this manuscript.

16. Building on the writing of Michael Burawoy (2009) and Imre Lakatos (1978), Zachary Levenson and I argue that research programs are "constituted by a 'hard core' of fundamental and unfalsifiable worldviews surrounded by a 'protective belt' made of testable, and therefore adjustable and replaceable, auxiliary hypotheses" (Levenson and Seim 2024: 9). With this in mind, I hold that the "hard core" of street-level bureaucracy theory is the fundamental assumption that policy is materialized by living workers at ground level. I see "discretion,"

which is no doubt a key theme, as an auxiliary hypothesis in the protective belt of this theory. The point of theory-driven research, as Levenson and I see it, is to "target the protective belts through empirical investigation—but investigation guided by hypotheses as methodological orientations. The idea is to continually modify the protective belts with novel predictions uncovered through theoretically guided research" (Levenson and Seim 2024: 9). My theory of proletarianized public servants is a reconstruction of street-level bureaucracy theory.

17. Bartram (2022: 11), drawing on a study of a different kind of public servant (building inspectors), notes, "To take a stab at justice is to take aim at immediate and small-scale goals. . . . While they stem from normative ideals, they are less likely to be geared toward wholesale change. Instead, stabs at justice are efforts to make things fairer in the moment at hand." Of course, a sense of "fairness" on the frontlines is not objective but rather dependent in part on the worldviews—and thus world positionings—of the workers.

18. SEIU 721 2021b.

19. Hasenfeld 1972.

20. Hasenfeld 1972. See also Hasenfeld 2010, where he explicitly considers workfare in Los Angeles as a people-changing effort.

21. Handler 2009; Soss, Fording, and Schram 2011.

22. START is the new name for GROW (General Relief Opportunities for Work). The program was rebranded in 2023.

23. Watkins-Hayes 2009.

24. Whereas Watkins-Hayes (2009: 344) observed an effort to mix eligibility and WTW work under a regime of "unified case management" in Massachusetts, I encountered a split of this labor rooted in welfare efficiency reforms enacted in California in the late 1960s. In the Golden State, eligibility determination labor was firmly separated from social work functions across the county welfare departments in 1968. The job of means testing has long been separated from the job of program brokering (see chapter 3 for details). Even so, what Watkins-Hayes calls efficiency engineering remains the dominant orientation across both eligibility and WTW workers—a testament to the relevance of her analysis across time and space.

25. Watkins-Hayes 2009: 13.

26. Watkins-Hayes 2009: 118–20.

27. See also Zacka (2017: 12) and the "family of dispositions" of "indifference, enforcement, and caregiving" he examined in an ethnography of an antipoverty agency in the northeastern United States. Relatedly, Dubois (2010), building on the work of Pierre Bourdieu, also gives us a theory of habitus and street-level bureaucracy in his ethnography of a French welfare office.

28. Levenson and Seim 2024.

29. Mills 1959: 8.

30. Wright and Singelmann 1982: 176. The full quote also emphasizes an erosion of "responsibility" ("less autonomy and responsibility for the worker"). I argue, however, that reduced autonomy is often accompanied by forces that place a unique form of responsibilization on workers—such as pressures that enforce the personal responsibility to work quickly (more on this in chapter 5). The key aspect of proletarianization, though, is its tendency to strip workers of autonomy over both the products and processes of their labor.

31. As sociologist Charles Derber (1983: 312) notes, "Marx theorized that the worker, forced to sell his or her labor power to others, lacks control in two senses: control, first, over the process of his or her labor and, second, over the uses of the product." Derber refers to the former as "technical control" and the latter as "ideological control." The workers in this study have generally always lacked ideological control over the products of their labor as they are tasked with materializing goals set by managers and lawmakers from above. I will demonstrate, however, that their technical control over the labor process has narrowed. Consistent with Derber (1983), I argue that the combination of low ideological control and low technical control justifies the label of proletarianization even for so-called white-collar professionals.

32. Oppenheimer 1972: 213. He adds a propensity toward collective bargaining as fourth feature of proletarianization, but I see that as a *potential* outcome rather than a defining feature. See also Larson 1980; Harris 2019.

33. Beyond my case, radical social work scholars, especially in the United Kingdom and during the time of Lipsky's book, were focused on the lack of discretion among frontline social service providers (Alaszewski and Manthorpe, 1993; Simpkin 1983; for summary, see Harris 2019). But this was not as much of a concern across the Atlantic. One exception is socialist thinker Bill Patry (1978) who, writing about a case in Texas, warned of an emergence of "Taylorism" in welfare offices.

34. The narrowing of discretion, and particularly the lowering of technical control over the labor process, is also a key point among those focused on the proletarianization of social work and related occupations (Patry 1978).

35. The labor process concept has long been folded into, for example, theories of sexism, racism, and their intersections with capitalism (Crowley 2013; Green 2001; Oksala 2016; Thomas 1982; Weeks 2007).

36. The Lakatosian "hard core" of labor process theory concerns, in my view, the conversion of labor power (the capacity to work) into actual productive activity. This conversion, and whether or not this power is commodified, depends on the

mode of production and especially its property relations (Marx [1847] 1978: 205; Marx and Engels [1932] 1978: 149). Capitalism is distinctive in the commodification of labor power. As Marx ([1867] 1996: 115) states, "The capitalist buys labour-power in order to use it; and labour-power in use is labour itself." While *capitalists*, as Paul Thompson (2010: 10) reminds us, may need to convert labor power into "actual profitable work," not all employers under capitalism are capitalist. Just as I do not see "discretion" as part of a hard core in street-level bureaucracy theory, I do not see capital accumulation or profitability as part of a hard core in labor process theory. As I explain further in this introduction, the core of the capitalist labor process concerns the commodification of labor power and the employer-guided conversion of said power into actual productive activity. By stripping away the condition of profit, we are able to better account for public sector employment and overcome some of "this tradition's blindness to public work" under capitalism (Johnston 1988: 40).

37. Burawoy 1979: 15. See also Seim 2017: 452.

38. The contradictory pressures of austerity and legal demand in contemporary public services is detailed most explicitly by Lara-Millán (2021). But where he shows how such pressures motivate a "redistribution of the poor" across different organizations, I show how these same pressures often intensify the extraction of labor effort from frontline workers within them.

39. Esbenshade et al. 2015; Harvey 2007; Hilgers 2012.

40. Connell et al. 2009; Moynihan 2006; Sanger 2004; Sears 1999.

41. Watkins-Hayes 2009.

42. "Executive Orientation to Minority Cultures, Session IV: The Chicano," March 27, 1970, Alicia Escalante Papers, Box 4, Folder 2; "Bureau Affirmative Action Plan," July 7, 1976, Los Angeles County Department of Public Social Services Records, Box 5.

43. See also Seim and DiMario 2023.

44. Haney 2002: 7–8.

45. Social work scholar John Harris (2019: 141) makes a similar point. What I am calling assembly line welfare has reduced discretion, "but it is impossible to eliminate it altogether."

Chapter 2. The Good County Job

1. See the appendix for details.

2. United States Census Bureau 2024. Per the Los Angeles County salary schedule in December 2024, an Eligibility Worker II can expect a minimum

monthly salary of $4,335 and a maximum monthly salary of $5,533, while a GAIN Services Worker (the official title of services workers in START as well) can expect a minimum monthly salary of $4,292 and a maximum monthly salary of $6,448 (Los Angeles County 2024). The middle points between two salary ranges are approximately $59,000 and $64,000 respectively.

3. Kalleberg 2011.

4. Clergé 2019: 128. See also Collins 1983; Landry and Marsh 2011; Wilson and Roscigno 2015; 2016.

5. In 1970, for example, roughly 10 percent of the county population was Black, compared to over a quarter of those employed by DPSS ("DPSS Newsletter," June 1970, Los Angeles County Department of Public Social Services, Box 11, Folder 3).

6. When affirmative action rules were imposed by the County Board of Supervisors around this period, administrative concern was less about Black hiring and more about Black promotion ("DPSS Newsletter"). But, above all, managers were concerned with increasing the number of Mexican Americans, a demographic that was significantly underrepresented at the time. They increased the number of Mexican-American workers from roughly 1 percent of the payroll in 1968 to nearly 10 percent in 1970 (Ellis P. Murphy to Gordon T. Nesvig, May 14, 1971, Los Angeles County Department of Public Social Services Records, Box 11, Folder 3). By 1980, however, the department was more broadly tracking its efforts in hiring "underrepresented minorities" generally. In June of that year, for example, the department hired, promoted, or transferred in 112 workers, 102 of which were non-white and 98 of which were women ("Letter from Eddy S. Tanaka to Yvonne Brathwaite Burke," July 23, 1980, Yvonne Brathwaite Burke Papers, Box 86, Folder 3).

7. I generated these calculations from a public dataset of worker counts by select demographics (Los Angeles County 2023). These estimates are for the fourth quarter of 2022. Roughly 18 percent of workers were white and 14 percent were Asian. This is generally consistent with the racial demographics of county employees. In the fourth quarter of 2022, for example, 13,635 DPSS employees were classified as 18 percent white, 18 percent Black, 46 percent Latino, and 14 percent Asian. In that same quarter, 91,465 Los Angeles County employees were classified as 20 percent white, 18 percent Black, 42 percent Latino, and 14 percent Asian.

8. I generated these calculations from a public dataset of worker counts by select demographics (Los Angeles County 2023). These estimates are for the fourth quarter of 2022.

9. "[Deleted User]," "Eligibility Worker II?" R/AskLosAngeles, April 28, 2024, www.reddit.com/r/AskLosAngeles/comments/194bf1l/eligibility_worker_ii/.

10. "LegitimateScreen31," "Hiring Process with LA County: DPSS (Eligibility Worker II)," R/AskLosAngeles, December 13, 2023, www.reddit.com/r/Ask-LosAngeles/comments/lkux9p/hiring_process_with_la_county_dpss_eligibility/.

11. "StayCoolDude," "Eligibility Worker II," R/LosAngeles, April 23, 2022, www.reddit.com/r/LosAngeles/comments/rwwsm8/eligibility_worker_ll/.

12. "goddesslainey," "Hiring Process with LA County: DPSS (Eligibility Worker II)," R/AskLosAngeles, June 5, 2022, www.reddit.com/r/AskLosAngeles/comments/lkux9p/hiring_process_with_la_county_dpss_eligibility/.

13. For a brief history on the "utopian origins" of cubicles in American workplaces, see Franz 2008. Cubicles emerged not just as architectures of efficiency but also out of a dream of supplanting rigid hierarchies. Cubicles were framed by its boosters as good relative to the traditional office structures of the mid-century. They "seemed to lack the fixity, and the constraints of bureaucracy of the old office. . . . Empowering and humane, cubicles seemed to create a workplace with a soul" (Franz 2008: 133).

14. The Los Angeles County Department of Human Resources (2014) reports that their turnover rate is historically low. Nationally, per the United States Bureau of Labor Statistics (2024a), government jobs tend to also have the lowest annual total separation rates.

15. Harknett, Schneider, and Luhr 2022.

16. Bauman 2000: 144–5.

17. Burawoy 1979.

18. I borrow this language from sociologist Zygmunt Bauman. In *Liquid Modernity* (Bauman 2000), he argues that both the solid modern marriage and the Fordist job have been replaced by more flexible or "liquid" forms (e.g., cohabitation in the home and short-term employment at work).

19. I generated these calculations from a public dataset of worker counts by select demographics (Los Angeles County 2023). This dataset imposes federal job classifications that do not align with official titles provided by the county. What I am calling *frontline workers* incudes the categories of "clerical," "general service," "operatives," "paraprofessional," "protective and regulatory," "professional," and "technical." What I am calling *middle-ranked supervisors* includes the categories of "supervising protective and regulatory," "supervising technical," "supervising clerical," "supervising paraprofessional" (none were listed in "supervising administrative staff"). What I am calling *upper-level managers* includes the categories of "management," "executive management," and "management staff."

20. In an internal report published in 1975, management determined that "the highly skilled EW [eligibility worker] has limited opportunity for advancement"

and that the "promotional system does not identify the better workers suitable for promotion" ("Eligibility Worker Job Study," April 4, 1975, Los Angeles County Department of Public Social Services Records, Box 15, Folder 19). This motivated the development of more advanced positions (e.g., quality control workers) and more intensive examinations for merit based advancements ("Eligibility Worker Job Study"). Roughly three years later, in the wake of the Proposition 13 taxpayer revolt mentioned in the introduction, management recognized that "morale" was lowered because of both wage and promotion freezes (Berstein 1978).

21. I generated these calculations from a public dataset of worker counts by select demographics (Los Angeles County 2023). These estimates are for the fourth quarter of 2022. I merged the category of Filipino with Asian. Frontline worker racial demographics: 19 percent white, 18 percent Black, 45 percent Latino, and 18 percent Asian. Supervisor racial demographics: 20 percent white, 17 percent Black, 50 percent Latino, and 13 percent Asian. Management racial demographics: 16 percent white, 16 percent Black, 51 percent Latino, and 17 percent Asian. The number of employees classified as "two or more races" accounted for less than 1 percent of the dataset.

22. Los Angeles County Board of Supervisors 2024.

23. *Antelope Valley Times* 2022.

24. Per a retention guide published by the Los Angeles County Department of Human Resources (2014), roughly four times as many county employees move between units within a department or from one department to another than quit.

25. Burawoy 1979: 110.

26. The national public sector union membership rate in 2023 was 32.5 percent, while it was only 6 percent in the private sector (United States Bureau of Labor Statistics 2024b). Following a "mid-century boom," union density in the United States has generally declined, and beginning in the 1970s, public sector unionism began to outpace the private sector (Stepan-Norris and Kerrissey 2023: 155). Unionization was more likely in this sector in part because it "was less affected by the new dangers of displacement and contingent work" (Stepan-Norris and Kerrissey 2023: 209).

27. Grodin 1999.

28. "Organizing 535," October 1975, SEIU Local 535 Records, Box 2, Folder 13. See also Scanlon and Harding 2005.

29. "Minutes: Social Workers Union Executive Board Meeting," December 1967, SEIU Local 535 Records, Box 1, Folder 1.

30. This was especially true after the emergence of the eligibility worker classification, which grew rapidly in the early 1970s (more on that in the next

chapter). By 1977, eligibility workers constituted the largest unit in the Los Angeles chapter of Local 535 (SEIU Local 535 Newsletter, July–August, 1977, SEIU Local 535 Records, Box 5, Folder 16).

31. *Los Angeles Times* 1968; Bermudez 2019; Letter from Abe F. Levy to Employee Relations Commission, May 1, 1969, Los Angeles County Federation of Labor Collection, Box 338, Folder 4.

32. Letter from Abe F. Levy to Employee Relations Commission. It is worth noting that organizing like this between welfare workers and welfare rights activists was not without controversy. After union members invited Alicia Escalante, a prominent welfare rights activist, to speak at a regularly scheduled union meeting in a district office in January 1969, management responded by suspending thirty-eight workers for one day without pay (Untitled Bulletin by Ellis P. Murphy, January 23, 1969, Los Angeles County Federation of Labor Collection, Box 338, Folder 3). Managers referred to this as the "Escalante incident" (Memo from Ellis P. Murphy to Sigmund Arywitz, June 25, 1969, Los Angeles County Federation of Labor Collection, Box 338, Folder 4). Union organizers subsequently pressured management to reconcile the matter and allow union meetings to include outside speakers (Local 535 Newsletter, January 1969, Los Angeles County Federation of Labor Collection, Box 338, Folder 3). The pressure succeeded: DPSS management retroactively revoked the suspensions and paid these workers all the wages they lost (Memo from Ellis P. Murphy to Civil Service Commission, April 2, 1969, Los Angeles County Federation of Labor Collection, Box 338, Folder 3). Managers were also apparently frustrated that union members participated in a picket line with Escalante and other welfare activities (Letter from Abe F. Levy to Employee Relations Commission, May 1, 1969, Los Angeles County Federation of Labor Collection, Box 338, Folder 4).

33. In 1966, the Bureau of Public Assistance was rebranded as DPSS. This symbolic change was followed by a material change the next year. The County Board of Supervisors, seeking more standardization in welfare services throughout the county during the "Great Society" expansions of food stamps and health insurance, imposed a top-down reorganization of welfare administration that increased both the density and the pay of managers (Goff 1967). Rather than focus on thickening frontline labor, county leaders responded by thickening administration. This was, as one labor organizer told the Board of Supervisors, a shift that would exacerbate the "miserable working conditions" of a "rotten welfare system" (*Los Angeles Times* 1967). But that was probably a bit hyperbolic. For all the increases in managerial power, which generally continued in the succeeding decades, DPSS has always been a "union shop" bureaucracy—a

fact that has been key to the preservation of relative material security on the frontlines.

34. Quote of Superior Court Judge Bernard Jefferson in a case involving Local 535, as summarized by David Novogrodsky ("Statement on Labor-Management Relations in Los Angeles County," April 8, 1968, Los Angeles County Federation of Labor Collection, Box 338, Folder 4).

35. For some time in the late 1970s, there was a jurisdiction dispute between Local 535 and Local 660 in Los Angeles. This was resolved with the latter covering eligibility workers ("Minutes of the State Executive Board," March 1978, SEIU Local 535 Records, Box 1, Folder 11). Local 660 eventually covered all DPSS workers entirely until Local 721 took over in 2006 (Johnson 2007).

36. For brief history of welfare rights activism in the United States, see Mittelstadt 2005: 155–73.

37. Johnson 2007; Therolf 2010.

38. Los Angeles County Board of Supervisors meeting transcript, May 13, 2015, https://bos.lacounty.gov/media-archive/.

39. Houston 2000; Moynihan and Pandey 2007; Perry et al. 2017.

40. du Gay 2000: 76. Weber, according to du Gay (2000: 75), "makes it quite clear that the bureau comprises a particular ethos. He insists it be assessed in its own right as a moral institution and that the ethical attributes of the bureaucrat be viewed as the contingent and often fragile achievements of that socially organized sphere of moral existence."

41. For more on how this Weberian "ethics of office" perspectives complicates street-level bureaucracy theory, see Møller, Pedersen, and Pors 2022. And, for a more Bourdieusian approach that challenges the myths of impersonal welfare bureaucracy, see Dubois (2010) 2016.

42. As one leader from Maximus explained to me at a welfare conference, Maximus administers GAIN in the San Fernando Valley and Antelope Valley, but it subcontracts the former region to Jewish Vocational Services (JVS), a nonprofit organization. I treat both regions as "privatized GAIN" run by Maximus even though some of these workers technically receive paystubs from JVS.

43. "The Public Cost of Private Contracting," April 1991, Gloria Molina Papers, Box 714, Folder 2.

44. The archival record suggests that Maximus has long made its bids in Los Angeles competitive by offering lower wages and benefits to its employees relative to those working for the county ("The LA Gain Management Bid: Why Poor Employment Standards Makes Maximus 'Competitive,'" n.d., Gloria Molina Papers, Box 717, Folder 2).

45. *Los Angeles Times* 1974. Inflation adjusted using CPI Inflation Calculator provided by the United States Bureau of Labor Statistics (2024c) (December 1974 to December 2024).

46. Per the Los Angeles County salary schedule in December 2024, an Eligibility Worker II could expect a minimum monthly salary of $4,335 (Los Angeles County 2024). That is approximately $52,000 a year.

47. The 1974 figure is technically for a lower-ranked position (Eligibility Worker I), but that was the standard entry-level rank at the time. The department now primarily hires at the rank of Eligibility Worker II, but even so, the wages are lower when adjusting for inflation. Management has recently began hiring more at the Eligibility I rank, which does not require a BA, but most opportunities for promotion and transfer require a four-year college degree.

48. Los Angeles County Board of Supervisor meeting transcript, September 22, 2015, https://bos.lacounty.gov/media-archive/.

49. Los Angeles County Board of Supervisor meeting transcript, March 28, 2003, https://bos.lacounty.gov/media-archive/.

50. Weberian theories of the bureaucratic "life order" assume entry and promotion within bureaucracies to be dependent on lengthy training in a technical expertise (du Gay 2000: 43–4). While there has been an inflation in general educational requirements (increased expectations that incoming eligibility workers have a bachelor's degree), there has been a decline in in-house, job-specific trainings as the work has become more standardized. That, at least, is the impression I get when comparing my ethnographic and interview data with archival evidence. The latter, especially from the 1970s and 1980s, includes multiple references to short classes like "Alcoholism," "Cultural Awareness," "Domestic Violence," "Incest," "Victimology," "Working with the Depressed Client," "Working with Gang Members," "Effective Communications," and much more ("Bureau of Program Planning and Development, Staff Development Division Quarterly Statistical Report," July 1981, Los Angeles County Department of Public Social Services Records, Box 16, Folder 1).

51. Wilson and Roscigno 2015; 2016. See also Laird 2017.

Chapter 3. Seeing Customers

1. Rank, Eppard, and Bullock 2021.

2. Based on a January 2025 statistical report published by DPSS (Los Angeles County Department of Public Social Services 2025).

3. Los Angeles County Department of Public Social Services 2024b; "Commission for Public Social Services, Agenda," December 16, 1992, California Social Welfare Archives Miscellaneous Publications, Box 8.

4. Los Angeles County Department of Public Social Services 2025.

5. For more on Medi-Cal churn, see Danielson and McConville 2023.

6. Based on a January 2025 statistical report published by DPSS (Los Angeles County Department of Public Social Services 2025).

7. Los Angeles County Department of Public Social Services 2024a. These program counts are for January 2024. DPSS also administers a small cash assistance program for immigrants (which covers roughly 8,000 persons) and a refugee cash assistance program (which covers roughly 1,500).

8. Los Angeles County Department of Public Social Services 2024a, emphasis added.

9. This conference was titled "Shaking Up Reentry: A Collaborative Approach to Reentry in L.A. County," and it was held on May 30, 2019.

10. According to Cohen (2003: 397), these "government customers" judged "public services and tax assessments much like other purchased goods, by the personal benefits they derived from them." In turn, state officials judged "potential actions by whether or not they lowered costs for consumer/citizens."

11. Rivera 1997a.

12. See also Esbenshade et al. 2015.

13. It is worth noting that while DPSS customers do not purchase anything, in 1993, the County Board of Supervisors did seriously consider imposing a $10 fee for each application submitted; this was never implemented ("Pamela D. Williams' Proposal—Budget Revenues Growth: Application Fee Proposal," Papers of Edmund D. Edelman, Box 456, Folder 1).

14. Lipsky 1980.

15. Camila explained to me that, as a dedicated lobby worker, she's not supposed to hold a case longer than a day. But she frequently does. "If a customer says they'll give paperwork tomorrow or something, I'll hold onto it," she told me. She explained that "it's just cleaner" to handle it that way. Things get messier as more workers touch the same case, so she actively tries to minimize that even though it means doing more work than is technically required of her.

16. For more on the department's implementation of call center technology, see Ortiz 2022.

17. Halushka 2020; Herd and Moynihan 2019. See also Paik 2021.

18. Consider a notoriously annoying errand mandated of CAPI customers. They must first apply for Supplemental Security Income (SSI) via the social security administration even though they know they are ineligible for such assistance due to their immigration status. They must then submit proof of their denial in order to be considered for CAPI.

19. Herd and Moynihan 2019: 2.

20. Peeters 2019: 578–80. See his four typologies of administrative burden: "formal + unintentional," "formal + intentional," "informal + unintentional," and "informal + unintentional" (2019: 572). Most of what I observed in the field could be classified as "formal + intentional" or "formal + unintentional." As I encountered it in the field, most relevant informal and intentional conduct among workers was oriented toward reducing administrative burdens and "sharing the runaround."

21. As Robert M. Emerson (1983: 425) rightly notes, "social control agents process and respond to cases in relation to, or as part of, some larger, organizationally determined *whole*" (emphasis in original). Welfare workers, even when proletarianized, may exercise some discretion over who gets extra assistance or scrutiny, but these decisions are based less on the individual case and more on the larger circumstances in which that case (or task) is embedded. Camila admits as much when she says she is less likely to share the runaround when the line is long.

22. Scott 1999.

23. Scott 2021: 513.

24. Scott 2021: 513.

25. Greenberg 2020: 872.

26. Greenberg 2020: 872.

27. Prottas 1978: 289.

28. Paik 2021: 3.

29. The customer "officially" has a week, but Kayla explained she "really" has thirty days before the application is denied.

30. Direct quote from CW2200 (California Department of Social Services 2024a). The "sponsor statement form" is for green card-holding immigrants.

31. Consider another example of how legibility preconditions eligibility. In an internal document responding to a series of complaints about benefit denials in 1980, a district office director mostly blamed clients for failing to make and maintain themselves as legible subjects for accurate eligibility determination. The report highlighted the following issues: "delinquent recertification," "evasive" applicants, "altered" (and potentially fraudulent) documents, missing information in the department's computer system, and other problems that prevented

eligibility workers from being able to "establish eligibility" (John Cliburn Letter to Marcine Shaw and Kenneth Hahn, Yvonne Brathwaite Burke Papers, Box 86, Folder 3).

32. Hunter 1971: 6.

33. This model was established before DPSS split from the Department of Charities and became a separate agency ("Operation Big City: Report of Administrative Review Findings," July 1965, California Social Welfare Archives Miscellaneous Publications, Box 1).

34. Gilbert 1966; Handler and Hasenfeld 2007: 186.

35. "Assembly of Human Services Interim Hearing, Welfare Eligibility Gridlock: A Study of Caseloads," November 27, 1989, California State Assembly of Human Services Committee Records, LP404.571.

36. Burton 1991: 102.

37. In Los Angeles, eligibility workers were generally expected to hold an associate of arts degree while social workers could hold either a bachelors or a masters (the latter coming with more pay) ("DPSS Personnel Manual," November 30, 1978, Los Angeles County Department of Public Social Services Records, Box 7, Folder 1).

38. Burton 1991.

39. Memo from Ellis P. Murphy to Gordon T. Nesvig, May 14, 1971, Los Angeles County Department of Public Social Services Records, Box 11, Folder 3. And, as union organizers at the time framed it, such work was easier to take advantage of because the state did not impose any standard workload maximums for those assigned to means testing (Letter from David Novogrodsky to Carley V. Porter, May 19, 1969, Los Angeles County Federation of Labor Collection, Box 338, Folder 4).

40. "DPSS Operations Handbook," May 28, 1974, Los Angeles County Department of Public Social Services Records, Box 11, Folder 5.

41. Author's calculations for 2017 (last year with reliable data) (Los Angeles County Auditor-Controller 2023).

42. Timnick 1984.

43. Handler and Hasenfeld 2007: 3.

44. Dow 2019: 137–8.

45. Yi 2000.

46. See also Watkins-Hayes 2009: 39–40.

47. See also Handler and Hasenfeld 2007: 195–6.

48. This increase was not linear. In 1978, DPSS set a departmental record of aiding a million persons—a number that soon declined to around nine hundred

thousand after Sacramento, under Reagan, tightened the state budget ("Public Assistance Caseload Growth," March 25, 1990, Collection of Kenneth Hahn, Box 343, Folder 6). But by 1990, the department had again surpassed the million mark, even as it grew at a rate slower than the overall population ("Public Assistance Caseload Growth"). The "welfare dependency rate" (total persons aided divided by county population) in the county declined from 13.7 percent to 11.4 percent. The number of cases rapidly grew in the first half of the 1990s, reaching roughly 1.8 million in 1994 before dipping to around 1.5 million by the end of 1998 ("DPSS Statistical Report," November 1999, California Social Welfare Archives Miscellaneous Publications, Box 9). Cases then began to climb in 1999, and the new millennium came with increased growth; it now stands at over four million. Today, the department no longer reports a "dependency rate;" if they did, it would stand at roughly 44 percent.

49. Freedman et al. 2000; Los Angeles County Department of Public Social Services 2025. Note that cases are different than individuals.

50. The number of In-Home Supportive Services customers also increased throughout the 1990s ("DPSS Statistical Report," November 1999, California Social Welfare Archives Miscellaneous Publications, Box 9).

51. Desilver 2023.

52. California Department of Health Care Services 2015; Insure the Uninsured Project 2021.

53. In early 1978, the total a number persons aided was 1,020,171, the highest recorded up to that point ("Welfare Caseloads Increase in August, 1980," Yvonne Brathwaite Burke Papers, Box 86, Folder 3). Meanwhile, the department workforce was "trimmed from 14,000 to 11,500 between 1975 and 1978" (Berstein 1978).

54. "Impending Workforce Reduction," July 15, 1995, California Social Welfare Archives Miscellaneous Publications, Box 8; Meyer 1995; Tobar 1992. Some local news articles reported staffing as low as roughly five thousand in the early 1990s, but this is not consistent with the material I encountered in the archives (Cedillo 1994; Stolberg 1991).

55. O'Shaughnessy 1989; Merl 1981; Tobar 1992. In 1989, DPSS director Eddy Tanaka summarized this issue to the press in this way: "The problem is not getting any simpler; the caseload is not decreasing. But the resources to administer the caseload are going down" (O'Shaughnessy 1989).

56. O'Shaughnessy 1989; Simon 1989. In 1989, for example, director Eddy Tanaka noted in a letter to the Board of Supervisors, "During the past ten years, caseloads have remained stable or slightly increased, while Departmental staff

has been reduced from 9500 positions in FY 1980/81 to 7600 positions in FY 1989/90, a 20% workforce reduction. The net effect has been repeated periods of higher worker caseloads" (Letter from Eddy S. Tanaka to Los Angeles County Board of Supervisors, September 18, 1989, Papers of Edmund D. Edelman, Box 455, Folder 2).

57. The end of the millennium also brought a significant and surprising surplus in welfare funding in Los Angeles County and throughout the nation. TANF block grants at the state level were dependent on 1994 caseloads, which were historically high in most places, but by the late 1990s the cash aid caseload had dropped significantly, leaving a kind of welfare reform windfall (Rivera 1999). How much this windfall directly contributed to staffing increases is not clear, especially when such funding has major strings attached, but it likely helped.

58. "Summary of Major Departmental Changes," Carl Washington Papers, LP488:243; Los Angeles County Department of Public Social Services 2024a.

59. "Training Programs on Staff Relationships with Ethnic Groups," February 28, 1974, Los Angeles County Department of Public Social Services Records, Box 11, Folder 7. Author's calculations for 2017 (Los Angeles County Auditor-Controller 2023).

60. "Commission for Public Social Services, Agenda," June 12, 1996, California Social Welfare Archives Miscellaneous Publications, Box 8; "DPSS Reception Room Overcrowding," August 25, 1989, Collection of Kenneth Hahn, Box 343, Folder 6. Even county supervisors recognized the problem since it was apparently lifting the welfare error rate in the county. As Kenneth Hahn stated in 1989, "Fewer welfare workers are now supervising a tremendously large number of cases, yet the resources to administer the huge caseloads continue to decrease" (Untitled Motion by Supervisor Kenneth Hahn, August 22, 1989, Collection of Kenneth Hahn, Box 343, Folder 6).

61. Los Angeles County Board of Supervisor meeting transcript, June 22, 2015, https://bos.lacounty.gov/media-archive/.

62. This is especially apparent when management and organized labor work together to fight against top-down commands to trim staffing. In the midst of a county budget crisis in the early 1990s, for example, administrators and union officials worked together to protect existing positions. A lettergram to Supervisor Edmund Edelman notes that DPSS director Eddy Tanaka "has been working together with Ansell (Local 535) as well as Dan Savage (Local 660) on the budget concerns . . . . Tanaka's *highest priority* is to secure the $4 million restoration in order to preserve current staff levels and services" ("Eddy Tanaka's Comments on the DPSS Budget Issues Raised by Phil Ansell," August 31, 1994, Papers of

Edmund D. Edelman, Box 456, Folder 7). The administration's desire to hire more employees is also evident when managers argue that pockets of additional funds should be used to secure more frontline workers, like when DPSS director Bryce Yokomizo requested that the Board of Supervisors approve hiring more GAIN workers to "reduce the yardstick" (caseload) and increase the likelihood of federal compliance (Los Angeles County Board of Supervisor meeting transcript, September 26, 2006, https://bos.lacounty.gov/media-archive/).

63. In 2024, for example, DPSS managers emphasized to the press and the Board of Supervisors that staffing levels have not risen proportionally with expansions in Medi-Cal. While the state is providing funds to help with the surge of cases, it is doing so through a one-time allocation (Reyes 2023). This is not ideal according to management because they want to hire permanent staff (Reyes 2023).

64. This is not my formula. Roughly 175 years before I began observing welfare workers, Karl Marx ([1847] 1978: 211–2) theorized the following dynamics of competitive capitalism:

> One capitalist can drive another from the field and capture his capital only by selling more cheaply. In order to be able to sell more cheaply without ruining himself, he must produce more cheaply, that is, raise the productive power of labour as much as possible. But the productive power of labour is raised, above all, by a *greater division of labour*, by a more universal introduction and continual improvement of *machinery* . . . . Hence, a general rivalry arises among the capitalists to increase the division of labour and machinery and to exploit them on the greatest possible scale.

In many ways, this seems like an irrelevant quote. It has nothing to do with welfare offices, let alone the specific kind of workers this book concerns. There's no effort to "sell more cheaply" at DPSS, because cash aid, food stamps, medical insurance, and the like aren't really for sale (even if DPSS administrators insist on calling their clients "customers"). DPSS managers are also not capitalists, and they are not positioned in the kind of competitive field described above. There is no general rivalry, for example, between DPSS administrators and their peers in other counties. And while the next chapter will complicate things a bit, DPSS has no interest in driving private safety net organizations out of business. Yet at the heart of this statement is a simple equation that remains relevant: *more division of labor + more machinery = more productivity.*

65. Wright 2000: 1563.

66. This is a key formula in the literature on proletarianized social workers specifically and proletarianized professionals more generally (Carey 2007; Harris 2019; Larson 1980; Oppenheimer 1972).

67. Miller 2013; 2019.

68. "DPSS Objectives and Goals for Fiscal Year 1977–78," 1977, Los Angeles County Department of Public Social Services Records. Box 5; "Report on the Ramifications of Implementing an Electronic Benefit Transfer (EBT) System in Los Angeles County," April 25, 1994, Papers of Edmund D. Edelman, Box 455, Folder 1.

69. "Report on the Ramifications of Implementing an Electronic Benefit Transfer (EBT) System in Los Angeles County."

70. The Welfare Case Management Information System (WCMIS) in the mid-1970s was justified because it streamlined processes for determining whether a client had active benefit cases. This increased legibility and speed of processing ("WCMIS Procedural Instruction P-52," September 30, 1977, Los Angeles County Department of Public Social Services Records, Box 6).

71. "WCMIS Procedural Instruction P-52"; "Minutes of the Meeting of the Los Angeles County Commission to Review Public Social Services," January 20, 1975, Los Angeles County Department of Public Social Services Records, Box 11, Folder 10.

72. "DPSS Newsletter," December 1974, Los Angeles County Department of Public Social Services Records, Box 14, Folder 14.

73. Keppel 1976.

74. Keppel 1976.

75. Letter from J. R. Distaso (TRW Technologies) to Supervisor Edelman, May 17, 1994, Papers of Edmund D. Edelman, Box 455, Folder 1.

76. Carol Matsui Letter to Sylvia Novoa, October 24, 1994, Gloria Molina Papers, Box 724, Folder 2. The plan was then to restructure and reassign those in data-entry clerk positions. Managers also justified automation to relieve overcrowded district offices (Eddie Tanaka Letter to Los Angeles County Board of Supervisors, April 2, 1992, Gloria Molina Papers, Box 724, Folder 2).

77. California Statewide Automated Welfare System 2024; County Welfare Directors Association of California 2024; Ortiz 2022.

78. As one public administration scholar notes in his admiration of DPSS's implementation of LRS, "Unlike the conventional process by which a social worker had to manually determine whether an individual qualified for the various

nutrition social services, with the new system, the details of an individual can quickly be fed into the system. Through internal system and algorithms, the systems can easily determine whether the individual falls into the respective categories. This has greatly lessened the time taken by social service providers to determine eligibility criteria" (Ortiz 2022: 175).

79. For more on how information technology social services have led to a contradictory mixture of upskilling and deskilling, see Carey 2007.

80. Wark 2019: 13.

81. The Work Number program is also justified for increasing accuracy and efficiency (Equifax 2022).

82. Lara-Millán 2021.

83. Los Angeles County Department of Public Social Services 2024a; "Case Transfers Under First Contact Resolution," Bureau of Workforce Services, September 1, 2021, obtained by a California Public Records Act request.

84. Giannella et al. 2024.

85. The Children's Partnership 2024. And, according to another report, roughly a quarter of calls made to the DPSS customer service center in 2022 were abandoned by callers (Reyes 2023).

86. SEIU 721 2021b.

87. Esbenshade et al. 2015; Eubanks 2018; Gadzo 2015; Hulsey et al. 2023; Greenblatt 1979.

88. Los Angeles County Board of Supervisor meeting transcript, September 26, 2017, https://bos.lacounty.gov/media-archive/.

89. "Eligibility Study Team Report Number Three," March 14, 1973, Los Angeles County Department of Public Social Services Records, Box 14, Folder 19.

90. "DPSS Newsletter," June 1973, Los Angeles County Department of Public Social Services Records, Box 14, Folder 14.

91. Gadzo 2015: 23-4.

92. According to two purchase orders (April 2021 and May 2018) obtained by a California Public Records Act request.

93. Change and Innovation Agency 2024.

94. Ritzer 1983: 100.

95. Ritzer 1983.

96. Dustin 2007. See also Carey 2007.

97. Miller 2019: 145.

98. Leidner 1993: 49.

99. Esbenshade et al. 2015.

100. Miller 2019: 128-9.

101. Miller 2019: 128-9.
102. Miller 2013: 7, 29.
103. Miller 2013: 85.

Chapter 4. Making Participants

1. Based on a January 2025 statistical report published by DPSS (Los Angeles County Department of Public Social Services 2025). That month, DPSS aided 4,136,130 unduplicated persons across all its programs. Of these, 2,507,592 were between the ages of eighteen and sixty-six, with 121,750 on General Relief and 68,097 on CalWORKs. When we take the working-age population (eighteen and sixty-six) on either General Relief or CalWORKs (189,847)—the only population mandated to participate in welfare-to-work programs—and divide that by the total number of DPSS customers within that same age range, we get an adult workfare rate of 7.6 percent. But even that statistic is inflated considering that a minority of those who are mandated to participate in such welfare-to-work programs are exempted from participation. Such exemptions are discussed later in this chapter.

2. Peck 2001: 13-4. See also Collins and Mayer 2010 and Morgen, Acker, and Weigt 2010.

3. Collins 2000; Dow 2019: 138.

4. United States Government Accountability Offices 2020.

5. Center on Budget and Policy Priorities 2022; Sanzenbacher 2023.

6. Drawing again on theorizations of the state provided by Lynne Haney (2002: 8), we can see schoolfare, medfare, and housefare as overlapping and mutually dependent zones in a fragmented network of "local bodies that shape clients' lives and interpret their need in direct and immediate ways."

7. I focus both on GAIN and START workers, but more on the former than the latter. GAIN is a larger program and one that I was able to observe more both in the field and in the archives. Indeed, workfare has been more explicitly and dramatically imposed on CalWORKs participants than General Relief recipients. That said, there are more similarities than difference in the frontline labor of GAIN and START and collapsing them into a single chapter is not unlike collapsing different eligibility workers into a single chapter. The core variation of importance, given what extant theory tells us about public services in general and welfare offices specifically, is between eligibility workers and WTW workers.

8. This manager also told me that there are two units of eight or nine workers in some "side rooms" in the building.

9. Sometimes, Tracy is directly handed cases from CalWORKs eligibility workers from the district offices or call centers, although she mentioned that this is pretty rare.

10. Tracy told me she had seventy cases on this particular day. Four were in "good cause exemption" because of homelessness, COVID, or something else. Roughly a dozen were in "no activity" because they had yet to be appraised or because they had been appraised but hadn't yet signed or updated their welfare-to-work contract.

11. DPSS administrators, upon reading this paragraph, asked that I include the following note: "All [WTW workers] receive initial training by the DPSS Training Academy. They also receive ongoing refresher training by their respective offices on the programs and resources offered to their participants." However, like Tracy, the WTW workers I met told me this training did not provide much insight into the exact interventions being performed. Tracy said she mostly learned about what the programs were "really like" from what her participants reported back to her.

12. See Collins and Mayer (2010: 141) for more on welfare-to-work contracts and how they afford a "measure of protection from the vagaries of the labor market at the cost of certain aspects of legal personhood."

13. Tracy confirmed that she would have mailed this contract to Hannah even before COVID.

14. Tracy told me that she often needs a "moment at home" after her shifts to shed the affectual weight of her work. Referring to the duration of this "moment," her preteen son is now in the habit of greeting her after work by asking, "You need ten minutes today or sixty minutes?"

15. Not all CalWORKs extenders participate in GAIN, but those that do are sorted into specialized supportive services and family stabilization units. Those on CalWORKs can get extenders *and* be exempt from GAIN under other conditions (e.g., disability) (California Department of Social Services 2024c).

16. Center on Budget and Policy Priorities 2022.

17. The case could also be made that a mental health referral was easier than a domestic violence referral *for Tracy*, since the former wouldn't require her to schedule a new appointment. However, I did not witness anything to suggest that she was motivated by this potential benefit. Tracy asked, more than once, which of the two options would be easier for Olivia. She even offered to still initiate a referral for domestic violence services after an extender was established via mental health. In short, Tracy seemed to be motivated more by client advocacy than a desire to reduce her workload.

18. "Social Services Manual," n.d., Los Angeles County Department of Public Social Services Records, Box 11, Folder 9.

19. As Juan Donaldo Hernández, a community organizer who presented to DPSS administrators in 1970, noted, the agency at the time was largely committed to a "traditional social work approach" in which workers "'trouble-shoot' difficult case problems brought to them by clients and do so by consulting with appropriate personnel, researching the problem, suggesting resolutions, and recommending on noted patters;" he continued, "this is a supplemental, rehabilitative consultive service to assist districts in meeting needs and ameliorating problems" ("Executive Orientation to Minority Cultures, Session IV: The Chicano," March 27, 1970, Alicia Escalante Papers, Box 4, Folder 2). He distinguished this from a "radical social work approach" characterized by deeper ties between civil society actors—namely, community consultants—and welfare workers ("Executive Orientation to Minority Cultures").

20. More on this in the Proletarianizing the Program Brokers section of this chapter.

21. Referralfare is always ostensibly in service of workfare, as one county CalWORKs implementation document makes clear: "The availability of quality supportive services is vitally important to ensuring the CalWORKs participants reach their employment goals" ("CalWORKs Implementation Plan," December 3, 1997, California Social Welfare Archives Miscellaneous Publications, Box 9).

22. In January 2020, 20,519 CalWORKs adult recipients were exempt from GAIN while 30,906 were enrolled in the program and 2,876 were deemed noncompliant (California Department of Social Services 2024e). I do not include exempt or noncompliant subjects in the subsequent calculations of activity percentages.

23. Employment-related activities include the following categories: job search and job readiness assistance, unsubsidized employment, self-employment, subsided private sector employment, subsidized public sector employment, on-the-job training, work study, supported work or transitional employment, community service, and job skills training directly related to employment.

24. Education-related activities include the following categories: vocational education training, education directly related to employment, adult basic education, and self-initiated programs (SIPs). The latter refer to school enrollment "initiated" by the participant but then registered as GAIN activity hours. In these cases, participants enroll in school independent of any assistance from a GAIN worker, and then they request to have their current and ongoing coursework count toward their GAIN programming.

25. Services include the following categories: mental health services and substance abuse services.

26. As DPSS administrators reminded me in an open comment to this manuscript, participants are first sent a notice of noncompliance and given twenty days to comply before being sanctioned. The sanction is only applied to the noncompliant participant and not to the whole case. In other words, if aid is cut, it is only cut for the GAIN participant and not their dependents or others on the case.

27. "Social Services Manual," n.d., Los Angeles County Department of Public Social Services Records, Box 11, Folder 9.

28. Schoolfare is also distinguished from workfare by Lødemel (2002:31). See also Sheared's (1998) analysis of edfare. What I label *schoolfare* is different from what others sometimes call learnfare (e.g., Corbett et al. 1989), which focuses on the school attendance and performance of minors on cash grant cases. Schoolfare focuses on the education of primary participants (not their offspring), and it was far more common than anything resembling learnfare in the GAIN units I observed.

29. Planning documents for GAIN clearly state DPSS workers would refer participants to LACOE services ("Greater Avenues for Independence County Plan for Fiscal Year 1988–89," May 1987, Los Angeles County Department of Public Social Services Records, Box 38, Folder 6). Some programs today are contracted to other county agencies but delivered in partnership with LACOE, like the financial literary services classes provided by the Los Angeles County Department of Consumer and Business Affairs ("MOU Between Department of Public Social Services and Department of Consumer and Business Affairs to Provide Financial Literacy Services," July 2023, obtained by a California Public Records Act request).

30. LACOE staff and administrators helped design the standardized educational assessment tools that GAIN workers use during their initial appraisal of new cases ("MOU Between Department of Public Social Services"). It is also worth noting another variety of schoolfare: mandating parents receiving AFDC under the age of nineteen to participate in a diploma program via "Cal-Learn" (launched in 1994) (Eddy Tanaka Letter to Los Angeles County Board of Supervisors, October 26, 1993, Gloria Molina Papers, Box 710, Folder 5).

31. This has been true since the inception of GAIN ("GAIN Program Interpretation Handbook," April 1988, Los Angeles County Department of Public Social Services Records, Box 38, Folder 2).

32. As I learned through my fieldwork in the GAIN offices, all community colleges in Los Angeles County have at least one designated CalWORKs counselor.

Among other things, these counselors help students make their credit hours legible to GAIN, and they're available for GAIN workers to contact should they have questions about a participant's progress.

33. Los Angeles County Office of Education 2024.

34. Freedman, Mitchel, and Navarro 1999: 5.

35. Sheared 1998: 135.

36. Seim and DiMario 2023. For more on the medical governance of poverty in California generally and Los Angeles specifically, see Barnard 2023 and Gong 2024.

37. A similar procedure exists in the START program ("MOU Between the Department of Public Social Services and the Department of Mental Health to Provide Mental Health Disability Assessments for General Relief Applicants and Participants in the General Relief District Offices," July 2017, obtained by a California Public Records Act request).

38. "MOU Between Department of Public Social Services and Department of Public Health to Provide General Relief Mandatory Substance Use Disorder Recovery Program Services," July 2022, obtained by a California Public Records Act request.

39. Quote from the San Fernando Valley Community Mental Health Center's (2024) description of services available to those referred by GAIN. The description also notes that "treatment staff works closely and collaboratively with each client in order to identify strengths and access barriers to obtaining and sustaining employment."

40. For more on how post-1996 welfare has become increasingly medicalized, see Hansen, Bourgois, and Drucker 2014.

41. DPSS, for example, contracts with the Los Angeles County Department of Public Health, who in turn subcontracts with local providers to administer domestic violence supportive services for eligibility GAIN and GROW/START participants. These providers are tasked with helping victims of domestic violence "overcome barriers that would limit and/or import their ability to become self-sufficient through employment and/or participation in (welfare-to-work) activities" ("MOU Between Department of Public Social Services and Department of Public Health to Administer Domestic Violence Supportive Services," July 2021, obtained by a California Public Records Act request).

42. Per a DPSS Factsheet about CalWORKs homeless assistance, participants can also use these funds for paid shelter or to pay another person with whom the participant "has entered into a short-term lease, sub-lease, or shared housing agreement" (Los Angeles County Department of Public Social Services 2024c). I mostly encountered this program in the field, however, as "hotel money."

43. This supplementation program is known as the Temporary Homeless Assistance Program ("THAP+14") (Los Angeles County Department of Public Social Services 2024c). Participants can use both the state and county temporary assistance programs once a year.

44. The largest of these programs is "once-in-a-lifetime" eviction protection assistance funded by Los Angeles County, which can reach a maximum of $5,000 per family to pay for past rent, overdue utilities, and more. The moving assistance program, which is also a once-in-a-lifetime opportunity, is capped at $2,500 (or up to two times the total rent) and covers eligible move-in costs (e.g., security deposit, utility deposit, truck rental). Finally, the once-in-a-lifetime rental assistance program is capped at $500 a month (based on family size) for a maximum of four consecutive months. Los Angeles County Department of Public Social Services 2024c.

45. Los Angeles County Department of Public Social Services 2024d.

46. Los Angeles County Department of Public Social Services 2024d.

47. Similar behavioral expectations are imposed on General Relief recipients who are referred for housing aid (i.e., General Relief Housing Subsidy) via the START Program (Los Angeles County Department of Public Social Services 2024e).

48. Los Angeles County Department of Public Social Services 2024e.

49. Los Angeles County Department of Public Social Services 2024e.

50. Los Angeles County Department of Public Social Services 2024f.

51. "CRIB Program—Community Resource Information Bank," January 27, 1975, Los Angeles County Department of Public Social Services Records, Box 11, Folder 9.

52. "CalWORKs Implementation Plan," December 3, 1997, California Social Welfare Archives Miscellaneous Publications, Box 9. DPSS Director Lynn Bayer (1998) articulated a similar point in a letter to the *Los Angeles Times*: "Beginning April 1, the managers and staff at the Department of Public Social Services began transforming an agency of over 10,000 employees, which for decades was focused almost exclusively on issuing welfare payments, into a client-centered service organization with a much broader mission—to help families become economically self-sufficient." And, in a letter to the Board of Supervisors that same year, she promised a "dramatic break from the social service system of the past in which the primary mission of DPSS was to determine eligibility and to deliver benefits" (Lynn Bayer letter to Los Angeles County Board of Supervisors, February 24, 1998, Gloria Molina Papers, Box 702, Folder 5). However, as I make clear

in this chapter, such a "people-changing" mission predates late 1990s welfare reform and was mostly a failed effort anyway.

53. Officially called Assembly Bill 2580 (California Legislative Analyst's Office 1985).

54. Marchevsky and Theoharis 2008: 79.

55. For more on the contradictions of "people processing" and "people changing" in the neoliberal welfare office and the "myth that the welfare department has been transformed into an employment agency," see Handler and Hasenfeld 2007: 235.

56. Sweeney 1972. Workfare efforts have a fairly long history in America generally and Los Angeles in particular. We tend to forget that the spectacle of work-oriented welfare interventions predates not only President Clinton but also Governor Reagan. In 1948, the Bureau of Public Assistance implemented a work program for General Relief recipients, and six years before it became DPSS that same bureau began pushing job placement services for all "potentially employable persons" ("The Road Ahead Through Job Training and Placement," 1966, Los Angeles County Department of Public Social Services Records, Box 23, Folder 7). These efforts focused, according to internal reports, on "the rehabilitation of employable recipients" ("The Road Ahead"). Similar eligibility limits were imposed across California by the state legislature in 1951 (Mittelstadt 2005: 61–2). Then, in 1965, the bureau launched the Community Work and Training Program (CWTP), which aimed to remove welfare recipients from the rolls by way of connecting them to formal employment opportunities. This could be achieved, according to managers at the time, through the intensive "counseling and guidance" of social workers (Mittelstadt 2005: 61–2). The next year, the union representing social workers at DPSS also published a report recommending an expansion of "rehabilitation programs" for unemployed fathers receiving AFDC, though this focused more on voluntary programming and ancillary support for job training ("The Aid to Families With Dependent Children-With Unemployed Parents (AFDC-U) Program in Los Angeles County," January 14, 1966, Los Angeles County Federation of Labor Collection, Box 338, Folder 3). Then, in the late 1960s and throughout the 1970s, DPSS administered the Work Incentive Program (WIN), which was funded under Title IV-C of the Social Security Act (1967) and provided "services to persons receiving AFDC aimed at assisting them to obtain immediate employment." This program also came with a kind of referralfare where "DPSS social workers" would "arrange for the provision of service needs such as child care, family planning, health related services and housing improve-

ment services to make the registrant employment ready" ("The Aid to Families with Dependent Children-With Unemployed Parents [AFDC-U] Program"). But such programming was ultimately more supplemental than mandatory. The GAIN Bill was a more significant wrench thrown into the people-processing machinery of DPSS.

57. "Workfare: An Analysis," January 17, 1984, California State Senate Industrial Relations Records, LP341:208. Subsequently, the Family Support Act of 1988 and the Personal Responsibility and Work Reconciliation Act of 1996 fueled GAIN programming by imposing work requirements on recipients of AFDC and TANF, respectively ("CalWORKs Implementation Plan," December 3, 1997, California Social Welfare Archives Miscellaneous Publications, Box 9).

58. "California Welfare Reform," September 28, 1987, California State Senate Industrial Relations Records, LP341:228.

59. This dual emphasis on increasing state legitimacy while decreasing state budget via GAIN was made most explicit during the proposal stage. Bureaucrats with the state-level agency overseeing welfare operations insisted that GAIN would save taxpayers "$136 million per year ($48.3 million General Fund, $73.9 million federal funds, and $13.8 million county funds)" (William G. Hamm Letter to Assemblyman Tom Bates, August 20, 1985, California State Senate Industrial Relations Records, LP341:206). These estimates were contested through a legislative analysis that warned that GAIN could inadvertently increase costs due to programming logistics. But, even so, the proposal was generally supported because it would presumably increase the following: employability and thus "self-esteem" for recipients, "positive role model(s)" for children, and "the value of the work performed by participants" for "society" (William G. Hamm Letter to Assemblyman Tom Bates). It is also worth noting that a political "crisis" of welfare legitimacy likely motivated California Democrats in the state legislature to endorse workfare programming. In the early 1980s, they struck down a proposal from Governor Deukmejian to force all AFDC recipients to search for work in the private sector or work off their benefits in public service jobs. But once a ballot initiative shortly thereafter nearly passed to cut welfare benefits in half, "Democrats in Sacramento began to have real fears about facing 'soft on welfare' charges in upcoming elections" ("California Welfare Reform," September 28, 1987, California State Senate Industrial Relations Records, LP341:228).

60. "Assembly Republican Caucus Press Release," July 17, 1985, California State Senate Industrial Relations Records, LP341: 206. This is also called the "San Diego Job Search and Work Experience Program" ("California Welfare Reform," September 28, 1987, California State Senate Industrial Relations Records, LP341:228).

61. Statements of Paul Eckert Before the Assembly of Human Resources Committee, August 20, 1985, California State Senate Industrial Relations Records, LP341:206.

62. "California Welfare Reform," September 28, 1987, California State Senate Industrial Relations Records, LP341:228.

63. "Final Report on the San Diego Job Search and Work Experience Demonstration," February 1986, California State Senate Industrial Relations Records, LP341:213.

64. "California Welfare Reform," September 28, 1987, State Senate Industrial Relations Records, LP341:228.

65. "California Welfare Reform"; "Final Report on the San Diego Job Search and Work Experience Demonstration," February 1986, California State Senate Industrial Relations Records, LP341:213. It is also worth noting that reduced AFDC grants in the San Diego project tended to be offset by employment-related deductions available in the program (e.g., deductions for childcare).

66. Deukmejian 1990.

67. "GAIN Appraisal Program, Second Report," November 1987, California State Senate Industrial Relations Records, LP341:229; "Fact Sheet AB 312 Provisions," January 1991, California Social Welfare Archives Miscellaneous Publications, Box 8. The Los Angeles County supervisors, and Kenneth Hahn especially, were particularly focused on integrating education and skill-based training into GAIN. In his words, "For these young people to succeed in life and become productive citizens, they must be given training in their chosen fields" (Untitled Press Release, February 8, 1988, Collection of Kenneth Hahn, Box 343, Folder 6).

68. "CalWORKs Implementation Plan," December 3, 1997, California Social Welfare Archives Miscellaneous Publications, Box 9.

69. "L.A. County Plan for GAIN Program," 1988, California State Senate Industrial Relations Records, LP341:239.

70. "L.A. County Plan for GAIN Program."

71. In an official response to the claim that DPSS would be the "best qualified agency to administer the GAIN program," Tanaka's DPSS stated that the agency "appreciates the statement of support for its ability to administer the GAIN program. However, as GAIN is a new and unique program in the welfare field, DPSS has no prior experience with GAIN" ("County of Los Angeles Department of Public Social Services, Public Hearing, Greater Avenues for Independence Plan Update," January 4, 1989, California State Senate Industrial Relations Records, LP341:231).

72. "The LA GAIN Case Management Bid: Why Poor Employment Standards Makes Maximus 'Competitive,'" n.d., Gloria Molina Papers, Box 717, Folder 2.

Contracting can therefore be thought of as another managerial response to the contradictions of austerity and legal demand. It is a kind of "redistribution" strategy (Lara-Millán 2021). However, because redistribution is not legally possible for frontline eligibility determination in the district offices, I argue the primary strategy is still to squeeze more productivity out of labor by advancing a division of labor and introducing more machinery into the productive process. Indeed, increased public servant productivity is more common than increased redistribution/contracting, even in the GAIN program.

73. Letter from Linda McMahon to Eddy Tanaka, December 3, 1986, California State Senate Industrial Relations Records, LP341:226.

74. "County of Los Angeles Department of Public Social Services, Public Hearing, Greater Avenues for Independence Plan Update," January 4, 1989, California State Senate Industrial Relations Records, LP341:231.

75. Roderick 1988.

76. "County of Los Angeles Department of Public Social Services, Public Hearing, Greater Avenues for Independence Plan Update," January 4, 1989, California State Senate Industrial Relations Records, LP341:231.

77. "County of Los Angeles Department of Public Social Services, Public Hearing, Greater Avenues for Independence Plan Update."

78. In 1990, Maximus GAIN ran offices in Panorama, Bell, Rancho Dominguez, Los Angeles, and El Monte ("A Public-Private Partnership in Human Services," 1990, Gloria Molina Papers, Box 718, Folder 5).

79. "JTPA SDA Coordination Committee Meeting," April 13, 1987, California State Senate Industrial Relations Records, LP341:229.

80. "GAIN Program Model," August 1986, Los Angeles County Department of Public Social Services Records, Box 38, Folder 3; "GAIN: Los Angeles County Plan Update for Fiscal Year 1992–1993," April 2, 1992, Los Angeles County Department of Public Social Services Records, Box 38, Folder 3.

81. "GAIN Program Model," August 1986, Los Angeles County Department of Public Social Services Records, Box 38, Folder 3.

82. "GAIN Program Model."

83. "GAIN Program Model."

84. "County of Los Angeles Department of Public Social Services, Public Hearing, Greater Avenues for Independence Plan Update," January 4, 1989, California State Senate Industrial Relations Records, LP341:231; Phil Ansell Letter to Gloria Molina, February 8, 1993, Gloria Molina Papers, Box 718, Folder 5.

85. Quote from Gary Pettigrew, Assistant Secretary of California Health and Welfare Agency, provided in an attached transcript (Delaine Eastin Letter

to Clifford Allenby, October 20, 1988, Gloria Molina Papers, Folder 718, Folder 5).

86. Delaine Eastin Letter to Clifford Allenby; Shuit 1990.

87. Roderick 1988.

88. Roderick 1988.

89. Shuit 1990.

90. Harris 1988; *Los Angeles Times* 1989.

91. Riccardi 2000.

92. Gloria Molina Letter to Dahlia Cornejo, July 8, 1993, Gloria Molina Papers, Box 718, Folder 4.

93. Lynn Bayer Letter to Los Angeles County Board of Supervisors, June 7, 2000, Gloria Molina Papers, Box 715, Folder 5.

94. Lynn Bayer Letter to Los Angeles County Board of Supervisors, May 9, 2000, Gloria Molina Papers, Box 715, Folder 5.

95. The drama over contracting has continued throughout the past twenty-five years, with union officials leading the charge against GAIN privatization whenever the contract is up for renewal. In the beginning the union accused Maximus of being less efficient than the county, but this was always a contentious claim (Los Angeles County Board of Supervisors meeting transcript, November 18, 2008; July 17, 2012). Eventually, their focus shifted toward admitting that Maximus may be efficient but at the cost of good county jobs. Bart Diener, representing SEIU 721 in a comment to the Board of Supervisors in late 2021, noted "Maximus and JVS [a subcontractor] achieved cost savings by significantly lowering labor standards where salaries that start at the bare county contractor minimum, health benefits that do not nearly cover the employee's own costs, much less those of her family, and little or no retirement benefits at all. In other words, the savings are achieved by replacing good stable county jobs with high turnover subsistence jobs" (Los Angeles County Board of Supervisors meeting transcript, November 16, 2021).

96. "Recommendation to Award Contract to Maximus Services Inc., for Greater Avenues for Independence Case Management Services," November 16, 2021, obtained by a California Public Records Act request.

97. "California Workfare Reporter," February–March, 1987, California State Senate Industrial Relations Records, LP341:227.

98. Freedman et al. 1996.

99. The average difference in total earnings for all six studied counties (Alameda, Butte, Los Angeles, Riverside, San Diego, and Tulare) was $2,853 across sixty months (Freedman et al. 1996).

100. The average difference in total AFDC payments received for all six counties studied was $1,496 across sixty months (Freedman et al. 1996).

101. The average difference in total AFDC payments received for Los Angeles County was –$1,383 across sixty months (Freedman et al. 1996).

102. Peck 2001: 169. See also Handler and Hasenfeld 2007.

103. It is worth noting, however, that Los Angeles County GAIN, having been inspired by Riverside, had also pivoted from prioritizing schoolfare toward a harder work-first approach in 1993 (DPSS Press Release, August 20, 1998, Gloria Molina Papers, Box 714, Folder 3).

104. The average difference in total earnings for Riverside County was $5,038 across sixty months. The average difference in total AFDC payments received for Riverside County was –$2,705 across sixty months (Freedman et al. 1996).

105. Handler and Hasenfeld 2007: 198. Behind the scenes, department managers are usually praised for running a "successful" GAIN program that increases "cost effectiveness" and the vague image of "self-sufficiency" (Eloise Anderson Letter to Eddy Tanaka, January 29, 1996, California State Assembly of Human Services Committee Records, LP404:679). There is generally little to no concern over how such programming might seriously affect material hardship.

106. Peck 2001: 188.

107. "CalWORKs: A Tough but Fair Program to End Welfare Dependency and Put Californians to Work," August 4, 1997, Carl Washington Papers, LP488:243.

108. Alameda County Social Services Agency 2024.

109. By the end of the millennium, the CalWORKs rolls had decreased by 28 percent since the 1996 reforms were implemented, but as reported in the *Los Angeles Times*, most did not enter "self-sustaining" work and remained "dependent" on food stamps, Medi-Cal, subsidized childcare, and more (Rivera 2000). And many researchers and commentators suggested the decrease in CalWORKs had more to do with a tight low-wage labor market combined with tightened rules for cash assistance (Rivera 2000).

110. Felder 2006.

111. *Los Angeles Post* 2023.

Chapter 5. Disciplining the Line

1. Marchevsky and Theoharis 2008: 79. Marchevsky and Theoharis draw on in-depth-interview data collected from Mexican immigrant welfare recipients in Los Angeles and their families between 1998 and 2000. Like this book, their study mentions not only district offices but also the GAIN program, which im-

poses different punitive strategies like "chastising (clients) for their low motivation and self-esteem." While no doubt significant and quote worthy, it is important to note that their analysis suffers from two major inaccuracies. First, they estimate an increase in discretion among welfare workers; but, as chapters 3 and 4 in the book demonstrate, discretion has generally narrowed. Second, they describe an elimination of casework in the district offices at a period in which it was actually alive and well (per interviews and archival evidence). I assume these missteps in their analysis are linked to their focus on the clientele. As far as I can tell, they never interviewed or observed workers at DPSS. But while they fall short in accounting for the worker experience, I fall short in accounting for clientele experience. Our studies pair well together in this regard.

2. For more on the punitive and carceral dynamics of contemporary welfare offices and related spaces, see the following: Abramovitz 2023; Headworth 2021; Simon 2007; Wacquant 2009.

3. In a letter to the Board of Supervisors, DPSS director Eddy Tanaka claimed there was an "upsurge" in "security incidents." He reluctantly advocated for a sort of carceral strategy: "Our responses continue to be appropriate yet prudent, avoiding any appearance of turning our local offices into armed fortresses. However, the balance is becoming considerably more challenging to maintain. We employ metal detectors routinely in our reception areas, and we are confiscating weapons and narcotics at a startling rate. We are attempting to preserve the dignity and maintain the safety of our staff and clientele, but I am extremely concerned that we have experienced almost 100 violent incidents in our offices during 1990" ("Upsurge of Violent Incidents in DPSS Offices," December 18, 1991, Papers of Edmund D. Edelman, Box 455, Folder 2). While, according to the letter, this was double the number of incidents that occurred in 1989, one hundred was still a small number considering the hundreds of thousands of cases being processed by over a dozen offices. Nonetheless, two years later, the department budgeted a 25 percent increase in office security ("DPSS Final Revised Budget," July 15, 1993, Papers of Edmund D. Edelman, Box 456, Folder 7).

4. Hazlett and Farr 1980.

5. Hazlett and Farr 1980. See also Yi 2000. Fingerprinting was first implemented in the General Relief program in 1991 and was then expanded to AFDC in 1994 and food stamps in 1996 ("CalWORKs Implementation Plan," December 3, 1997, California Social Welfare Archives Miscellaneous Publications, Box 9). According to an internal report in 1994, roughly 1.6 percent of approved cash aid cases were terminated because of noncompliance with fingerprinting requirements. Only fifty-four (out of more than three hundred thousand fingerprinted

files) matched more than one case and were referred to the district attorney for further investigation. "Second Progress Report—AFDC AFIRM Federal Demonstration Project," September 28, 1994, Papers of Edmund D. Edelman, Box 457, Folder 5. Interviews with veteran employees suggest that fingerprinting was dropped a decade or so ago.

6. Ray White Letter to Yvonne Burke, June 30, 1993, Papers of Edmund D. Edelman, Box 456, Folder 1.

7. "Alleged DPSS Employee Misconduct," September 21, 1994, Papers of Edmund D. Edelman, Box 455, Folder 6.

8. Foucault (1975) 1995.

9. Mik-Meyer and Villardsen 2012; Powell and Biggs 2000; Whitworth and Carter 2014.

10. Soss, Fording, and Schram 2011.

11. Soss, Fording, and Schram 2011: 48.

12. Foucault (1975) 1995: 170

13. Foucault (1975) 1995: 194.

14. Foucault (1975) 1995: 218–221.

15. Foucault (1975) 1995: 170.

16. Foucault (1975) 1995: 170-7.

17. Foucault (1975) 1995: 183.

18. Foucault (1975) 1995: 184.

19. Soss, Fording, and Schram 2011: 81.

20. Soss, Fording, and Schram 2011: 2.

21. Soss, Fording, and Schram 2011: 209.

22. Soss, Fording, and Schram 2011: 230.

23. As Schram et al. (2010: 746) note, "the new welfare system is perhaps best understood as a decentralized chain of disciplinary relationships which runs from the federal government down to states, down to local regional boards, down to contracted service providers, down to frontline workers, and ultimately down to welfare clients. At each point in this cascade, benchmarks for outcomes are established and monitored, and managerial techniques, incentives, and penalties are used to discipline actors below." See also Morgen, Acker, and Weigt 2010: 64-6.

24. Watkins-Hayes 2009.

25. In bridging Foucault's theory of disciplinary power with Black feminist thought, Patricia Hill Collins (2000: 280-3) reminds us that when work becomes increasingly done by Black and brown women, the close monitoring and scrutiny of that work tends to also increase.

26. Author's calculations for 2017 (last year with reliable data) (Los Angeles County Auditor-Controller 2023). As noted in the introduction, there are more than six thousand eligibility workers and roughly one thousand WTW workers at DPSS. This does not, however, account for those WTW workers employed by Maximus in the San Fernando and Antelope valleys.

27. At the time, Carmen was instructed by her supervisors to add incoming calls to Current, the task-bank software program the department implemented for a short period (see chapter 3).

28. This county-specific app shut down shortly after I completed fieldwork in 2022. At the time of publication, customers were using the web portal Benefits-Cal, which they could access through a browser on their smartphones.

29. Foucault (1975) 1995: 182.

30. Foucault (1975) 1995: 189.

31. For more on the "managerial gaze," see McKinlay and Starkey 1997.

32. Department protocols seem to acknowledge this variation in intimacy. While customers in the district office are not as closely monitored as eligibility workers, the information collected is generally seen as more "private." That is why when there are workers who are also customers (i.e., eligibility workers on food stamps), their cases are assigned to specialized units that better protect their files from others in the organization.

33. Most remote workers at DPSS (and Los Angeles County generally) are expected to submit a manually completed work log that accounts for all minutes in a shift (Alamillo 2020). Such logs must detail the emails sent, the calls made, and so on. However, supervisors I spoke to in the field told me these logs are generally redundant since the digitalization of welfare work has increased opportunities for labor monitoring even when workers "log on" from home using their county-issued computers. Either way, there seems to be a general sense that workers are more closely surveilled when they work from home. As Gabe, a twenty-six-year-old eligibility worker explained, "When I'm at home I have to do a telework log, so they do monitor me in that way versus when I'm working in the office where they don't ask for a telework log. So, I could work even less cases [tasks] while I'm working in the office and I'll be totally fine. But when I'm working at home, it's like, 'Okay, there isn't much time to have a break.'"

34. The temporal pressure is even more intense for eligibility workers assigned to the main customer service hotline: They are generally expected to spend no more than three minutes between calls.

35. Auyero (2012: 8–9) also draws on Foucault's theory of disciplinary power as "productive power" to understand how client waiting and the runaround helps

manufacture particular "subjects" of the state: those who *"patiently comply with the seemingly arbitrary, ambiguous, and always changing state requirements"* (emphasis in original).

36. Collins 2000.

37. Consider a parallel example: airport security. Who is more intensely examined, the travelers or the agents? While the agents gain special insight into travelers' personal lives—including not only their bags but also their bodies via X-ray machines—the former are more intensely observed by management. Yes, much of this is a qualitative difference, with managers examining labor rather than luggage, but there is also a quantitative difference in the form of temporal exposure. The TSA agent is monitored longer by their managers than they themselves monitor any given traveler.

38. It is worth noting that according to protocol, Ella could, and perhaps should, have been processed for a START exemption by a General Relief eligibility worker. Rosa, however, did not place blame on the unknown means tester who let Ella "slide by." As a former eligibility worker herself, Rosa told me she understood the intake question about workfare exemption to be brief. She told me that "many people" enter START only to later realize they should have been medically exempted by eligibility workers first. Other WTW workers said similar things. I do not know, however, how many such cases exist. All of them presumably add to the runaround that General Relief customers confront.

39. DiMario 2022: 861, emphasis in original.

40. For more on the failures of welfare-to-work programming, see chapter 4.

41. Near this was a smaller poster that read, "It takes only one person to change your life . . . you."

42. Mounk 2017.

43. Foucault (1975) 1995: 170.

44. Soss, Fording, and Schram 2011: 209.

Chapter 6. Dis/Connected

1. Durkheim (1893) 2014; Marx (1847) 1978.

2. Marx (1844) 1978: 72, emphasis in original.

3. Durkheim (1893) 2014.

4. Durkheim (1893) 2014: 49, emphasis added.

5. Durkheim (1893) 2014: 50.

6. Pugh 2022.

7. Pugh 2022: 23.

8. Bernstein 1967.

9. "Discussion Leader's Guide to a Courtesy Awareness Program for Public Contact Employees," June 1975, Los Angeles County Department of Public Social Services Records, Box 11, Folder 3.

10. Yelp, "Los Angeles County DPSS," retrieved October 18, 2022, https://www.yelp.com/biz/los-angeles-county-dpss-los-angeles.

11. "Proposal to Develop a Pilot Ethnic Rapport Training Program," November 20, 1974, Los Angeles County Department of Public Social Services Records, Box 11, Folder 7; "Courtesy—A Requirement for the Social Worker" and "Proposal for Public Employee Courtesy Training," March 19, 1975, Los Angeles County Department of Public Social Services Records, Box 11, Folder 19.

12. "Discussion Leader's Guide to a Courtesy Awareness Program for Public Contact Employees," June 1975, Los Angeles County Department of Public Social Services Records, Box 11, Folder 3.

13. "L.A. County Department of Public Social Services: Cultural Awareness Task Force Report," October 10, 1975, Los Angeles County Department of Public Social Services Records, Box 11, Folder 3; "Executive Staff Orientation to Minority Cultures and Problems," 1970, Los Angeles County Department of Public Social Services Records, Box 11, Folder 3.

14. "Cultural Awareness and Affirmative Action Training Schedule," n.d., Los Angeles County Department of Public Social Services Records, Box 11, Folder 4.

15. Norma Ross quoted by Hector Tobar (1991).

16. Antonia Jiménez quoted in an undated interview in the Civilla (2022) blogpost.

17. Los Angeles County Department of Public Social Services 2016.

18. Eubanks 2018: 74.

19. SEIU Local 721 2022.

20. SEIU Local 721 2022.

21. SEIU Local 721 2022.

22. For more on "controlling images" generally and "welfare dependency" specifically, see Collins's (2000) *Black Feminist Thought*, especially chapter 4. She notes how the image of the "welfare queen" was conjured under an interlocking system of capitalism, racism, and sexism to "mask the effects of cuts in government spending on social welfare programs." Building on Collins, Hancock (2003) finds compelling evidence that controlling images of dependency were used to justify and frame late twentieth-century welfare reforms focused on discourses of self-sufficiency.

23. Soss, Fording, and Schram 2011.

24. Los Angeles County Department of Public Social Services 2022a.

25. Quotes from an informational video posted on GAIN webpage (Los Angeles County Department of Public Social Services 2022b).

26. Moffit 2002; Soss, Fording, and Schram 2011. More specific to Los Angeles, a randomized case control evaluation in the late 1980s, for example, concluded that GAIN increased employment but did little to increase overall earnings (Riccio, Friedlander, and Freedman 1994).

27. Phil Ansell quoted by Rivera (1997b).

28. See especially chapter 6, "Advocacy and Alienation in Street-Level Work," in *Street-Level Bureaucracy* (Lipsky 1980: 71–80).

29. Lipsky 1980: 71–80.

30. Pugh 2022.

Conclusion

1. Based on a January 2025 statistical report published by DPSS (Los Angeles County Department of Public Social Services 2025).

2. Los Angeles County Department of Public Social Services 2025.

3. Seim and DiMario 2023.

4. As Ken Miller puts it in one of the handouts given to me by a Change and Innovation Agency representative, "Human services faces a phenomenal capacity crisis—there is way more work than resources available."

5. For more on penal-state abolition and calls to invest in a less punitive social safety net, see Davis 2003, Gilmore 2022, and Kaba 2021.

6. For a comparable discussion of the "insufficiency of self-sufficiency" in the American welfare state and the need to emphasize alternative policies of "self-realization," see Gowayed 2022: 50–2, 127.

7. For more on poverty governance in the US during the COVID-19 pandemic see Parolin 2023.

Appendix

1. Lipsky 1980; Watkins-Hayes 2009.

2. Seim 2024.

3. Seim 2016; Seim 2020. For more on the methods concerning these projects, see Seim 2024 and Gibson-Light and Seim 2020.

4. For more on historically embedded ethnography, see the methodological appendix in *Redistributing the Poor* (Lara-Millán 2021).

5. Online Archive of California 2024.

6. Benzecry, Deener, and Lara-Millán 2020: 298.

7. Burawoy 2009; Levenson and Seim 2024.

References

Abramovitz, Mimi. 2023. "From the Welfare State to the Carceral State: Whither Social Reproduction?" *Affilia* 38(1):20–39.

Addams, Jane. 1911. *Twenty Years at Hull-House, with Autobiographical Notes*. New York: Macmillan.

Alameda County Social Services Agency. 2024. "Employment & Training." *Employment & Training: CalWORKs Welfare-to-Work*. Retrieved Aug. 27, 2024. https://www.alamedasocialservices.org/our-services/Work-and-Money/Employment-and-Training/Welfare-to-work

Alamillo, Joanna Victoria. 2020. "Teleworking Benefits for Los Angeles County Employees." MPA thesis, Northridge, Tseng College, California State University, Northridge.

Alaszewski, Andy, and Jill Manthorpe. 1993. "Quality and the Welfare Services: A Literature Review." *The British Journal of Social Work* 23(6):653–65.

Antelope Valley Times. 2022. "Jury Awards $3.5 Million to DPSS Worker Who Protested Workplace Segregation." November 1.

Auyero, Javier. 2012. *Patients of the State: The Politics of Waiting in Argentina*. Durham, NC: Duke University Press.

Baldassare, Mark, Michael A. Shires, Christopher Hoene, and Aaron Koffman. 2000. *Risky Business: Providing Local Public Services in Los Angeles County*. San Francisco: Public Policy Institute of California.

Barnard, Alex V. 2023. *Conservatorship: Inside California's System of Coercion and Care for Mental Illness*. New York: Columbia University Press.

Bartram, Robin. 2022. *Stacked Decks: Building Inspectors and the Reproduction of Urban Inequality*. Chicago: University of Chicago Press.

Bauman, Zygmunt. 2000. *Liquid Modernity*. Cambridge, UK: Polity Press.

Bayer, Lynn. 1998. "Welfare-to-Work Program." *Los Angeles Times*, October 17, Letters Desk.

Beckett, Katherine, and Bruce Western. 2001. "Governing Social Marginality Welfare, Incarceration, and the Transformation of State Policy." *Punishment & Society* 3(1):43–59.

Benzecry, Claudio E., Andrew Deener, and Armando Lara-Millán. 2020. "Archival Work as Qualitative Sociology." *Qualitative Sociology* 43(3): 297–303.

Bermudez, Rosie Cano. 2019. "Doing Dignity Work: Alicia Escalante and the East Los Angeles Welfare Rights Organization, 1967–1974." PhD dissertation, University of California, Santa Barbara.

Bernstein, Harry. 1967. "Watts Area Relief Rolls 'Skyrocket' Since Riots." *Los Angeles Times*, July 17, A6.

Berstein, Sid. 1978. "County Employees: The Word Is Angry; Morale Shot, Many Leaving in Wake of Prop. 13 Cutbacks." *Los Angeles Times*, October 19, p. 2.

Bohn, Sarah, Caroline Danielson, Sara Kimberlin, Patricia Malagon, and Christopher Wimer. 2023. "Poverty in California." *Public Policy Institute of California*. Retrieved September 6, 2024. https://www.ppic.org/publication/poverty-in-california/

Bovens, Mark, and Stavros Zouridis. 2002. "From Street-Level to System-Level Bureaucracies: How Information and Communication Technology Is Transforming Administrative Discretion and Constitutional Control." *Public Administration Review* 62(2):174–84.

Brady, David. 2009. *Rich Democracies, Poor People: How Politics Explain Poverty*. Oxford: Oxford University Press.

Brady, David. 2021. *American Poverty Should Be Measured Relative to the Prevailing Standards of Our Time*. Washington, DC: The Century Foundation.

Braverman, Harry. 1974. *Labor and Monopoly Capital: The Degradation of Work in the Twentieth Century*. New York: Monthly Review Press.

Buffat, Aurélien. 2015. "Street-Level Bureaucracy and E-Government." *Public Management Review* 17(1):149–61.

Burawoy, Michael. 1979. *Manufacturing Consent: Changes in the Labor Process Under Monopoly Capitalism*. Chicago: University of Chicago Press.

Burawoy, Michael. 2009. *The Extended Case Method: Four Countries, Four Decades, Four Great Transformations, and One Theoretical Tradition*. Oakland: University of California Press.

Burton, Alice. 1991. "Dividing Up the Struggle: The Consequences of 'Split' Welfare Work for Union Activism." In *Ethnography Unbound: Power and*

Resistance in the Modern Metropolis, edited by Michael Burawoy, 85–101. Berkeley: University of California Press.

California Department of Health Care Services. 2015. "Medi-Cal Statistical Brief." Retrieved September 6, 2024. https://www.dhcs.ca.gov/dataandstats /statistics/Documents/Historic-Growth-Brief.pdf

California Department of Social Services. 2024a. "Request for Verification." Retrieved August 26, 2024. https://www.cdss.ca.gov/cdssweb/entres/forms /english/cw2200.pdf

California Department of Social Services. 2024b. "CALWORKS 48-Month Time Limit." Retrieved August 26, 2024. https://www.cdss.ca.gov/cdssweb/entres /forms/english/cw2184.pdf

California Department of Social Services. 2024c. "CalWORKs Data Tables." Retrieved May 1, 2024. https://www.cdss.ca.gov/inforesources/research-and-data/calworks-data-tables

California Legislative Analyst's Office. 1985. *Final Summary of Major Financial Legislation Enacted During 1985*. Sacramento: California Legislative Analyst's Office.

California Statewide Automated Welfare System. 2024. "History of Statewide Automated Welfare." Retrieved September 6, 2024. https://www.calsaws .org/about-us/history/

Carey, Malcolm. 2007. "White-Collar Proletariat? Braverman, the Deskilling /Upskilling of Social Work and the Paradoxical Life of the Agency Care Manager." *Journal of Social Work* 7(1):93–114.

Cedillo, Gilbert. 1994. "Food Stamp Fraud." *Los Angeles Times*, February 16, VYB14.

Center on Budget and Policy Priorities. 2022. "Policy Basics: Temporary Assistance for Needy Families." Retrieved September 6, 2024. https://www.cbpp .org/research/family-income-support/policy-basics-an-introduction-to-tanf

Change and Innovation Agency. 2024. "Current: Manage Work + Staff Capacity." Retrieved August 27, 2024. https://changeagents.info/current/

Chief Executive Offices of Los Angeles. 2023. "2023–24 Final Budget." Retrieved May 10, 2024. https://ceo.lacounty.gov/wp-content/uploads/2023/12/LA-County-2023–24-Final-Budget-Book.pdf

Chief Executive Offices of Los Angeles. 2024. "Understanding the LA County Budget." Retrieved May 10, 2024. https://ceo.lacounty.gov/budget/

The Children's Partnership. 2024. "Medi-Cal Call Wait Times Survey Report." Retrieved July 1, 2025. https://childrenspartnership.org/research/medi-cal-call-wait-times-survey-report/

Civilla. n.d. "Cutting Through Bureaucracy." Retrieved October 21, 2022. https://civilla.org/stories/interview-antonia-jimenez

Clergé, Orly. 2019. *The New Noir: Race, Identity, and Diaspora in Black Suburbia.* Oakland: University of California Press.

Cohen, Lizabeth. 2003. *A Consumers' Republic: The Politics of Mass Consumption in Postwar America.* New York: Knopf Doubleday.

Collins, Jane L., and Victoria Mayer. 2010. *Both Hands Tied: Welfare Reform and the Race to the Bottom in the Low-Wage Labor Market.* Chicago: University of Chicago Press.

Collins, Patricia Hill. 2000. *Black Feminist Thought: Knowledge, Consciousness, and the Politics of Empowerment.* New York: Routledge.

Collins, Sharon M. 1983. "The Making of the Black Middle Class." *Social Problems* 30(4):369–82.

Comfort, Megan. 2007. "Punishment Beyond the Legal Offender." *Annual Review of Law and Social Science* 3:271–96.

Connell, Raewyn, Barbara Fawcett, and Gabrielle Meagher. 2009. "Neoliberalism, New Public Management and the Human Service Professions: Introduction to the Special Issue." *Journal of Sociology* 45(4):331–38.

Corbett, Thomas, Jeannette Deloya, Wendy Manning, and Liz Uhr. 1989. "Learnfare: The Wisconsin Experience." *Focus* 12(2).

County Welfare Directors Association of California. 2024. "LEADER Replacement System Deployment Begins." Retrieved Aug. 27, 2024. https://www.cwda.org/featured-content/leader-replacement-system-deployment-begins

Crowley, Martha. 2013. "Gender, the Labor Process and Dignity at Work." *Social Forces* 91(4):1209–38.

Danielson, Caroline, and Shannon McConville. 2023. "As Medi-Cal Enters a Post-Pandemic Phase, Keeping Eligible Californians Enrolled Is a Key Concern." *Public Policy Institute of California.* Retrieved September 6, 2024. https://www.ppic.org/blog/as-medi-cal-enters-a-post-pandemic-phase-keeping-eligible-californians-enrolled-is-a-key-concern/

Davis, Angela. 2003. *Are Prisons Obsolete?* New York: Seven Stories Press.

Davis, Mike. 1990. *City of Quartz: Excavating the Future in Los Angeles.* New York: Verso Books.

Derber, Charles. 1983. "Managing Professionals: Ideological Proletarianization and Post-Industrial Labor." *Theory and Society* 12(3):309–41.

DeSilver, Drew. 2023. "What the Data Says About Food Stamps in the U.S." *Pew Research Center.* Retrieved September 6, 2024. https://www.pewresearch

.org/short-reads/2023/07/19/what-the-data-says-about-food-stamps-in -the-u-s/

Deukmejian, George. 1990. "California Commentary: Clear Away Obstacles to Workfare: The State's Program is Making Progress, but Putting People in Jobs Must Become the Top Priority." *Los Angeles Times*, July 27, p. 7.

DeVerteuil, Geoffrey. 2015. *Resilience in the Post-Welfare Inner City: Voluntary Sector Geographies in London, Los Angeles and Sydney*. Bristol: Policy Press.

DeVerteuil, Geoffrey, Woobae Lee, and Jennifer Wolch. 2002. "New Spaces for the Local Welfare State? The Case of General Relief in Los Angeles County." *Social & Cultural Geography* 3(3):229–46.

DiMario, Anthony. 2022. "To Punish, Parent, or Palliate: Governing Urban Poverty Through Institutional Failure." *American Sociological Review* 87(5):860–88.

Dow, Dawn Marie. 2019. *Mothering While Black: Boundaries and Burdens of Middle-Class Parenthood*. Oakland: University of California Press.

Dubois, Vincent. (2010) 2016. *The Bureaucrat and the Poor: Encounters in French Welfare Offices*. New York: Routledge.

Du Bois, W. E. B. 1899. *The Philadelphia Negro: A Social Study*. Philadelphia: University of Pennsylvania Press.

du Gay, Paul. 2000. *In Praise of Bureaucracy: Weber—Organization—Ethics*. Thousand Oaks, CA: Sage.

Durkheim, Émile. (1893) 2014. *The Division of Labor in Society*. New York: Free Press.

Dustin, Donna. 2007. *The McDonaldization of Social Work*. Burlington, VT: Ashgate.

Emerson, Robert M. 1983. "Holistic Effects in Social Control Decision-Making." *Law & Society Review* 17(3):425–55.

Engels, Friedrich. (1845) 1892. *Conditions of the Working Class in England*. London: Swan Sonnenschein.

Equifax. 2022. "Case Study: Los Angeles County Department of Public Social Services." Retrieved September 6, 2024. https://assets.equifax.com/wfs /theworknumber/assets/TWN_Case_Study_LA_County.pdf

Esbenshade, Jill, Matt Vidal, Gina Fascilla, and Mariko Ono. 2015. "Customer-Driven Management Models for Choiceless Clientele? Business Process Reengineering in a California Welfare Agency." *Work, Employment and Society* 30(1): 77–96.

Eubanks, Virginia. 2018. *Automating Inequality: How High-Tech Tools Profile, Police, and Punish the Poor*. New York: St. Martin's.

Felder, Henry E. 2006. *DPSS Trend in the Era of Welfare Reform: 1998–2006.* Los Angeles: California Department of Public Social Services.

Foucault, Michel. (1975) 1995. *Discipline and Punish: The Birth of the Prison.* New York: Vintage Books.

Franz, David. 2008. "The Moral Life of Cubicles: The Utopian Origins of Dilbert's Workspace." *The New Atlantis* (19):132–39.

Freedman, Stephen, Daniel Friedlander, Winston Lin, and Amanda Schweder. 1996. *Five-Year Impacts on Employment, Earnings, and AFDC Receipt.* New York: Manpower Demonstration Research Corporation.

Freedman, Stephen, Jean Tansey Knab, Lisa A. Gennetian, and David Navarro. 2000. *The Los Angeles Jobs-First GAIN Evaluation: Final Report on a Work First Program in a Major Urban Center.* New York: Manpower Demonstration Research Corporation.

Freedman, Stephen, Marisa Mitchell, and David Navarro. 1999. *The Los Angeles Jobs-First GAIN Evaluation: First-Year Findings on Participation Patterns and Impacts.* New York: Manpower Demonstration Research Corporation.

Gadzo, Ryan. 2015. "SNAP and TANF Administration in New York State Counties: Comparing Case-Based, Mixed Methods and Task-Based Processes." MPA thesis, Department of Political Science, Public Administration, and Planning, Buffalo State University.

Giannella, Eric, Tatiana Homonoff, Gwen Rino, and Jason Somerville. 2024. "Administrative Burden and Procedural Denials: Experimental Evidence from SNAP." *American Economic Journal: Economic Policy* 16(4):316–40.

Gibson-Light, Michael, and Josh Seim. 2020. "Punishing Fieldwork: Penal Domination and Prison Ethnography." *Journal of Contemporary Ethnography* 49(5):666–90.

Gilbert, Charles E. 1966. "Policy-Making in Public Welfare: The 1962 Amendments." *Political Science Quarterly* 81(2):196–224.

Gilmore, Ruth Wilson. 2022. *Abolition Geography: Essays Towards Liberation.* New York: Verso.

Goff, Tom. 1967. "County Welfare Reorganization to Be Proposed: Plan Based on 10-Month Study Aims at Improved Controls Plus Economies Incomplete Source." *Los Angeles Times*, March 6, SF7 & 3.

Gong, Neil. 2024. *Sons, Daughters, and Sidewalk Psychotics: Mental Illness and Homelessness in Los Angeles.* Chicago: Chicago University Press.

Gordon, Eric, John Harlow, Samantha A. Whitman, and Myeong Lee. 2024. "Data Discretion: Screen-Level Bureaucrats and Municipal Decision-Making." *Digital Government: Research and Practice.* doi: 10.1145/3652950.

Gouldner, Alvin W. 1954. *Patterns of Industrial Bureaucracy*. New York: Free Press.

Gowayed, Heba. 2022. *Refuge: How the State Shapes Human Potential*. Princeton: Princeton University Press.

Green, Venus. 2001. *Race on the Line: Gender, Labor, and Technology in the Bell System, 1880–1980*. Durham, NC: Duke University Press.

Greenberg, Max A. 2021. "Not Seeing Like a State: Mandated Reporting, State-Adjacent Actors and the Production of Illegible Subjects." *Social Problems* 68(4):870–85.

Greenblatt, Michael. 1979. *Public Welfare: Notes from Underground*. Cambridge, MA: Routledge.

Grodin, Joseph R. 1999. "Public Employee Bargaining in California: The Meyers-Milias-Brown Act in the Courts." *Hastings Law Journal* 50(4): 717–59.

Halpern-Meekin, Sarah, Kathryn Edin, Laura Tach, and Jennifer Sykes. 2015. *It's Not Like I'm Poor: How Working Families Make Ends Meet in a Post-Welfare World*. Oakland: University of California Press.

Halushka, John M. 2020. "The Runaround: Punishment, Welfare, and Poverty Survival after Prison." *Social Problems* 67(2):233–50.

Hancock, Ange-Marie. 2003. "Contemporary Welfare Reform and the Public Identity of the 'Welfare Queen.'" *Race, Gender & Class* 10(1):31–59.

Handler, Joel F. 2009. "Welfare, Workfare, and Citizenship in the Developed World." *Annual Review of Law and Social Science* 5(5):71–90.

Handler, Joel F., and Yeheskel Hasenfeld. 2007. *Blame Welfare, Ignore Poverty and Inequality*. Cambridge, UK: Cambridge University Press.

Haney, Lynne. 2002. *Inventing the Needy: Gender and the Politics of Welfare in Hungary*. Berkeley, CA: University of California Press.

Hansen, Helena, Philippe Bourgois, and Ernest Drucker. 2014. "Pathologizing Poverty: New Forms of Diagnosis, Disability, and Structural Stigma Under Welfare Reform." *Social Science & Medicine (1982)* 103:76–83.

Harknett, Kristen, Daniel Schneider, and Sigrid Luhr. 2022. "Who Cares If Parents Have Unpredictable Work Schedules? Just-in-Time Work Schedules and Child Care Arrangements." *Social Problems* 69(1):164–83.

Harris, John. 2019. "From Seebohm Factories to Neoliberal Production Lines? The Social Work Labour Process." In *What is the Future of Social Work?*, edited by M. Lavalette, 123–42. Bristol, England: Bristol University Press.

Harris, Scott. 1988. "Row with State Threatens County Workfare Project." *Los Angeles Times*, September 23, p. 3.

Harvey, David. 2007. *A Brief History of Neoliberalism*. New York: Oxford University Press.

Hasenfeld, Yeheskel. 1972. "People Processing Organizations: An Exchange Approach." *American Sociological Review* 37(3):256–63.

Hasenfeld, Yeheskel. 2010. "Organizational Responses to Social Policy: The Case of Welfare Reform." *Administration in Social Work* 34(2):148–67.

Hazlett, Bill and Bill Farr. 1980. "L.A. County Planning Computer Setup to Foil Welfare Cheaters." *Los Angeles Times*, December 20, OCA1.

Headworth, Spencer. 2021. *Policing Welfare: Punitive Adversarialism in Public Assistance*. Chicago: Chicago University Press.

Herd, Pamela, and Donald P. Moynihan. 2019. *Administrative Burden: Policy-making by Other Means*. 1st edition. New York: Russell Sage Foundation.

Hernandez, Marjorie, and Matthew Sedacca. 2023. "Iconic Venice Beach Boardwalk Continues to Be Occupied by Homeless Groups During Spiraling Crisis." *New York Post*. July 15. https://nypost.com/2023/07/15/iconic-venice-beach-boardwalk-continues-to-be-occupied-by-homeless-groups-during-spiraling-crisis/

Hilgers, Mathieu. 2012. "The Historicity of the Neoliberal State." *Social Anthropology* 20(1):80–94.

Houston, David J. 2000. "Public-Service Motivation: A Multivariate Test." *Journal of Public Administration Research and Theory* 10(4):713–28.

Hunter, Maude. 1971. "A Study of Eligibility Worker Attitudes Toward the Dissatisfied Client." MSW thesis, School of Social Work, Fresno State College.

Hulsey, Lara, Kevin Conway, Andrew Gothro, Rebecca Kleinman, Megan Reilly, Scott Cody, and Emily Sama-Miller. 2023. *The Evolution of SNAP Modernization Initiatives in Five States*. Washington, DC: United States Department of Agriculture.

Insure the Uninsured Project. 2021. "Health Care Coverage and Enrollment During the Pandemic." Retrieved September 6, 2024. https://www.itup.org/nff-blog-series-health-care-coverage-and-enrollment-during-the-pandemic/

Johnson, William. 2007. "Service Employees Union Mergers Lead to Conflict in California." *Labor Notes*, June, p. 8.

Johnston, Paul. 1988. "The Politics of Public Work: A Theory of Public Work and Labor Struggle." *Berkeley Journal of Sociology* 33:37–71.

Kaba, Mariame. 2021. *We Do This 'Til We Free Us: Abolitionist Organizing and Transforming Justice*. Chicago: Haymarket Books.

Kaiser Family Foundation. 1996. "Medicaid Update: Expenditures and Beneficiaries in 1996; Policy Brief." Retrieved Feb. 19, 2025. https://www.kff.org/medicaid/issue-brief/medicaid-update-expenditures-and-beneficiaries-in-1994-2/

Kalleberg, Arne L. 2011. *Good Jobs, Bad Jobs: The Rise of Polarized and Precarious Employment Systems in the United States, 1970s to 2000s*. New York: Russell Sage Foundation.

Keppel, Bruce. 1976. "County Welfare Agency Trims Fat by Computer." *Los Angeles Times*, November 28, 1976, C1.

Laird, Jennifer. 2017. "Public Sector Employment Inequality in the United States and the Great Recession." *Demography* 54(1):391–411.

Lakatos, Imre. 1978. *The Methodology of Scientific Research Programmes*. Cambridge, UK: Cambridge University Press.

Landry, Bart, and Kris Marsh. 2011. "The Evolution of the New Black Middle Class." *Annual Review of Sociology* 37(1):373–94.

Landsbergen, David. 2004. "Screen Level Bureaucracy: Databases as Public Records." *Government Information Quarterly* 21(1):24–50. doi: 10.1016/j.giq.2003.12.009.

Lara-Millán, Armando. 2021. *Redistributing the Poor: Jails, Hospitals, and the Crisis of Law and Fiscal Austerity*. New York: Oxford University Press.

Larson, Magali Sarfatti. 1980. "Proletarianization and Educated Labor." *Theory and Society* 9(1):131–75.

Leidner, Robin. 1993. *Fast Food, Fast Talk: Service Work and the Routinization of Everyday Life*. Berkeley, CA: University of California Press.

Levenson, Zachary, and Josh Seim. 2024. "Cracking the Iron Ceiling: On Ethnography as Theory." *Critical Sociology* 50(6):997–1004. doi: 10.1177/08969205241263546.

Lipsky, Michael. 1980. *Street-Level Bureaucracy: Dilemmas of the Individual in Public Service*. New York: Russell Sage Foundation.

Lødemel, Ivar. 2002. *Workfare in Six European Nations: Findings from Evaluations and Recommendations for Future Development*. Tøyen, Oslo: Fafo.

Los Angeles County. 2023. "County of Los Angeles Employee Counts and Demographics Dataset." Retrieved June 15, 2024. https://data.lacounty.gov/datasets/bb365027d03747eb8744bcb9fc4ee34a_0/explore

Los Angeles County. 2024. "Los Angeles County Class and Salary Listing Alphabetical Order." Retrieved July 15, 2024. https://file.lacounty.gov/SDSInter/lac/1043266_alpha.pdf

Los Angeles County Auditor-Controller. 2023. "LA County Employee Salaries."
Retrieved July 1, 2024. https://data.lacounty.gov/datasets/1fefbd3af4cf41fda
827f2c23a1fe09b/explore

Los Angeles County Board of Supervisors. 2024. "Celebrating Women's History
Month: Closing the Gender Pay Gap." Retrieved September 6, 2024. https://
file.lacounty.gov/SDSInter/bos/supdocs/189649.pdf

Los Angeles County Department of Human Resources. 2014. "STAY Interview
Guide: An Employee Retention Strategy for Supervisors." Retrieved
September 6, 2024. https://employee.hr.lacounty.gov/wp-content/uploads
/2015/10/StayInterviewGuide_9.26.14.pdf

Los Angeles County Department of Public Social Services. 2016. *DPSS Annual
Report*. Los Angeles: Los Angeles County Department of Public Social
Services.

Los Angeles County Department of Public Social Services. 2022a. "General
Relief Opportunities for Work (GROW)." Retrieved October 21, 2022.
https://dpss.lacounty.gov/en/jobs/grow.html

Los Angeles County Department of Public Social Services. 2022b. "Greater
Avenues for Independence (GAIN)." Retrieved October 21, 2022. https://
dpss.lacounty.gov/en/jobs/gain.html

Los Angeles County Department of Public Social Services. 2024a. *Strategic Plan
2022–2027*. Los Angeles: Los Angeles County Department of Public Social
Services.

Los Angeles County Department of Public Social Services. 2024b. "General
Relief." Retrieved August 27, 2024. https://dpss.lacounty.gov/en/cash/gr.html

Los Angeles County Department of Public Social Services. 2024c. "CalWORKs
Homeless Programs." Retrieved September 6, 2024. https://dpss.lacounty
.gov/en/cash/calworks/homeless.html

Los Angeles County Department of Public Social Services. 2024d. "GR Housing
Subsidy and Case Management Program." Retrieved July 19, 2024. https://
dpss.lacounty.gov/en/cash/gr/housing.html

Los Angeles County Department of Public Social Services. 2024e. "Child Care."
Retrieved July 19, 2024. https://dpss.lacounty.gov/en/jobs/childcare.html

Los Angeles County Department of Public Social Services. 2024f. "Domestic
Violence." Retrieved September 6, 2024. https://dpss.lacounty.gov/en/jobs
/gain/sss/domestic-violence.html

Los Angeles County Department of Public Social Services. 2025. "DPSS
Statistical Report." Retrieved February 21, 2025. https://myapps.dpss
.lacounty.gov/pls/apexprod/f?p=AAGT:AAGT

Los Angeles County Office of Education. 2024. "LACOE GAIN—Providing Career Services to Welfare-to-Work Participants." Retrieved August 27, 2024. https://lacoegain.org/

Los Angeles Post. 2023. "DPSS Unveils New Name for Grow Program: Introducing the START Program." Retrieved September 6, 2024. https://lapost.us/?p=59228

Los Angeles Times. 1967. "Welfare Reorganization OK'd Despite Opposition by Union: County Supervisors Give Unanimous Approval to Plan for Top-Level Reshuffle in Overriding Critic's Attack Supervisors OK Reshuffle for Welfare." Newspaper editorial. March 8, pp. 3 & 19.

Los Angeles Times. 1968. "Welfare Rights Group Pickets, Renews Yule Bonus Demands." Newspaper editorial. December 24, p. 1.

Los Angeles Times. 1974. "Classified Ad 28." Newspaper editorial. December 29, p. 11.

Los Angeles Times. 1989. "U.S. Approves Private Pact for Workfare." Newspaper editorial. January 21, VY4.

Lytle Hernández, Kelly. 2017. *City of Inmates: Conquest, Rebellion, and the Rise of Human Caging in Los Angeles, 1771–1965 (Justice, Power, and Politics)*. Chapel Hill: University of North Carolina Press.

Marchevsky, Alejandra, and Jeanne Theoharis. 2008. "Dropped from the Rolls: Mexican Immigrants, Race, and Rights in the Era of Welfare Reform." *Journal of Sociology and Social Welfare* 35(3):71–96.

Marx, Karl. (1844) 1978. "Economic and Philosophic Manuscripts of 1844." In *The Marx-Engels Reader*, edited by Robert C. Tucker, 66–132. New York: W.W. Norton.

Marx, Karl. (1847) 1978. "Wage Labour and Capital." In *The Marx-Engels Reader*, edited by Robert C. Tucker, 203–17. New York: W.W. Norton.

Marx, Karl. (1867) 1996. *Das Kapital: A Critique of Political Economy*. Washington DC: Regnery.

Marx, Karl, and Friedrich and Engels (1932) 1978. "The German Ideology: Part I." In *The Marx-Engels Reader*, edited by Robert C. Tucker, 146–200. New York: W.W. Norton.

McCabe, Joshua T. 2018. *The Fiscalization of Social Policy: How Taxpayers Trumped Children in the Fight Against Child Poverty*. Oxford: Oxford University Press.

McDonnell, Erin Metz. 2020. *Pathwork Leviathan: Pockets of Bureaucratic Effectiveness in Developing States*. Princeton: Princeton University Press.

McKinlay, Alan, and Ken Starkey. 1997. *Foucault, Management and Organization Theory: From Panopticon to Technologies of Self.* Thousand Oaks, CA: Sage.

Menendian, Stephen, and Samir Gambhir. 2021. *National Segregation Report.* Berkeley, CA: Othering & Belonging Institute.

Merl, Jean. 1981. "Cuts in L.A. County Leave Many Jobless." *Los Angeles Times,* July 27, OCA1.

Meyer, Josh. 1995. "County Employees Stop Work to Protest Cutbacks." *Los Angeles Times,* July 12, VYB8.

Meyers, Joan S. M. 2022. *Working Democracies: Managing Inequality in Worker Cooperatives.* Ithaca, NY: Cornell University Press.

Mik-Meyer, Nanna, and Kaspar Villardsen. 2012. *Power and Welfare: Understanding Citizens' Encounters with State Welfare.* London: Routledge.

Miller, Ken. 2013. *We Don't Make Widgets: Overcoming the Myths That Keep Government from Radically Improving.* Washington, DC: Governing Books.

Miller, Ken. 2019. *Extreme Government Makeover: Increasing Our Capacity to Do More Good.* Washington, DC: Governing Books.

Mills, C. Wright. 1959. *The Sociological Imagination.* New York: Oxford University Press.

Mittelstadt, Jennifer. 2005. *From Welfare to Workfare: The Unintended Consequences of Liberal Reform, 1945–1965.* Chapel Hill: The University of North Carolina Press.

Moffitt, Robert. 2002. "From Welfare to Work: What the Evidence Shows." *Brookings,* January 2. https://www.brookings.edu/research/from-welfare-to-work-what-the-evidence-shows/

Møller, Anne Mette, Kirstine Zinck Pedersen, and Anja Svejgaard Pors. 2022. "The Bureaucratic Ethos in Street-Level Work: Revitalizing Weber's Ethics of Office." *Perspectives on Public Management and Governance* 5(2):151–63.

Morgen, Sandra, Joan Acker, and Jill Weigt. 2010. *Stretched Thin: Poor Families, Welfare Work, and Welfare Reform.* Ithaca, NY: Cornell University Press.

Mounk, Yascha. 2017. *The Age of Responsibility: Luck, Choice, and the Welfare State.* Cambridge, MA: Harvard University Press.

Moynihan, Donald P. 2006. "Managing for Results in State Government: Evaluating a Decade of Reform." *Public Administration Review* 66(1):77–89.

Moynihan, Donald P., and Sanjay K. Pandey. 2007. "The Role of Organizations in Fostering Public Service Motivation." *Public Administration Review* 67(1):40–53.

Office of Family Assistance. 2019. "Caseload Data 1994 (AFDC Total)." Retrieved February 19, 2025. https://acf.gov/ofa/data/caseload-data-1994-afdc-total

Oksala, Johanna. 2016. "Affective Labor and Feminist Politics." *Signs: Journal of Women in Culture and Society* 41(2):281–303.

Online Archive of California. 2024. "About OAC." Retrieved October 23, 2024. https://oac.cdlib.org/about/

Oppenheimer, Martin. 1972. "The Proletarianization of the Professional." *The Sociological Review* 20(S1):213–27.

Ortiz, Samuel. 2022. "The Impact of Technology on the Delivery of Social Services." PhD dissertation, Department of Public Administration, University of La Verne.

O'Shaughnessy, Lynn. 1989. "Millions Misspent on Welfare." *Los Angeles Times*, August 13, OC3.

Paik, Leslie. 2021. *Trapped in a Maze: How Social Control Institutions Drive Family Poverty and Inequality*. Oakland: University of California Press.

Parolin, Zachary. 2023. *Poverty in the Pandemic: Policy Lessons from COVID-19*. New York: Russell Sage Foundation.

Patry, Bill. 1978. "Taylorism Comes to the Social Services." *Monthly Review*, October 1978.

Peck, Jamie. 2001. *Workfare States*. New York: Guilford Press.

Peeters, Rik. 2020. "The Political Economy of Administrative Burdens: A Theoretical Framework for Analyzing the Organizational Origins of Administrative Burdens." *Administration & Society* 52(4):566–92.

Perry, James L., Robert K. Christensen, and Laurie Paarlberg. 2017. "Public Service Motivation Research: Lessons for Practice Theory to Practice." *Public Administration Review* 77(4):529–42.

Piven, Frances Fox, and Richard A. Cloward. 1971. *Regulating the Poor: The Functions of Public Welfare*. New York: Vintage Books.

Powell, Jason, and Simon Biggs. 2000. "Managing Old Age: The Disciplinary Web of Power, Surveillance and Normalization." *Journal of Aging and Identity* 5(1):3–13.

Prottas, Jeffrey. 1978. "The Power of the Street-Level Bureaucrat in Public Service Bureaucracies." *Urban Affairs Quarterly* 13(3): 285–312.

Pugh, Allison. 2022. "Emotions and the Systematization of Connective Labor." *Theory, Culture, and Society* 39(5):23–42.

Rank, Mark Robert, Lawrence M. Eppard, and Heather E. Bullock. 2021. *Poorly Understood: What America Gets Wrong About Poverty*. New York: Oxford University Press.

Reyes, Emily Alpert. 2023. "A Scramble to Keep Benefits as Medicaid Rules Change." *Los Angeles Times*, May 4, 2023, A1.

Riccardi, Nicholas. 2000. "Political Struggle Centers on Welfare-to-Work Contractor." *Los Angeles Times*, June 20, B-1 & B-7.

Riccio, James, Daniel Friedlander, and Stephen Freedmen. 1994. "GAIN: Benefits, Costs, and Three-Year Impacts of a Welfare-to-Work Program." *Manpower Demonstration Research Corporation*. Retrieved October 21, 2022. https://www.mdrc.org/sites/default/files/gain_benefits_costs_fr.pdf

Ritzer, George. 1983. "The 'McDonaldization' of Society." *Journal of American Culture* 6(1):100–107.

Rivera, Carla. 1997a. "Effects of County Welfare Changes Will Be Profound." *Los Angeles Times*, August 23, VYA1.

Rivera, Carla. 1997b. "Changing the Way Welfare Works." *Los Angeles Times*, December 1, VYB1.

Rivera, Carla. 1999. "Welfare Drop Leaves County with Surplus." *Los Angeles Times*, January 30, VYA1.

Rivera, Carla. 2000. "Mothers Try to Make Leap from Welfare to Work." *Los Angeles Times*, October 16, VYB9.

Roderick, Kevin. 1988. "State Officials Castigate L.A. County Over GAIN Project." *Los Angeles Times*, October 08, p. 10.

San Fernando Valley Community Mental Health Center. 2024. "CalWORKS Mental Health Supportive Services." Retrieved Aug. 27, 2024. https://www.movinglivesforward.org/program/calworks-mental-health-supportive-services/

Sanger, Mary Bryna. 2004. *The Welfare Marketplace: Privatization and Welfare Reform*. Lanham, MD: Rowman & Littlefield.

Sanzenbacher, Geoffrey. 2023. "Did Welfare-to-Work Policy Actually Work?" *Progress-Less*. Retrieved September 12, 2024. https://progressless.org/2023/06/27/did-welfare-to-work-policy-actually-work/

Scanlon, Edward, and Scott Harding. 2005. "Social Work and Labor Unions: Historical and Contemporary Alliances." *Journal of Community Practice* 13(1):9–30.

Schram, Sanford F., Joe Soss, Linda Houser, and Richard C. Fording. 2010. "The Third Level of US Welfare Reform: Governmentality Under Neoliberal Paternalism." *Citizenship Studies* 14(6):739–54.

Scott, Austin. 1978. "Welfare Cuts May Come at a High Price." *Los Angeles Times*, June 21, B1.

Scott, James C. 1999. *Seeing Like a State: How Certain Schemes to Improve the Human Condition Have Failed*. New Haven, CT: Yale University Press.

Scott, James C. 2021. "Further Reflections on Seeing Like a State." *Polity* 53(3): 507–14.

Sears, Alan. 1999. "The 'Lean' State and Capitalist Restructuring: Towards a Theoretical Account." *Studies in Political Economy* 59(1): 91–114.

Sears, David and Jack Citrin. 1982. *Tax Revolt: Something for Nothing in California*. Cambridge, MA: Harvard University Press.

Seim, Josh. 2016. "Short-Timing: The Carceral Experience of Soon-to-Be-Released Prisoners." *Punishment & Society* 18(4):442–58. doi: 10.1177 /1462474516641377.

Seim, Josh. 2017. "The Ambulance: Toward a Labor Theory of Poverty Governance." *American Sociological Review* 82(3):451–75.

Seim, Josh. 2020. *Bandage, Sort, and Hustle: Ambulance Crews on the Front Lines of Urban Suffering*. Oakland: University of California Press.

Seim, Josh. 2024. "Participant Observation, Observant Participation, and Hybrid Ethnography." *Sociological Methods & Research* 53(1):121–52.

Seim, Josh, and Anthony DiMario. 2023. "City of Gauze: Medicine and the Governance of Urban Poverty." *Social Problems* spad041. doi: 10.1093 /socpro/spad041.

SEIU Local 721. 2021. "September-October 2021 President's Report to the Members of SEIU 721." Retrieved May 15, 2024. https://www.seiu721.org /wp-content/uploads/2021/10/September-October-2021-Presidents -Report-8.5x11-final2.pdf

SEIU Local 721. 2021b. "DPSS Director Acknowledges Issues with 'Task-Based' Work System After Hundreds Rally at Agency Headquarters." Retrieved October 21, 2022. https://www.seiu721.org/2021/09/dpss-massive- demonstration.php

Sheared, Vanessa. 1998. *Race, Gender, and Welfare Reform: The Elusive Quest for Self-Determination*. Milton Park: Taylor & Francis.

Shuit, Douglas P. 1990. "Budget Cuts Threaten to Undermine GAIN Welfare: The State's Ambitious Education and Training Program is Designed to End Dependency by Teaching Job Skills; A Battle is Shaping Up to Keep the Money Flowing." *Los Angeles Times*, March 20, A3 & A28.

Simon, Jonathan. 2007. *Governing Through Crime: How the War on Crime Transformed American Democracy and Created a Culture of Fear*. New York: Oxford University Press.

Simon, Richard. 1989. "Lawyers Assail Welfare System in L.A. County," *Los Angeles Times*, September 6, OCA8.

Simpkin, Mike. 1983. *Trapped Within Welfare: Surviving Social Work*. 2nd ed. London: Macmillan.

Sommeiller, Mark Price, and Ellis Wazeter. 2016. *Income Inequality in the U.S. by State, Metropolitan Area, and County*. Washington, DC: Economic Policy Institute.

Soss, Joe, Richard C. Fording, and Sanford Schram. 2011. *Disciplining the Poor: Neoliberal Paternalism and the Persistent Power of Race*. Chicago: University of Chicago Press.

Stanford Center on Poverty and Inequality. 2021. "California Policy Measure." Retrieved September 6, 2024. https://inequality.stanford.edu/data /california-poverty-measure

Stepan-Norris, Judith, and Jasmine Kerrissey. 2023. *Union Booms and Busts: The Ongoing Fight Over the U.S. Labor Movement*. New York: Oxford University Press.

Stolberg, Sheryl. 1991. "County Workers Union Threatens More Walkouts." *Los Angeles Times*, November 2, VYB1.

Sweeney, Joan. 1972. "Relief Seekers Forced to Work Without Pay." *Los Angeles Times*, March 30, A3.

Talking About Organizations podcast. 2021. "78: Patterns of Bureaucracy; Alvin Gouldner." Retrieved Sep. 12, 2024. https://www.talkingaboutorganizations. com/78-patterns-of-bureaucracy-alvin-gouldner/

Taylor, Mac. 2018. "Rethinking the 1991 Realignment." Retrieved October 10, 2024. https://lao.ca.gov/Publications/Report/3886

Terrell, Paul. 1981. "Adapting to Austerity: Human Services After Proposition 13." *Social Work* 26(4):275–81.

Therolf, Garrett. 2010. "L.A. County Chief Calls for Job Cuts; His Budget Plan would Eliminate Many Empty Positions; 100 Layoffs Might Be Needed." *Los Angeles Times*, April 20, AA1.

Thomas, Robert J. 1982. "Citizenship and Gender in Work Organization: Some Considerations for Theories of the Labor Process." *American Journal of Sociology* 88:S86–112.

Thompson, Paul. 2010. "The Capitalist Labour Process: Concepts and Connections." *Capital & Class* 34(1):7–14.

Timnick, Lois. 1984. "Supervisors Vote to Create Children's Services Agency." *Los Angeles Times*, April 11, B1.

Tobar, Hector. 1991. "Sickout at Welfare Office Creates Chaos on 'Check Day.'" *Los Angeles Times*, October 8, VYB1.

Tobar, Hector. 1992. "Officials Find Solace in Simple Fiscal Survival," *Los Angeles Times*, December 23, VCB5.

United States Bureau of Labor Statistics. 2024a. "Table 20: Annual Average Total Separations Rates by Industry and Region, Not Seasonally Adjusted." Retrieved May 18, 2024. https://www.bls.gov/news.release/jolts.t20 .htm

United States Bureau of Labor Statistics. 2024b. "Union Members—2023." Retrieved September 6, 2024. https://www.bls.gov/news.release/pdf /union2.pdf

United States Bureau of Labor Statistics. 2024c. "CPI Inflation Calculator." Retrieved September 6, 2024. https://data.bls.gov/cgi-bin/cpicalc.pl

United States Census Bureau. 2024. "Los Angeles County, California—Census Bureau Profile." Retrieved September 12, 2024. https://data.census.gov /profile/Los_Angeles_County,_California?g=050XX00US06037

United States Department of Agriculture. 2024. "A Short History of SNAP." Retrieved February 19, 2025. https://www.fns.usda.gov/snap/history#1994

United States Government Accountability Offices. 2020. "Federal Social Safety Net Programs: Millions of Full-Time Workers Rely on Federal Health Care and Food Assistance Programs." Retrieved September 12, 2024. https:// www.gao.gov/products/gao-21-45

University of Southern California Program for Environmental Regional Equity. 2017. *An Equity Profile of the Los Angeles Region: Summary*. Los Angeles: USC Program for Environmental & Regional Equity.

Wacquant, Loïc J. D. 2009. *Punishing the Poor: The Neoliberal Government of Social Insecurity*. Durham, NC: Duke University Press.

Wark, McKenzie. 2019. *Capital Is Dead: Is This Something Worse?* New York: Verso.

Watkins-Hayes, Celeste. 2009. *The New Welfare Bureaucrats: Entanglements of Race, Class, and Policy Reform*. Chicago: University of Chicago Press.

Weber, Max. 1978. *Economy and Society: An Outline of Interpretative Sociology*. Berkeley, CA: University of California Press.

Weeks, Kathi. 2007. "Life Within and Against Work: Affective Labor, Feminist Critique, and Post-Fordist Politics." *Ephemera: Theory and Politics in Organization* 37(7):233-49.

Whitworth, Adam, and Elle Carter. 2014. "Welfare-to-Work Reform, Power and Inequality: From Governance to Governmentalities." *Journal of Contemporary European Studies* 22(2):104-17.

Wilson, George, and Vincent Roscigno. 2015. "End of an Era? Managerial Losses of African American and Latinos in the Public Sector." *Social Science Research* 54:36–49.

Wilson, George, and Vincent Roscigno. 2016. "Public Sector Reform and Racial Occupational Mobility." *Work and Occupations* 43(3):259–93.

Wright, Erik Olin. 2000. "Class, Exploitation, and Economic Rents: Reflections on Sørensen's 'Sounder Basis.'" *American Journal of Sociology* 105(6):1559–71. doi: 10.1086/210464.

Wright, Erik Olin. 2002. "The Shadow of Exploitation in Weber's Class Analysis." *American Sociological Review* 67(6):832–53.

Wright, Erik Olin, and Joachim Singelmann. 1982. "Proletarianization in the Changing American Class Structure." *American Journal of Sociology* 88:S176–209.

Yi, Daniel. 2000. "Most Recipients Unfazed by Law Requiring Photos, Fingerprints: Policy; Few Who Get Welfare or Food Stamps Have Dropped from the Rolls; Critics of the New Rules Had Predicted Otherwise." *Los Angeles Times*, October 9, A3 & A10.

Zacka, Bernardo. 2017. *When the State Meets the Street: Public Service and Moral Agency.* Cambridge, MA: Harvard University Press.

Index

Addams, Jane, 2

administrative burden: defined, 5; reduction of, 192, 193, 194, 224n20; from resource constraints and legal pressures, 14; runarounds and, 69, 70, 71, 224n20

administrative discipline, 15, 148, 155, 156, 166, 170, 190

Adriana (supervisor), 98

adult basic education services, 119, 233n24

AFDC (Aid to Families with Dependent Children) program: AFDC recipients, 128, 211n20, 234n30, 237n56; fingerprinting in, 243n5; GAIN program and, xiii–xiv; payments, 135, 237n56, 242nn100,101,104; replacement of, 83, 103, 135–36; San Diego project grants, 239n65; schoolfare and, 118, 234n30; TANF and, 135, 147; workfare and, 127, 128, 237n56, 238n57

affirmative action initiatives, 32, 36, 217n6

Affordable Care Act of 2010, 84, 85

airport security analogy, 246n37

Alameda County, 48, 136, 241n99

alienation: increase in, 96; of labor, 8, 59, 190; producer-product alienation, 168; worker-client relations and, 96, 175, 185–87, 187

Alvarez, Marcos, 93

Amber (eligibility worker), 35–36

ambulance services, 4

Andrea (eligibility worker), 39, 96

Ansell, Phil, 185, 227n62

Antelope Valley, xiv, 55, 104, 133, 145, 206, 221n42, 245n26

approval side, xiii, 27, 45, 65, 86, 90, 106–7, 168

Arsen (eligibility worker), 40

artificial intelligence, 191

assembly lines: classic formula for, 85; direct managerial power and, 10; form of, 9; types of, 8. *See also* people changing; people processing; welfare assembly line

austerity: budgetary, 6, 32, 90; GAIN as welfare austerity program, 129; pressures of, 100, 189, 216n38; responses to, 191, 240n72. *See also* budgets; funding automation: continuation of, 191; discretion and, 17; disempowerment through, 195; increase in, 7, 8, 212n32; justification of, 229n76; McDonaldization and, 98; in means testing, 86; people processing and less, 9; productivity and, 86; taskwork and, 177; unions and, 49; updating of, 87; welfare assembly line and, 189, 190, 191; welfare work and, 8, 13, 14, 105, 190. *See also* CalSAWS (California Statewide Automated Welfare System); digital case management systems; welfare assembly line

autonomy: bureaucracy and, 5; casework and, 95; connective labor theory and, 190; disciplinary power theory and, 190; of eligibility workers, 21, 22, 138, 159–60, 162; In-Home Supportive Services (IHSS) work and, 83; proletarianization and, 29, 33, 34, 215n30; reduction of, 215n30; relative autonomy, 18, 22, 68, 162; street-level bureaucracy and, 26, 30; taskwork and, 56, 69, 95; welfare assembly line and, 190; of welfare workers, 9, 13–14, 190; workfare and, 138, 189; of WTW workers, 26, 131, 138, 159–60, 162. *See also* connective labor theory; disciplinary power theory

Auyero, Javier, 155, 245n35

Baldassare, Mark, 211n27
Bandage, Sort, and Hustle (Seim), 4, 202
Bartram, Robin, 23, 214n17
Basma (eligibility worker), 46, 89
Bauman, Zygmunt, 44, 218n18

Bayer, Lynn, 236n52
benefits: amount of people receiving, 4; average benefit amounts, 3; denials, 224nn29,31; DPSS and delivery of, 3, 189, 236n52; of eligibility workers, 36; from welfare offices, 4, 192; of welfare work, 36–38, 60, 189; to WTW workers, 36
Benefits-Cal (web portal), 245n28
black box referrals, 59, 108–9, 137, 160. *See also* referralfare
Black Feminist Thought (Collins), 244n25, 247n22
Board of Supervisors, 5, 49, 58, 85, 93, 105, 133, 193, 220n33
Bourdieu, Pierre, 214n27
Brady, David, 3, 210n6
Brianna (worker), 49
budgets: decreasing state budgets, 127; DPSS concerns over, 85, 227n62; legal demand and austerity of, 6; limited staff budgets, 195; public funds and, 5; tightening of, 82, 226n48. *See also* austerity; funding
Buffat, Aurélien, 213n11
Burawoy, Michael, 44, 47, 208, 213nn2,16
bureaucracy: of DPSS, 220n33; federal government and, 5; as order, 52–54; patterns of, 211n22; screen-level, 64, 213n11; state government, 5–6; street-level, 9, 17–18, 27–28, 64, 189, 213n11, 214nn16,27
Bureau of Labor Statistics, 218n14, 219n26, 222n45
Bureau of Public Assistance: as DPSS, 48, 80, 220n33, 237n56; strike, 48; work requirements and, 237n56. *See also* DPSS (Department of Public Social Services)

Cash Assistance Program for Immigrants (CAPI), 65, 66, 224n18
Cassandra (eligibility worker), 19–21, 26
Change and Innovation Agency, 97, 98, 191, 201, 248n4
childcare: after 1996 reforms, 242n109; contracting of, 130; housefare and, 105, 117*tab.*, 123, 128; provision for, 43, 237n56; referrals, 112, 125, 192; specialists and, 130; as supplemental service, 135
Cisco Finesse, 76, 98, 152
Citrin, Jack, 212n28
Clergé, Orly, 36
clients: client-on-employee violence, 140; client-to-worker ratios, 188; discouraging connectivity with, 174–78; policy administration and, 18; rising numbers of, 8; worker-client connections, 15, 167–70; worker-client disconnections, 15, 167–70. *See also* connectivity
Clinton, Bill, 27, 82, 125–26, 184–85, 237n56
Cohen, Lizabeth, 63, 223n10
collective bargaining, 194, 215n32. *See also* unions
Collins, Patricia Hill, 103, 155, 244n25, 247n22
Community Work and Training Program (CWTP), 237n56
compliance: ancillary assistance to enable, 25, 118; compliance costs, 69; discipline power and, 146; expectations of, 56; federal, 228n62; maintaining, 182; malicious compliance, 130; patience and, 245n35. *See also* noncompliance
Comrie, Keith, 88, 212n31
connective labor theory, 169–70, 190

connectivity: directing, 184–85, 187; discouraging, 174–78, 186; on welfare assembly line, 185–87; worker-client connections, 10, 167–70; worker-client disconnect, 167–70
contracting: additional work from, 55–56; debates over, 133, 241n95; as managerial response, 240n72. *See also* Maximus; privatization
COVID-19 pandemic: CalFresh customers and, 84; contact reduction before, 177, 232n13; effects on methodology, 198; expansion of remote work, 194; good cause exemption for, 232n10; relaxation of rules, 115, 116, 194; sanctions paused for, 24; temporary reactions to, 194
Current (task-bank software), 97, 98, 100, 152, 155, 201, 245n27
customer (term), 63, 212n41

Davis, Mike, 1, 6, 211n26
deception, 23, 76, 141, 150, 155, 158
demographics, 46, 199, 206, 207, 217n7, 218n19, 219n21
Department of Charities, 225n33
Department of Children and Family Services, 47, 82, 84
Department of Human Resources, 218n14, 219n24
Department of Mental Health (DMH), 47, 113, 122–23, 161, 235n37
dependency, 17, 23, 44, 123, 125, 127–28, 158, 163. *See also* self-sufficiency discourse
Derber, Charles, 215n31
deskilling/upskilling, 89, 190
Deukmejian, George, 127, 128, 132, 238n59

Diener, Bart, 241n95
digital case management systems, 212n32, 245n33
DiMario, Anthony, 163
disability: benefits, 79; CalWORKs and, 232n15; claims as welfare, 4, 121; Department of Aging and Disability, 47; temporary disability screenings, 105
disciplinary power: administrative discipline, 15, 148, 155, 155–56, 156, 166, 170, 190; paternalistic discipline, 15, 146, 148, 162–63, 166, 170, 190; proletarianized public servants and, 166
disciplinary power theory, 15, 143–45, 152, 165, 190, 244n25, 245n35
Disciplining the Poor (Soss, Fording, and Schram), 143, 145–47
discretion: application of, 224n21; data discretion, 213n11; of frontline workers, 17, 64, 189, 190; increase in, 193, 243n1; lack of, 215n33; narrowing, 59, 81, 129–34, 189, 215n34
distant managerial gaze, 159
division of labor: advancing of, 10, 14, 23, 240n72; complexity in, 107; disempowerment through, 195; increase in, 8, 83–90, 91, 100, 168, 228n64; proletarianization and, 29. *See also* welfare assembly line
domestic violence supportive services: benefits and, 111, 125; extenders and, 111, 113; for GAIN and START participants, 25, 106, 108–12, 235n41; housefare and, 105, 108, 117*tab.*, 123; program brokers and, 129; referrals and, 116, 232n17; requirements of, 111; self-sufficient clients and, 12; standardization

and, 112; welfare workers and, 10, 107
Dow, Dawn Marie, 103
Dubois, Vincent, 214n27
Du Bois, W. E. B., 2
du Gay, Paul, 54, 57, 221n40
Durkheim, Émile, 168, 169
Dustin, Donna, 98

Earned Income Tax Credit, 3, 4
Eckert, Paul, 127–28
Edelman, Edmund D., 203*tab.*, 227n62
education: adult basic education services, 119, 233n24; civil rights protests against racism in, 80; contracting and, 130; edfare, 234n28; GAIN program and, 25, 108, 233n24, 239n67; opportunities for women and, 120; referralfare and, 116; referrals and, 114, 125, 131, 135, 192; schoolfare and, 118–20, 128; welfare office and, 80; welfare work and, 222n50; WTW workers and, 119, 157, 158, 159, 160. *See also* GED program; LACOE (Los Angeles County Office of Education); schoolfare
efficiency: administrative efficiency, 163; advocacy and, 186; automation and, 49; autonomy and, 189; client-to-worker ratios and, 188; connectivity and, 176; cost of increase in, 96, 128; cubicles and, 218n13; disciplinary power and, 146, 165; effectiveness and, 190, 194; efforts to increase, 80; increased emphasis on government efficiency, 63; McDonaldization and, 98; people processing and, 148; productivity and, 86, 87; reduction of worker's control over, 7; standards and, 67,

SNAP (Supplemental Nutritional Assistance Program)

Fording, Richard, 165, 210n10

Fordism, 14, 44, 47, 49, 50, 100

for-profit government services companies, xiv

Foucault, Michel, 143, 143–45, 152, 165, 244n25, 245n35

fraud, 76, 82, 87–88, 136, 141–42, 150, 164, 224n31

frontline labor: computerization and, 213n11; demographics, 218n19; fairness and, 214n17; focus on administration over, 220n33; frontline eligibility determination, 240n72; of GAIN and START, 231n7

frontline workers: discretion of, 17, 64, 189, 190; at DPSS, 12; extraction of labor effort from, 7, 189, 216n38; labor process of, 9; problem solving and, 113–16; union for, xiv. *See also* DPSS workers; eligibility workers; SEIU 721 (Services Employee International Union 721); WTW (welfare-to-work) workers

funding: federal sources, 6; in Los Angeles County, 227n57; policy administration and, 18; Proposition 13 and, 6, 127, 211nn27,28, 219n20; state sources, 6; in United States, 227n57. *See also* austerity; budgets

Gabe (eligibility worker), 245n33

GAIN (Greater Avenues for Independence) program: CalWORKs and, xiii; CalWORKs recipients and, 107, 233n22; community colleges and, 234n32; contracting and, 240n72; cost effectiveness increases in, 242n105; defined, xiii–xiv; domestic

violence supportive services and, 235n41; DPSS and, 239n71; education and training in, 239n67; employment and earning from, 248n26; evaluation of, 134–37; exemption from, 232n15; LACOE service referrals and, 234n29; Maximus and, 221n42; operational hierarchy of, 106–8; privatization of, 241n95; punitive strategies of, 242n1; redistribution and, 240n72; service worker salaries, 216n2; state budget and, 238n59; TANF and, xiii; workfare and, 106–10; work-first approach of, 242n103; work requirements and, 238n57

GAIN Bill, 126, 129, 134, 135, 238n56

GAIN workers, 178–84; approval workers, 106; family stabilization units, 107, 232n15; focus on, 231n7; focus on workfare by, 25; housefare, 123–25; intake workers, 106; medfare, 120–23; referralfare, 116–18; schoolfare, 118–20; specialized supportive service workers, 107, 108. *See also* WTW (welfare-to-work) workers

GEARS (GAIN Employment Activity Reporting System), 131, 133

GED program: people changing focus and, 158; pressure to participate in, 180; as referralfare, 12, 25, 116–18; as schoolfare, 105; welfare workers and, 10; as workfare, 120

gender: disciplinary power and, 147; labor and, 28, 31, 39; poverty and, 191, 209n6; promotions and, 45; wage inequality and, 209n4; welfare work and, 32–33

general flow workers, 27

General Relief program: assistance offered by, 4; average benefit amount, 3, 62, 210n14; cash assistance through, 171, 188; defined, xiv; eligibility for, 170–73; eligibility workers, 170–74, 246n38; fingerprinting in, 243n5; recipients, xiv, 107, 231n7; START and, 103; statistics on persons on, 63, 231n1; work requirements and, 237n56. *See also* eligibility workers

ghost files, 91–92

Gloria (eligibility worker), 95

good cause exemptions, 232n10

Gouldner, Alvin W., 211n22

Gov-Tech vendors, 191

Great Recession, 84

Great Society, 220n33

Greenberg, Max, 75

GROW (General Relief Opportunities for Work): domestic violence supportive services and, 235n41; launch of, 136; START program as replacement for, xiv, 136–37, 214n22

habitus, 214n27

Hahn, Kenneth, 203*tab.*, 227n60, 239n67

Halpern-Meekin, Sarah, 4

Hancock, Ange-Marie, 247n22

Haney, Lynne, 33, 231n6

Hannah (client), 109–10, 115, 232n13

Hansen, Helena, 4

Harris, John, 216n45

health insurance, 84, 85, 220n33. *See also* Medicaid; Medi-Cal

Herd, Pamela, 5, 69

Hernández, Juan Donaldo, 233n19

Hernández, Kelly Lytle, 2

hierarchical observation, 145

homelessness: CalWORKs and, 235n42; good cause exemption for, 232n10; in Los Angeles County, 1, 209n2

Homemaker Chore Program, 81

hotel money (term), 235n42

hotline workers, 245n34

housefare: abolishing of, 193; as overlapping and mutually dependent, 231n6; welfare workers and, 10, 105; as workfare alternatives and supplements, 123–25

housing aid: eviction protection assistance, 236n44; General Relief recipients referred for, 236n47; housing improvement services, 237n56

IHSS (In-Home Supportive Services), 63, 81, 83, 226n50

incarceration, 2, 4

In-Home Supportive Services, 63, 81, 83, 226n50

intake side, xiii, 27, 45, 65, 86, 106–7, 168, 246n38

internet, 110, 213n11

Isabel (WTW worker), 24–27

Jenny (supervisor), 153–55, 161

Jeremy (eligibility worker), 96

Jewish Vocational Services (NPO), 221n42, 241n95

Jim (supervisor), 160–61

Jiménez, Antonia, 63, 92, 176, 177, 197

Job Club, 25, 31, 116, 119, 120

jobs: job readiness assistance, 102, 114, 119, 127, 233n23; job search assistance, 25, 107, 116, 119, 120, 128, 132, 135, 158, 233n23; job training, 10, 12, 130, 164, 180, 233n23, 237n56. *See also* START

Molina, Gloria, 203*tab.*
moving assistance program, 236n44
Moynihan, Donald, 5, 69

Natalie (eligibility worker), 51
negligence, 23, 150, 155, 158
New Welfare Bureaucrats, The
  (Watkins-Hayes, 27–28
noncompliance: CalWORKs
  recipients and, 233n22; notice of,
  234n26; sanctions for, 24; termination because of, 243n5. *See also*
  compliance
normalizing judgement, 145–46

Olivia (client), 110–13, 115, 232n17
online applications, 5
on-the-job training, 233n23
Oppenheimer, Martin, 29–30, 215n32

Paik, Leslie, 76
Pam (eligibility worker), 40
participant (term), 212n41
participatory gaze, 157, 159
paternalistic discipline, 15, 146, 148,
  162–63, 166, 170, 190
Peck, Jamie, 102, 135, 137–38
Peeters, Rik, 71, 224n20
people changing: paternalistic
  discipline and, 15; term usage,
  212n37; in welfare assembly line, 9;
  WTW workers and, 156–59
people processing: administrative
  discipline and, 15; eligibility
  workers and, 149–51; term usage,
  212n37; in welfare assembly line, 9
Personal Responsibility and Work
  Reconciliation Act of 1996, 238n57
poverty: gender and, 147; in Los
  Angeles County, 2, 209n6;
  maintenance of, 210n10; poverty

redistribution, 212n32; race and,
  191; safety net programs, 4;
  structural roots of, 103; welfare
  mission to alleviate, 54
poverty governance: fiscalization of;
  increased automation in, 191,
  212n32; medicalization of; nature of,
  2; priorities of, 191; scholarship on,
  3–4; theories on sociology of, 210n10
privatization, 32, 55–56, 104, 130,
  132–33, 221n42, 241n95
program brokers, 60, 125–29;
  disciplinary power and, 166;
  frontline workers as, 12–13; means
  testing and, 214n24
proletarianization: autonomy and,
  215n30; collective bargaining and,
  215n32; defined, 29; of frontline
  workers, 12, 13, 15, 61, 190; of
  professionals/social workers, 8,
  215nn31,34, 229n66; of program
  brokers, 125–29, 166; of public
  servants, 15, 29–34, 169, 187, 190,
  195, 214n16; taskwork model and,
  193; of welfare work, 14, 188–89
Proposition 13, 6, 127, 211nn27,28,
  219n20
Prottas, Jeffrey, 75
public servants: labor process of, 9;
  productivity increase of, 240n72;
  proletarianization of, 13, 15, 29–34,
  169, 187, 190, 195, 214n16; workfare
  programs and, 104. *See also*
  frontline workers; WTW (welfare-
  to-work) workers
public services: as contradictory,
  57–58; dependence on labor of, 191;
  government customers judgement
  of, 223n10; as labor process, 31–33;
  for the poor, 2–3; street-level
  bureaucracy in, 17

Public Welfare Amendments, 80
Pugh, Allison, 169–70, 186

race: disciplinary power and, 147; poverty and, 191, 210n6; promotions and, 45; segregation, 46, 209n4; wage inequality and, 1–2, 209n4; welfare queen image, 82, 102–3, 247n22; welfare work and, 32–33
Reagan, Ronald, 82, 133, 226n48, 237n56
redistribution strategies, 192, 212n32, 240n72
referralfare: AFDC and, 237n56; black box referrals, 59, 108–10, 137, 160; contracted programs and, 108–9; standardization and, 125, 137, 144; as workfare alternatives and supplements, 116–18; workfare and, 233n21
rehabilitation programs, 233n19, 237n56
remote workers, 19, 36, 57, 153, 194, 245n33
rental assistance program, 236n44
resources: ancillary aid, 118; connecting recipients to, 25, 80, 125; as constrained, 5, 14; decrease in, 7, 226n55, 227n60; as limited, 34, 181, 248n4; redirection of, 192; staffing resources, 189, 232n11; stretched, 129
responsibility: erosion of, 215n30; signage in welfare offices about, 163–66
Ritzer, George, 98, 99
Riverside County: AFDC payments, 242n104; earnings in, 241n99; GAIN program, 135–36; influence of, 242n103
Rocío (eligibility worker), 46–47

Rosa (WTW worker), 156–63, 246n38
Roscigno, Vincent, 60
Roxanne (eligibility worker), 51
runarounds, 69–74, 77–79, 96, 161, 173, 174, 188, 194, 224n20

safety net programs: CalFresh as, 3; California Poverty Measure and, 209n6; capitalism and, 228n64; Earned Income Tax Credit as, 4; expansion of, 192; frontline workers as, 167–68, 170; maintaining of, 110, 129; protection of, 48; SSI as, 4; as weak and fragmented, 10
sanctions: activity hours and, 103, 105, 117; autonomy and, 21; COVID-19 pandemic pause on, 24, 115, 116; discouraging connectivity and, 185; discretion and, 17, 34, 129, 130, 131; GAIN Bill and, 134; for noncompliance, 24, 118, 132, 234n26; of recipients, 8; records of, 146; standardization of, 27, 30; START sanctions, 158; taskwork and, 59; threat of, 25; workfare and, 140, 142, 158
San Diego County, 93, 99, 127, 136, 207, 238n60, 239n65, 241n99
San Fernando Valley, xiv, 55, 104, 133, 145, 206, 221n42, 245n26
San Fernando Valley Community Mental Health Center, 235n39
schoolfare: abolishing of, 193; as overlapping and mutually dependent, 231n6; varieties of, 234n30; welfare workers and, 10, 105; as workfare alternatives and supplements, 118–20; workfare and, 105, 109–10, 234n28
Schram, Sanford, 143, 165, 210n10, 244n23

Scott, James, 74–75
Sears, David, 212n28
segregation, 46, 209n4
SEIU (Services Employee International Union), xiv, 48, 55, 167
self-employment, 77, 78, 79, 233n23
self-initiated programs (SIPs), 233n24
Self-Sufficiency Centers, 136
self-sufficiency discourse: controlling images of dependency and, 103, 179, 247n22; domestic violence victims and, 235n41; people changing and, 9, 123; redirection to self-determination, 193; self-sustaining work, 242n109; vague image of, 242n105
semiannual review reports (SAR-7s), 72, 73, 86
Services Employee International Union (SEIU), xiv, 48, 55, 167
Shandra (eligibility worker), 47
Sheared, Vanessa, 120
SNAP (Supplemental Nutritional Assistance Program), xiii, 62, 195. See also CalFresh; food stamps
Social Security Act of 1967, 237n56
social unrest, 3, 191
social work: McDonaldization of, 98–101; mechanization of, 137–39; proletarianization of, 8, 80–83, 215n34, 229n66; as separate from eligibility determination, 214n24; social workers, 225n37, 237n56; traditional/radical approaches, 233n19
Sofia (GAIN worker), 178–84
Soss, Joe, 165, 210n10
specialization: automation and, 8; difficulties for workers from, 59–60; increase in, 7; people processing and less, 9; productivity

and, 86; welfare work and, 8, 10, 13, 14
staffing: as DPSS controllable resource, 6; DPSS on levels of, 227n62; levels of, 193, 226nn53,54; as limited resource, 189, 195; Medi-Cal and, 228n63; stagnant budget for, 8. See also welfare workers
standardization: difficulties for workers from, 59–60; discretion and, 17; disempowerment through, 195; of GAIN program, 131, 133; increase in, 7, 8; of referrals, 114, 125, 137; welfare work and, 13, 14. See also welfare assembly line
START (Skills and Training to Achieve Readiness for Tomorrow) program: aid amount, 137; defined, xiv, 125; directing connectivity and, 184; domestic violence supportive services for, 25, 106, 108–12, 235n41; DPSS and, xiii, 125, 142; exemptions, 246n38; frontline labor of, 231n7; GAIN program and, 103, 104, 105, 125; General Relief program and, 103, 107, 124; GROW as replaced by, xiv, 136–37, 214n22; mission of, 164–65; referrals and, 114–15; rule relaxation, 194; schoolfare and, 118; staffing, 137; standardization and, 180; taskwork and, 105; workfare through, 103–4. See also General Relief program
START workers: casework, 26, 107; connectivity and, 184, 187; disciplinary power and, 162–63; GAIN workers and, 231n7; housefare and, 124; internal labor market and, 46–47; management and, 159–62; medfare and, 121, 123;

START workers *(continued)*
people changing focus of, 156–59;
as program brokers, 26, 118;
referralfare and, 116, 117, 118;
schoolfare and, 119, 120; as WTW
workers, xiv. *See also* WTW
(welfare-to-work) workers
state legitimacy: demonstration of, 6;
directing connectivity and, 184;
expression of, 3, 191, 210n10;
increase in, 134, 238n59; state
budget and, 127, 238n59
Street-Level Bureaucracy (Lipsky), 17,
27, 185
Supplemental Nutritional Assistance
Program (SNAP). *See* SNAP
(Supplemental Nutritional
Assistance Program)
Supplemental Security Income (SSI),
65, 224n18
surveillance, 8, 26, 32, 87, 144, 145, 152,
154, 159, 245n33
Sydney (eligibility worker), 52

Talisa (eligibility worker), 39, 46
Tanaka, Eddy, 130–31, 226nn55,56,
227n62, 239n71, 243n3
TANF (Temporary Assistance for
Needy Families): AFDC and,
83–84, 135, 147; block grants,
227n57; CalWORKs, xiii, 62; federal
regulations for, 195; study of, 94;
work requirements, 238n57; WTW
programming for, 145, 147
taskwork model, 59, 90–100, 92–93,
193
technical control, 213n11, 215nn31,34
technology: benefits of, 194; call
centers and, 5, 68, 92, 177;
efficiency engineering and, 87, 88;
eligibility workers and, 88–89;

operational accuracy and efficiency
and, 87–88. *See also* automation;
internet
Temporary Homeless Assistance
Program (THAP+14), 236n43
Theoharis, Jeanne, 140, 242n1
Thompson, Paul, 216n36
Tiffany (client), 157–58, 160
Tracy (GAIN worker), 107–13, 115,
138, 232nn9,11, 232nn13,14,
232n17
transitional employment, 104,
233n23
Transitional Subsidized Employment
(TSE) programs, 182–83
Tre (eligibility worker), 36
Tulare County, 241n99

unified case management, 214n24
unions: appeals to Board of Supervisors, 58; automation and, 49;
collective bargaining and, 194,
215n32; eligibility workers and,
219n30; GAIN program and,
241n95; management and, 48–49;
Maximus and, 241n95; membership, 219n26; public sector
unionization, 48; on standard
workload maximums, 225n39;
welfare rights activists and, 220n32.
See also SEIU 721 (Services
Employee International Union
721)
unsubsidized employment, 233n23
upskilling, 89

Valentina (GAIN worker), 55, 56
Vanessa (eligibility worker), 170–74,
178, 179, 183
vocational education training, 105,
116, 117*tab.*, 120, 128, 233n24

voluntary programming, 113, 194, 237n56

Wacquant, Loïc, 2, 4, 210n10
Wark, McKenzie, 89
Washington, Carl, 204*tab*.
Watkins-Hayes, Celeste, 27–29, 31, 32, 147, 197, 214n24
Weber, Max, 5, 54, 98, 99, 211n22, 221n40, 222n50
welfare: changing nature of, 2–3; material deprivation and, 3; McDonaldization of, 98–101, 137–38, 192; need for protecting, 3; public opinion about, 211n28; as punitive, 4, 140, 192; welfare dependency rate, 225n48; welfare legitimacy, 238n59
welfare assembly line: about, 7–11; contradictions of, 10–11, 188; efficiencies of, 10–11, 189; in Los Angeles welfare offices, 8; people changing in, 9; people processing in, 9; reforming of, 192; WTW workers and, 105. *See also* automation; division of labor; standardization
Welfare Case Management Information Systems (WCMIS), 88, 229n70
Welfare Fraud Prevention and Investigations Section, 141
welfare offices: assembly-line model for, 8; benefits received from, 4, 192; bureaucracy and, 5; CalFresh and, 3; CalWORKs and, 3; disciplinary power in, 142, 143–48; General Relief and, 3; labor process and, 12; Medi-Cal and, 3; programs distributed through, 3, 188; proletarianization of, 14; securitization of, 140; signage about

responsibility, 163–66; taskwork in, 18–23; workfare and, 106–10, 192; WTW workers in, 105. *See also* call centers; frontline workers; public services; welfare workers
welfare policy: materialization of, 10; post-1996 policy, 166; street-level bureaucracy and, 17–18, 22
welfare queen image, 82, 102–3, 247n22
welfare recipients: bureaucracy and, 8; CWTP and, 237n56; dependency discourse and, 128; determination of, 8; disciplinary power and, 147; fingerprinting of, 82, 141, 243n5; immigrant, 242n1; means tested aid, 63, 103; monitoring of, 8, 141; private-sector job placement of, 135; punishment of fraudulent, 141; sanctioning of, 8; schoolfare and, 119; taskwork and, 193–94; welfare assembly line and, 118
welfare reform: Clinton-era reforms, 27, 184–85; dependency discourse and, 247n22; efficiency reforms, 126, 214n24; late 1990s reforms, 27, 63, 136, 140, 176, 227n57; people changing mission, 237n52
welfare rights activism: access to public benefits and, 147; diversity and, 32; GAIN Bill and, 134; Maximus contract and, 132; organizing and, 220n32; unionization and, 48, 220n32
welfare state: artificial intelligence in, 191; critique of, 98–101; as customer service state, 63; effectiveness and, 190; expansions of, 4; investments in the, 192; post-welfare state image, 103; problem solving and, 113; work-oriented interventions of, 127

welfare system: assault on, 6, 18, 220n33; capacity crisis in, 191; mission of, 125–26, 244n23; Proposition 13 and, 6; as punitive, 4. *See also* CalSAWS (California Statewide Automated Welfare System); funding

Welfare Transition (WT), 145

welfare work: application process for, 38–39; automation and, 8, 13, 14, 190; benefits of, 36–38, 60, 189; bureaucratic order of, 52–54; as calling, 50–52; difficulties of, 35–36, 189; internal decline from, 57–61; internal labor market, 44–47; internal state, 47–50; moral dimensions of, 54–57; proletarianization of, 8; security of, 42–44, 189; specialization and, 8, 10, 13, 14; standardization and, 13, 14. *See also* welfare assembly line; WTW (welfare-to-work) work

welfare workers: casework, 193, 226nn55,56, 227n60; connectivity and, 190; as customers, 245n32; directing connectivity, 184–85; discouraging connectivity with clients, 174–78; organizing and, 220n32; proletarianization of, 14, 188–89, 224n21; punishment of, 141–42; radical social work approach and, 233n19; worker-client connections, 15, 167–70, 193; workload, 192; WTW programming expansion and, 10. *See also* DPSS workers; eligibility workers; staffing; WTW (welfare-to-work) workers

Wendy (client), 180–84

Wilson, George, 60

workfare: abolishing of, 193; AFDC and, 127, 128, 237n56, 238n57;

autonomy and, 138, 189; Cal-WORKs recipients and, 231n7; COVID-19 and, 194; exemptions, 246n38; GAIN program as, xiii, 103–10; GAIN workers focus on, 25; GED program as, 120; General Relief recipients and, 231n7; motives of, 102–3; as persistent, 2; public servants and, 104; as punitive, 2; referralfare and, 233n21; responsibility and, 163–66; schoolfare and, 105, 109–10, 234n28; START program as, 103–6; statistics on, 231n1; welfare legitimacy and, 238n59; welfare offices and, 106–10, 192; welfare workers and, 10; Workfare Pilot Program, 127. *See also* GAIN (Greater Avenues for Independence) program; START (Skills and Training to Achieve Readiness for Tomorrow) program

workfare alternatives and supplements: housefare as, 123–25; medfare as, 120–23; referralfare as, 116–18; schoolfare as, 118–20

Workfare States (Peck), 102

work-first approach, 103, 115, 138, 242n103

Work Incentive Program (WIN), 237n56

work study, 233n23

Wright, Erik Olin, 86

WTW (welfare-to-work) contracts, 24, 102, 115, 117, 130, 146, 232n12

WTW (welfare-to-work) programs: assembly line conditions in, 105; CalWORKs and, 136, 184; connective labor and, 184; disciplinary power and, 143–48; domestic violence victims and,

235n41; DPSS customers mandated to participate in, 102, 231n1; employment at DPSS through, 40; expansion of, 10; GAIN program as, xiii, 184; Maximus and, 133; as mechanized social work, 83, 137–39; monitoring and incentivizing client activities for, 27; privatization of, 133; self-sufficiency discourse and, 115; START program as, xiv. *See also* GAIN (Greater Avenues for Independence) program; START (Skills and Training to Achieve Readiness for Tomorrow) program

WTW (welfare-to-work) work: casework in offices, 24–29; as different from eligibility work, 179–80; terms used in, 212n41; workfare and, 105–6

WTW (welfare-to-work) workers: autonomy of, 26; benefits, 36; career paths, 46–47; caseload of, 26–27; defined, xiv, 12–13; as different from eligibility workers, 12–13, 26, 104, 105–6, 181–82, 186, 231n7; directing connectivity, 184–85, 186–87; disciplinary power and, 14–15, 25–26, 143–49, 156–63; discouraging connectivity with clients, 174–78; discretion of, 26, 106, 129–34, 246n38; division of labor and, 107; at DPSS, 245n26; efficiency engineering and, 27–28, 214n24; employed by Maximus, 55–57, 245n26; extenders/exemptions, 110–13; GAIN Bill and, 134–37; labor process and, 30–31; people changing focus of, 14, 15, 105, 109, 156–63, 170; proletarianization of, 12–13, 105, 125–29; referrals and, xiv, 59, 108–10, 113–15, 116–25, 137, 160; responsibility and, 163–66; salaries, 36; training for, 232n11; welfare assembly line and, 9, 105, 137–39; worker-client connections, 15, 26, 64, 167–70; workfare and, 25, 104, 105–6, 106–10. *See also* GAIN workers; START workers; welfare workers; *specific workers*

Yokomizo, Bryce, 228n62

Founded in 1893,
UNIVERSITY OF CALIFORNIA PRESS
publishes bold, progressive books and journals
on topics in the arts, humanities, social sciences,
and natural sciences—with a focus on social
justice issues—that inspire thought and action
among readers worldwide.

The UC PRESS FOUNDATION
raises funds to uphold the press's vital role
as an independent, nonprofit publisher, and
receives philanthropic support from a wide
range of individuals and institutions—and from
committed readers like you. To learn more, visit
ucpress.edu/supportus.

www.ingramcontent.com/pod-product-compliance
Lightning Source LLC
Chambersburg PA
CBHW032345280326
41935CB00008B/452